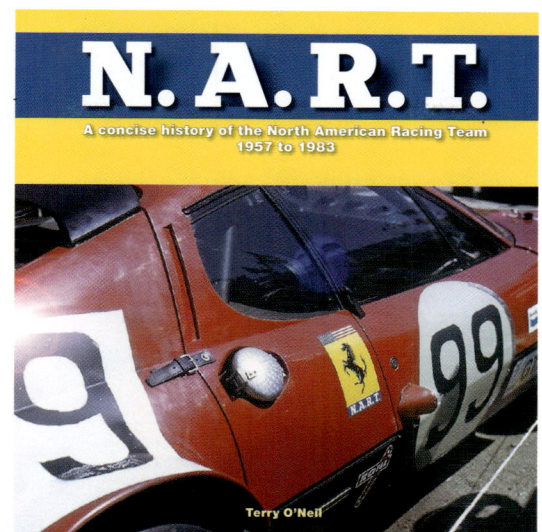

Biographies

A Chequered Life – Graham Warner and the Chequered Flag (Hesletine)
Amédée Gordini ... a true racing legend (Smith)
André Lefebvre, and the cars he created at Voisin and Citroën (Beck)
Chris Carter at Large – Stories from a lifetime in motorcycle racing (Carter & Skelton)
Cliff Allison, The Official Biography of – From the Fells to Ferrari (Gauld)
Edward Turner – The Man Behind the Motorcycles (Clew)
Driven by Desire – The Desiré Wilson Story
First Principles – The Official Biography of Keith Duckworth (Burr)
Inspired to Design – F1 cars, Indycars & racing tyres: the autobiography of Nigel Bennett (Bennett)
Jack Sears, The Official Biography of – Gentleman Jack (Gauld)
Jim Redman – 6 Times World Motorcycle Champion: The Autobiography (Redman)
John Chatham – 'Mr Big Healey' – The Official Biography (Burr)
The Lee Noble Story (Wilkins)
Mason's Motoring Mayhem – Tony Mason's hectic life in motorsport and television (Mason)
Raymond Mays' Magnificent Obsession (Apps)
Pat Moss Carlsson Story, The – Harnessing Horsepower (Turner)
Tony Robinson – The biography of a race mechanic (Wagstaff)
Virgil Exner – Visioneer: The Official Biography of Virgil M Exner Designer Extraordinaire (Grist)

General

11/2-litre GP Racing 1961-1965 (Whitelock)
AC Two-litre Saloons & Buckland Sportscars (Archibald)
Alfa Romeo 155/156/147 Competition Touring Cars (Collins)
Alfa Romeo Giulia Coupé GT & GTA (Tipler)
Alfa Romeo Montreal – The dream car that came true (Taylor)
Alfa Romeo Montreal – The Essential Companion (Classic Reprint of 500 copies) (Taylor)
Alfa Tipo 33 (McDonough & Collins)
Alpine & Renault – The Development of the Revolutionary Turbo F1 Car 1968 to 1979 (Smith)
Alpine & Renault – The Sports Prototypes 1963 to 1969 (Smith)
Alpine & Renault – The Sports Prototypes 1973 to 1978 (Smith)
Anatomy of the Works Minis (Moylan)
Armstrong-Siddeley (Smith)
Art Deco and British Car Design (Down)
Autodrome (Collins & Ireland)
Autodrome 2 (Collins & Ireland)
Automotive A-Z, Lane's Dictionary of Automotive Terms (Lane)
Automotive Mascots (Kay & Springate)
Bahamas Speed Weeks, The (O'Neil)
Bentley Continental, Corniche and Azure (Bennett)
Bentley MkVI, Rolls-Royce Silver Wraith, Dawn & Cloud/Bentley R & S-Series (Nutland)
Bluebird CN7 (Stevens)
BMC Competitions Department Secrets (Turner, Chambers & Browning)
BMW 5-Series (Cranswick)
BMW Z-Cars (Taylor)
BMW Boxer Twins 1970-1995 Bible, The (Falloon)
BMW Cafe Racers (Cloesen)
BMW Custom Motorcycles – Choppers, Cruisers, Bobbers, Trikes & Quads (Cloesen)
BMW – The Power of M (Vivian)
Bonjour – Is this Italy? (Turner)
British 250cc Racing Motorcycles (Pereira)
British at Indianapolis, The (Wagstaff)
British Cars, The Complete Catalogue of, 1895-1975 (Culshaw & Horrobin)
British Custom Motorcycles – The Brit Chop – choppers, cruisers, bobbers & trikes (Cloesen)
BRM – A Mechanic's Tale (Salmon)
BRM V16 (Ludvigsen)
BSA Bantam Bible, The (Henshaw)
BSA Motorcycles – the final evolution (Jones)
Bugatti Type 40 (Price)
Bugatti 46/50 Updated Edition (Price & Arbey)
Bugatti T44 & T49 (Price & Arbey)
Bugatti 57 2nd Edition (Price)
Bugatti Type 57 Grand Prix – A Celebration (Tomlinson)
Caravan, Improve & Modify Your (Porter)
Caravans, The Illustrated History 1919-1959 (Jenkinson)
Caravans, The Illustrated History From 1960 (Jenkinson)
Carrera Panamericana, La (Tipler)
Chrysler 300 – America's Most Powerful Car 2nd Edition (Ackerson)
Chrysler PT Cruiser (Ackerson)
Citroën DS (Bobbitt)
Classic British Car Electrical Systems (Astley)
Cobra – The Real Thing! (Legate)
Competition Car Aerodynamics 3rd Edition (McBeath)
Concept Cars, How to illustrate and design (Dewey)
Cortina – Ford's Bestseller (Robson)
Coventry Climax Racing Engines (Hammill)
Daily Mirror 1970 World Cup Rally 40, The (Robson)
Daimler SP250 New Edition (Long)
Datsun Fairlady Roadster to 280ZX – The Z-Car Story (Long)
Dino – The V6 Ferrari (Long)
Dodge Challenger & Plymouth Barracuda (Grist)
Dodge Charger – Enduring Thunder (Ackerson)
Dodge Dynamite! (Grist)
Dorset from the Sea – The Jurassic Coast from Lyme Regis to Old Harry Rocks photographed from its best viewpoint (Belasco)
Dorset from the Sea – The Jurassic Coast from Lyme Regis to Old Harry Rocks photographed from its best viewpoint (souvenir edition) (Belasco)
Draw & Paint Cars – How to (Gardiner)
Drive on the Wild Side, A – 20 Extreme Driving Adventures From Around the World (Weaver)
Ducati 750 Bible, The (Falloon)
Ducati 750 SS 'round-case' 1974, The Book of the (Falloon)
Ducati 860, 900 and Mille Bible, The (Falloon)
Ducati Monster Bible (New Updated & Revised Edition), The (Falloon)
Dune Buggy, Building A – The Essential Manual (Shakespeare)
Dune Buggy Files (Hale)
Dune Buggy Handbook (Hale)
East German Motor Vehicles in Pictures (Suhr/Weinreich)
Fast Ladies – Female Racing Drivers 1888 to 1970 (Bouzanquet)
Fate of the Sleeping Beauties, The (op de Weegh/Hottendorff/op de Weegh)
Ferrari 288 GTO, The Book of the (Sackey)
Ferrari 333 SP (O'Neil)
Fiat & Abarth 124 Spider & Coupé (Tipler)
Fiat & Abarth 500 & 600 – 2nd Edition (Bobbitt)
Fiats, Great Small (Ward)
Fine Art of the Motorcycle Engine, The (Peirce)
Ford Cleveland 335-Series V8 engine 1970 to 1982 – The Essential Source Book (Hammill)
Ford F100/F150 Pick-up 1948-1996 (Ackerson)
Ford F150 Pick-up 1997-2005 (Ackerson)
Ford GT – Then, and Now (Streather)
Ford GT40 (Legate)
Ford Model Y (Roberts)
Ford Small Block V8 Racing Engines 1962-1970 – The Essential Source Book (Hammill)
Ford Thunderbird From 1954, The Book of the (Long)
Formula 5000 Motor Racing, Back then ... and back now (Lawson)
Forza Minardi! (Vigar)
France: the essential guide for car enthusiasts – 200 things for the car enthusiast to see and do (Parish)
From Crystal Palace to Red Square – A Hapless Biker's Road to Russia (Turner)
Funky Mopeds (Skelton)
Grand Prix Ferrari – The Years of Enzo Ferrari's Power, 1948-1980 (Pritchard)
Grand Prix Ford – DFV-powered Formula 1 Cars (Pritchard)
GT – The World's Best GT Cars 1953-73 (Dawson)
Hillclimbing & Sprinting – The Essential Manual (Short & Wilkinson)
Honda NSX (Long)
Inside the Rolls-Royce & Bentley Styling Department – 1971 to 2001 (Hull)
Intermeccanica – The Story of the Prancing Bull (McCredie & Reisner)
Italian Cafe Racers (Cloesen)
Italian Custom Motorcycles (Cloesen)
Jaguar, The Rise of (Price)
Jaguar XJ 220 – The Inside Story (Moreton)
Jaguar XJ-S, The Book of the (Long)
Jeep CJ (Ackerson)
Jeep Wrangler (Ackerson)
Karmann-Ghia Coupé & Convertible (Bobbitt)
Kawasaki Triples Bible, The (Walker)
Kawasaki Z1 Story, The (Sheehan)
Kris Meeke – Intercontinental Rally Challenge Champion (McBride)
Lamborghini Miura Bible, The (Sackey)
Lamborghini Urraco, The Book of the (Landsem)
Lambretta Bible, The (Davies)
Lancia 037 (Collins)
Lancia Delta HF Integrale (Blaettel & Wagner)
Land Rover Series III Reborn (Porter)
Land Rover, The Half-ton Military (Cook)
Laverda Twins & Triples Bible 1968-1986 (Falloon)
Lea-Francis Story, The (Price)
Le Mans Panoramic (Ireland)
Lexus Story, The (Long)
Little book of microcars, the (Quellin)
Little book of smart, the – New Edition (Jackson)
Little book of trikes, the (Quellin)
Lola – The Illustrated History (1957-1977) (Starkey)
Lola – All the Sports Racing & Single-seater Racing Cars 1978-1997 (Starkey)
Lola T70 – The Racing History & Individual Chassis Record – 4th Edition (Starkey)
Lotus 49 (Oliver)
Marketingmobiles, The Wonderful Wacky World of (Hale)
Maserati 250F In Focus (Pritchard)
Mazda MX-5/Miata 1.6 Enthusiast's Workshop Manual (Grainger & Shoemark)
Mazda MX-5/Miata 1.8 Enthusiast's Workshop Manual (Grainger & Shoemark)
The book of the Mazda MX-5 Miata – The 'Mk1' NA-series 1988 to 1997 (Long)
Mazda MX-5 Miata Roadster (Long)
Maximum Mini (Booij)
Meet the English (Bowie)
Mercedes-Benz SL – R230 series 2001 to 2011 (Long)
Mercedes-Benz SL – W113-series 1963-1971 (Long)
Mercedes-Benz SL & SLC – 107-series 1971-1989 (Long)
Mercedes-Benz SLK – R170 series 1996-2004 (Long)
Mercedes-Benz SLK – R171 series 2004-2011 (Long)
Mercedes-Benz W123-series – All models 1976 to 1986 (Long)
MGA (Price Williams)
MGB & MGB GT– Expert Guide (Auto-doc Series) (Williams)
MGB Electrical Systems Updated & Revised Edition (Astley)
Micro Caravans (Jenkinson)
Micro Trucks (Mort)
Microcars at Large! (Quellin)
Mini Cooper – The Real Thing! (Tipler)
Mini Minor to Asia Minor (West)
Mitsubishi Lancer Evo, The Road Car & WRC Story (Long)
Montlhéry, The Story of the Paris Autodrome (Boddy)
Morgan Maverick (Lawrence)
Morgan 3 Wheeler – back to the future!, The (Dron)
Morris Minor, 60 Years on the Road (Newell)
Moto Guzzi Sport & Le Mans Bible, The (Falloon)
Motor Movies – The Posters! (Veysey)
Motor Racing – Reflections of a Lost Era (Carter)
Motor Racing – The Pursuit of Victory 1930-1962 (Carter)
Motor Racing – The Pursuit of Victory 1963-1972 (Wyatt/Sears)
Motor Racing Heroes – The Stories of 100 Greats (Newman)
Motorcycle Apprentice (Cakebread)
Motorcycle GP Racing in the 1960s (Pereira)
Motorcycle Road & Racing Chassis Designs (Noakes)
Motorhomes, The Illustrated History (Jenkinson)
Motorsport In colour, 1950s (Wainwright)
MV Agusta Fours, The book of the classic (Falloon)
N.A.R.T. – A concise history of the North American Racing Team 1957 to 1983 (O'Neil)
Nissan 300ZX & 350Z – The Z-Car Story (Long)
Nissan GT-R Supercar: Born to race (Gorodji)
Northeast American Sports Car Races 1950-1959 (O'Neil)
Nothing Runs – Misadventures in the Classic, Collectable & Exotic Car Biz (Slutsky)
Off-Road Giants! (Volume 1) – Heroes of 1960s Motorcycle Sport (Westlake)
Off-Road Giants! (Volume 2) – Heroes of 1960s Motorcycle Sport (Westlake)
Off-Road Giants! (volume 3) – Heroes of 1960s Motorcycle Sport (Westlake)
Pass the Theory and Practical Driving Tests (Gibson & Hoole)
Peking to Paris 2007 (Young)
Pontiac Firebird (Cranswick)
Porsche Boxster (Long)
Porsche 356 (2nd Edition) (Long)
Porsche 908 (Födisch, Neßhöver, Roßbach, Schwarz & Roßbach)
Porsche 911 Carrera – The Last of the Evolution (Corlett)
Porsche 911R, RS & RSR, 4th Edition (Starkey)
Porsche 911, The Book of the (Long)
Porsche 911SC 'Super Carrera' – The Essential Companion (Streather)
Porsche 914 & 914-6: The Definitive History of the Road & Competition Cars (Long)
Porsche 924 (Long)
The Porsche 924 Carreras – evolution to excellence (Smith)
Porsche 928 (Long)
Porsche 944 (Long)
Porsche 964, 993 & 996 Data Plate Code Breaker (Streather)
Porsche 993 'King Of Porsche' – The Essential Companion (Streather)
Porsche 996 'Supreme Porsche' – The Essential Companion (Streather)
Porsche Racing Cars – 1953 to 1975 (Long)
Porsche Racing Cars – 1976 to 2005 (Long)
Porsche – The Rally Story (Meredith)
Porsche: Three Generations of Genius (Meredith)
Preston Tucker & Others (Linde)
RAC Rally Action! (Gardiner)
RACING COLOURS – MOTOR RACING COMPOSITIONS 1908-2009 (Newman)
Racing Line – British motorcycle racing in the golden age of the big single (Guntrip)
Rallye Sport Fords: The Inside Story (Moreton)
Renewable Energy Home Handbook, The (Porter)
Roads with a View – England's greatest views and how to find them by road (Corfield)
Rolls-Royce Silver Shadow/Bentley T Series Corniche & Camargue – Revised & Enlarged Edition (Bobbitt)
Rolls-Royce Silver Spirit, Silver Spur & Bentley Mulsanne 2nd Edition (Bobbitt)
Runways & Racers (O'Neil)
Russian Motor Vehicles – Soviet Limousines 1930-2003 (Kelly)
Russian Motor Vehicles – The Czarist Period 1784 to 1917 (Kelly)
RX-7 – Mazda's Rotary Engine Sportscar (Updated & Revised New Edition) (Long)
Scooters & Microcars, The A-Z of Popular (Dan)
Scooter Lifestyle (Grainger)
SCOOTER MANIA! – Recollections of the Isle of Man International Scooter Rally (Jackson)
Singer Story: Cars, Commercial Vehicles, Bicycles & Motorcycle (Atkinson)
Sleeping Beauties USA – abandoned classic cars & trucks (Marek)
SM – Citroën's Maserati-engined Supercar (Long & Claverol)
Speedway – Auto racing's ghost tracks (Collins & Ireland)
Sprite Caravans, The Story of (Jenkinson)
Standard Motor Company, The Book of the
Subaru Impreza: The Road Car And WRC Story (Long)
Supercar, How to Build your own (Thompson)
Tales from the Toolbox (Oliver)
Tatra – The Legacy of Hans Ledwinka, Updated & Enlarged Collector's Edition of 1500 copies (Margolius & Henry)
Taxi! The Story of the 'London' Taxicab (Bobbitt)
Toleman Story, The (Hilton)
Toyota Celica & Supra, The Book of Toyota's Sports Coupés (Long)
Toyota MR2 Coupés & Spyders (Long)
Triumph Bonneville Bible (59-83) (Henshaw)
Triumph Bonneville!, Save the – The inside story of the Meriden Workers' Co-op (Rosamond)
Triumph Motorcycles & the Meriden Factory (Hancox)
Triumph Speed Twin & Thunderbird Bible (Woolridge)
Triumph Tiger Cub Bible (Estall)
Triumph Trophy Bible (Woolridge)
Triumph TR6 (Kimberley)
TT Talking – The TT's most exciting era – As seen by Manx Radio TT's lead commentator 2004-2012 (Lambert)
Two Summers – The Mercedes-Benz W196R Racing Car (Ackerson)
TWR Story, The – Group A (Hughes & Scott)
Unraced (Collins)
Velocette Motorcycles – MSS to Thruxton – New Third Edition (Burris)
Vespa – The Story of a Cult Classic in Pictures (Uhlig)
Volkswagen Bus Book, The (Bobbitt)
Volkswagen Bus or Van to Camper, How to Convert (Porter)
Volkswagens of the World (Glen)
VW Beetle Cabriolet – The full story of the convertible Beetle (Bobbitt)
VW Beetle – The Car of the 20th Century (Copping)
VW Bus – 40 Years of Splitties, Bays & Wedges (Copping)
VW Bus Book, The (Bobbitt)
VW Golf: Five Generations of Fun (Copping & Cservenka)
VW – The Air-cooled Era (Copping)
VW T5 Camper Conversion Manual (Porter)
VW Campers (Copping)
You & Your Jaguar XK8/XKR – Buying, Enjoying, Maintaining, Modifying – New Edition (Thorley)
Which Oil? – Choosing the right oils & greases for your antique, vintage, veteran, classic or collector car (Michell)
Works Minis, The Last (Purves & Brenchley)
Works Rally Mechanic (Moylan)

For post publication news, updates and amendments relating to this book, scan the QR code or visit: www.veloce.co.uk/books/V4787

www.velocebooks.com

First published in August 2015 by Veloce Publishing Limited, Veloce House, Parkway Farm Business Park, Middle Farm Way, Poundbury, Dorchester DT1 3AR, England. Fax 01305 268864 / e-mail info@veloce.co.uk / web www.veloce.co.uk or www.velocebooks.com.

ISBN: 978-1-845847-87-6 UPC: 6-36847-04787-0

© 2015 Terry O'Neil and Veloce Publishing. All rights reserved. With the exception of quoting brief passages for the purpose of review, no part of this publication may be recorded, reproduced or transmitted by any means, including photocopying, without the written permission of Veloce Publishing Ltd. Throughout this book logos, model names and designations, etc, have been used for the purposes of identification, illustration and decoration. Such names are the property of the trademark holder as this is not an official publication. Readers with ideas for automotive books, or books on other transport or related hobby subjects, are invited to write to the editorial director of Veloce Publishing at the above address. British Library Cataloguing in Publication Data – A catalogue record for this book is available from the British Library.
Typesetting, design and page make-up all by Veloce Publishing Ltd on Apple Mac. Printed in India by Replika Press.

N.A.R.T.

A concise history of the North American Racing Team 1957 to 1983

VELOCE PUBLISHING
THE PUBLISHER OF FINE AUTOMOTIVE BOOKS

Terry O'Neil

Contents

Author's foreword 6

Acknowledgements 8

Data sources 9

Introduction 10

1 CHAPTER 1
Luigi Chinetti 13

2 CHAPTER 2
1957-58
The formative period of NART 25

3 CHAPTER 3
1959-61
Expanding horizons 43

4 CHAPTER 4
1962-64
NART diversifies 75

5 CHAPTER 5
1965
Le Mans success for NART 121

CHAPTER 6
1966-69
A series of disappointments 135

CHAPTER 7
1970-72
Overcoming adversity 163

CHAPTER 8
1973-74
Further troubled times.. ..185

CHAPTER 9
1975
A very confused affair 194

CHAPTER 10
1976-77
The barren years.. 202

CHAPTER 11
1978-80
Limited participation. 205

CHAPTER 12
1981-83
The passing of an era 214

CHAPTER 13
Spyder
The NART 275 GTB4 220

Epilogue 224

CHAPTER 14
1957-1983
Statistical review.. 226

Index . .. .255

Author's foreword

The title alone possibly brings the reader to conjecture over the precise format and substance of this book. The answer is relatively simple, in so far that it is an overview of 26 years of history of the activities of the North American Racing Team. History never stops being created, and there is undoubtedly more that could be uncovered, there always is in a work such as this. The book records a view within a given time span, but is not attempting in any way to be the definitive article on the subject matter, and I have serious doubts as to whether that could ever be achieved now, due to the passing of time since events took place.

Napoleon Bonaparte was reported as saying "History is the version of past events that people have decided to agree upon." If only it could be that simple, but in this instance it is not. Although having no bias towards the subject matter, research into the subject has led to both opinion and the weight of evidence being factors that have contributed to the writing of this book.

There is another issue to take into consideration, that of chassis numbers. It was not unknown for Ferrari to make a 'slip of the pen' when making documentation out, so in certain instances the history of a few cars contained within this book is clouded, and chassis numbers are recorded to the best of my knowledge.

While research can reveal the written word, it alone does not guarantee that the 'facts' are those we believe to be so. In putting the book together, photographic records have been incorporated to support the written word – photographs taken at a time when the camera didn't lie.

The book has been constructed in a manner that takes in as many contributions as possible from the people who were connected with NART. However, the acknowledged danger that the reader must take into account is that, when looking back over 50 years, people's memories have possibly lapsed when it comes to recalling specific details.

So many of the details and stories have never been documented, for the subject was never designed to be recorded in the annals of time. The detail that some people consider important today, would have had little meaning or consequence at the time of it happening; the people concerned were too busy trying to win races.

Against a background of strong Italian influence, where actions spoke louder than words, it is not surprising that race records played an insignificant part within the NART organisation, at a time when perpetual movement of machinery around the Americas and Europe to meet race deadlines was the priority. Dick Fritz, team manager between 1967-76, said "Nobody cared a damn what the chassis number of the car was."

Whilst care has been taken to be as accurate as possible in recording race data, inevitably, doubt as to the authenticity of some information has been taken into account. Consequently, deciding what constitutes a NART race entry has been an ongoing problem.

NART was not a very tight-knit organisation, with many deals for race entry most likely conducted on an informal basis between Chinetti and a client, but not necessarily recorded. I have taken the following parameters for the purpose of defining a NART entry in this book.

- Chinetti would purchase a car from a manufacturer, enter the vehicle in an event, and employ the driver(s). Chinetti was reluctant to give drivers a contract, due to him not being able to guarantee the availability of the right kind of car at any one time in the season.
- A client would purchase a vehicle from Chinetti, but Chinetti would enter the car in a race on behalf of the client. The race package would include spares and the use of Chinetti's mechanics.
- A client could lease a vehicle from Chinetti on a race-by-race basis. It was not unusual for Chinetti to employ a well-known driver to accompany the client in endurance races.
- Expediency dictated it necessary for Chinetti to enter vehicles into certain races on behalf of the Ferrari factory team under the colours of NART. Inevitably personnel from the factory accompanied the cars.

Chinetti not only survived on this business strategy, but succeeded in accomplishing this feat during the years that are acknowledged to be the zenith of sports car racing, competing against the might of the official factory teams. Amateurs and professionals drove shoulder to shoulder, sportsmanship and fair play were predominant in most areas of the sport, and to some drivers the prize money came purely as a bonus. This was an era when racing was fun to participate in, fun to be involved in, even around the peripheries, and enthusiasm counted for everything.

NART was to become one of the premier acronyms in sports car racing over three decades. Certainly, no other race team was so inextricably linked with its creator, as the North American Racing Team was to Luigi Chinetti.

Terry O'Neil

Acknowledgements

A book of this scope and diversity relies upon the cooperation of the people who were actually involved with the North American Racing Team in one capacity or another.

I was fortunate to be able to either talk with or correspond with a number of these people whilst visiting America in the year 2000. In days long gone by, British gentry went on the European Grand Tour in search of valuable objects and works of art. For my research, I consider that I did the modern day equivalent, not for valuable objects but for valuable information for the contents of this book.

My journey lasted for three weeks, in which time I visited Bob Grossman at his home on Long island to talk about his career and look at some of his paintings, and then visited Bob Craige at Roslyn Heights, Long Island, where a chat was followed by lunch and a look at the film footage taken at Bonneville in 1974. Up in Connecticut, a visit to John Cuccio for lunch in Westport, a ride in his modified 365 GTB4, and some time reflecting on his memories, was followed the next day by a visit to see Peter Sachs and his amazing collection of Ferraris. François Sicard was generous enough to give me an overnight stay and an insight as to what it was like to work for Luigi Chinetti, and an afternoon at Dick Fritz's house outside of Ridgefield was very enlightening. It tested my navigational skills to find Alfredo Caiti out at Wallkill Airport in New York State, though it was a lot easier to find Sam Posey, who invited me to stay for lunch at his home in Sharon, Connecticut. I also visited Jean-Louis Lebreton at his workshop in Greenwich, and Ed Johnson in Riverside. I must also include Rick Anderson, who put me up overnight, and showed me some of the Ferraris stored at Lyme, together with paperwork relating to NART, and, of course, Luigi Chinetti Jr at his home near Lyme, Connecticut, where he generously gave of his time (and wine) sitting on the decking in the sunshine. At the end of our conversation he added that he was not in favour of me writing a book about the North American Racing Team...

To all of these individuals, who gave a valuable insight into what it was like to work with Luigi Chinetti Sr, I am thankful and most appreciative.

I also met with Stirling Moss and David Piper in England, Denise McCluggage at her home in New Mexico, Phil Hill at Watkins Glen at different times, and corresponded with Ed Hugus, all of whom drove for Luigi Chinetti at some point in their career.

In was inevitable that I should turn to the International Motor Racing Research Centre at Watkins Glen, and also to Dean Butler. They both played an important role in producing valuable information for me from the vast archives and collections in their possession. I am also grateful to the late Gerald Roush, who allowed me access to his library and document collection at his home in Georgia, and also patiently guided me through the many Ferrari minefields.

My thanks are extended to the following people for providing photographs for this publication.

Alexis Callier, Tim Hendley, Ed McDonough, Nick England (VIRhistory), Dave Nicholas (Barcboys) Gerald Roush, Tom Schultz, François Sicard, Jeff Taylor, Ted Walker (Ferret Fotographics), author's collection.

Data sources

The following list details those sources used during the preparation of the book, from which information has been extracted or referred to, and analysed, in order to form background information, race information, race results, and, wherever possible, chassis numbers.

Magazines
Autosport, Car and Driver, Cavallino, Competition Press, Ferrari, Motor, Modern Motor, Motoracing, Motor Sport, Motor Trend, National Speed Sport News, Pit Talk, Prancing Horse, Road and Track, Sports Car.

Newspapers
Used with appropriate caution, as there were some speculative articles about Chinetti receiving an engine from Ferrari to fit into an Indianapolis car project, and whilst these speculative articles bordered on the truth, further research resulted in digging out the facts of the Indianapolis-bound Ferrari of 1954.

Baltimore Sun, Boston Globe, Greenwich Times, Hartford Courant, Miami News, Nassau Guardian, New York Times, Washington Post.

Books
Dino, Nye, Doug
Ferrari, Tanner, Hans and Nye, Doug
Ferrari Dino SPs, Godfrey, John
Ferraris at Le Mans, Dominique Pascal
Ferrari 250 LM, Masini, Marcel
Time and Two Seats, Wimpffen, Janos

Research
Much of the research for this book has come from conversations with people who were in some way involved with the cars that are discussed in the book, together with the sources listed above. Every effort has been made to corroborate historical data, but such information, particularly when it involves chassis history, is subject to reasonable error and should be interpreted as such.

Introduction

Ferrari... the very name is evocative. Ferrari commands respect in a manner which is unique to this marque, and the name has become a modern legend. However, as with most legends, it suffers from embellishment as the years go by. Ordinary events from the past can be perceived as being important, as the story gains in magnitude. Past race achievements, irrespective of the opposition, are classified as magnificent triumphs, and failure, though not totally disregawrded, is put down to experience to learn from. As a result, truth is the victim, and has become tainted with fiction and exaggeration through subsequent years.

So it is that most things associated with Ferrari suffer in a similar fashion. The North American Racing Team is no exception to this phenomenon. The quotation "The only certainty about NART is that there are no certainties" is fairly accurate, in so far as the history of this famous racing team is concerned, and there remain some issues that are to be resolved beyond doubt.

In America during the late 1950s, the tide of change was transforming the traditional amateur sport into a professional activity. Historically the SCCA (Sports Car Club of America) had retained the sparse amount of money obtained from race spectators at its organised race events, and supposedly spent the money on track safety measures throughout America. While undoubtedly a large percentage of the money was put back into the sport, a minority of drivers were of the opinion that they should, as the entertainers, be entitled to either start money and/or prize money.

The SCCA National Officers and Committee were firmly against this idea, failing at the time to recognise the escalating cost of motor racing to the individual. They insisted on remaining an amateur organisation. With a membership of nearly 9000 in 1957, the organisation had clout, with the majority of members realising that despite the increasing costs, being professional would not bring them riches. That would fall to those teams, and a few lucky individuals, who could afford to purchase and maintain the best performing sports cars.

For years, the wealthy owners who 'employed' drivers, had paid them in one form or another, whether in money, jewellery, or jobs that commanded a salary but little work, and the SCCA had turned a blind eye to most of the indiscretions. Although in theory having to retain amateur status in America, these same people could race in other countries, and retain any prize money earned. Consequently, there had been a drain on the top drivers from local competition, as the likes of Phil Hill, Masten Gregory and Carroll Shelby plied their skills mainly in Europe.

The timing of the formation of the North American Racing Team coincided with a major restructuring of sports car racing in America, with the introduction of professional races run by the United States Automobile Club (USAC), an organisation that was already the sanctioning body for different formulas of professional motor sport. USAC's idea was to prise away the better sports car drivers from the SCCA with the lure of start money and prize money.

Was Chinetti's decision to form NART coincidental to what was happening in motor sport? Being a shrewd business man, the answer is probably not. Up until 1958 Chinetti would appear to have entered cars in his own name, mainly on behalf of customers who wished to enter major races such as Sebring, but required his expertise to look after the car.

As an importer of prestigious cars into America, Chinetti knew that sports cars were becoming more expensive to maintain in a competitive state, as they were constantly being updated. All of this cost money, more than he could manage off the back of a motor business without having financial backing, and more than some of his customers were willing to pay without the incentive of some monetary reward. A tin cup did not pay for the service bills!

With USAC opening the door to professionalism, Chinetti could see the opportunity to subsidise his expenditure on racing, by leasing cars to better known drivers from Indy car racing, who did not own their own sports cars. Albeit a long time SCCA supporter, Chinetti joined the Board of Directors of this new venture, so, in theory, he now had a foot in both the amateur and professional camps. This suited Chinetti's ambitions, as he could have his cars entered in either organisation's events in one guise or another, in the name of a client as a rent-a-car entry or, in the case of World Championship races, in his own name. Either way, it came under the banner of NART at the end of the day, and NART was to be Chinetti's answer to the manufacturer's teams through three decades of racing at the major events in America and Europe.

Leasing cars to other entrants was nothing new for Chinetti. He had used this practice in 1956, with cars going to John Edgar for Carroll Shelby to drive. Apart from the prestige, it was a useful source of income, for while NART grew in stature it was always short of money, and in that respect could not compete with the likes of Briggs Cunningham on the east coast, or John von Neumann and John Edgar on the west coast of America.

Irrespective of the grand sounding name, to imagine that NART was a large organisation would be incorrect, for many of the people involved in NART were predominantly employees of Chinetti Motors. When they had finished their day duties, attention was turned to preparing cars for races, and they were joined by a team of enthusiastic volunteers that would work long into the night. John Cuccio, a long-time friend of Chinetti, said "At Luigi Chinetti Motors there was no formal code or organisation. As a commercial venture it served mainly to help his ambition to race Ferraris. Customers and drivers would drop in and help prepare the race cars in an evening." In an interview with Alfredo Caiti, an ex-Ferrari employee who joined Chinetti in 1960, he indicated "Only four or five people went to the

Introduction

races, so any bad comments made by drivers criticising our procedures were not justified, as NART worked on a tight budget, unlike factory teams. It was well known that Chinetti had to improvise at some of the races he sent his cars to. Borrowing bits from production models in the car park was a practice carried out when necessary – but always leaving a note on the windscreen for the owner." Team manager Dick Fritz added "The logistics of a big race at Sebring or Daytona was a problem, with up to four sets of wheels and tyres per vehicle, plus spares (engines occasionally) and tools. Chinetti himself would sometimes get involved in doing pit work."

So, from humble beginnings and limited finance, Chinetti began to form a bond with Ferrari and his customers that would last over three decades. No, it was not the most efficient organisation, and yes, they did get it wrong sometimes, but with their enthusiasm they left an everlasting impression on customers and their competitors that was unparalleled in the sport in that golden era.

■■ The first design of the North American Racing Team decal, usually attached to the side and/or rear of the car.

■■ The second design of the North American Racing Team decal incorporating part of the American flag was adopted, as the design was thought to be more prominent than the previous version. (Many owners kept these decals on their car even if it was not entered in a race by Chinetti/NART.)

> During the relatively short period that Ferrari has been in existence, a few individuals have contributed significantly to the success of the marque in different parts of the world. In North America, Luigi Chinetti was one of those individuals.

Through his long friendship with Enzo Ferrari, his own enthusiasm, racing accomplishments and passion, he helped form the foundation of what has today become the largest and most important market in the world for Ferrari.

Luigi Chinetti was born on 17 July 1901 at 11 Via Volta, in the Porta Volta area of Milan, to Giuseppi, a master gunsmith, and Antoinette. He spent two years at a local polytechnic, dabbled with machine tools, and then, not yet 18, enlisted in the Italian Air Force as an engine mechanic during World War I. He was subsequently discovered to be underage, and told to leave.

In 1917 Chinetti went to work for Alfa Romeo as an engineer/mechanic, a position recommended by an uncle. Whilst at Portello he was assigned to fabricating the main journals on Giuseppe Merosi's engines, and then gradually worked his way up to the competition department, whereupon he began to witness Italian motor racing first-hand.

It was at Alfa Romeo, in 1918, that Luigi Chinetti met Enzo Ferrari, a symbolic association that would bring much success to both men in years to come. He remembered Vittorio Jano coming to Alfa Romeo from Fiat, and the immortal P2 Grand Prix car being developed from the blueprints that Jano brought with him.

Chinetti was with the Alfa Romeo team at the French Grand Prix in 1925, when Alfa's great champion Antonio Ascari spun off the track and was killed. He had travelled as a mechanic for the team, but decided not to make the trip back to his home in Milan. Disheartened by the rise of fascism in Italy, and always a man who lived life to the fullest, Chinetti decided to relocate to France as he felt 'at one' with the French lifestyle.

Chinetti, whose expertise with automobiles ranged from the arcane field of bearing fabrication to occasional race driving, moved to Paris where he planned to open a small exotic-car repair shop. He assisted Alfa's French sales and maintenance efforts from his base in Paris, and, through his continued association with Alfa Romeo, drove his first race in an Alfa Romeo 6C at Spa on 8 July 1928, with co-driver Rachewsky.

In 1931 Chinetti was instrumental in setting a number of speed records at Montlhéry. With two other drivers he drove 5000 miles in 33 hours, 6 minutes and 28 seconds, at an average speed of 93.8mph. The team also set a 48-hour record at 94.4mph. Chinetti's involvement was totally unplanned. He took the car being used by René Dreyfus on the track "I wanted just to prove the car was fast. I find out that not only was it fast, but I figure out it was fast enough to make the one-hour record," said Chinetti.

Within the two-year period from 1932 to 1934, Chinetti was credited with two victories and a second place in three 24-hour races at Le Mans. The first victory was in 1932, driving with Raymond Sommer at the wheel of an Alfa Romeo 8C 2300 LM, finishing two laps ahead of Franco Cortese and Giovanni Battista Guidotti in a similar car. Chinetti also entered Le Mans for a second time in 1933, finishing second in an exciting battle with Nuvolari. The lead changed twice in the last lap alone, with Nuvolari crossing the finish line a mere ten seconds ahead of Chinetti's Alfa Romeo 8C 2300, in the closest Le Mans finish to date. He was convinced that only his own Alfa's failing gearbox and his rival's alleged use of benzole fuel held him a few seconds behind Nuvolari at the end of the final lap.

Determined to avenge his defeat, he entered Le Mans again in 1934 with co-driver Philippe Étancelin, again in an Alfa Romeo 8C 2300. To add to his pressures a French film company approached Chinetti with the offer to star in their production *300 km an Hour*. For a fee of 30,000 Fr Francs they wanted to film everything he did within the 24-hour race, including pit stops, refuelling and "many other things." "Many other things?" questioned Chinetti, "Well also there's an actress in the movie – you have to do something with her," came the reply. Indirectly, Chinetti attributed his win to the film crew, because of the bright lighting; there were many repairs to carry out on the car, including one to the leaking fuel tank, which was repaired with chewing-gum – but with those bright lights the job was made all that much simpler. The Alfa finished 13 laps ahead of the second place car, a Riley 6/12 MPH.

In the late 1930s, France cut off trade with Italy in retaliation for Mussolini's military action in Africa, and Chinetti received a telegram demanding that he return to Italy and serve in the Army. He defiantly wired a reply that he had already served his country in World War I. Instead, he established a relationship with Anthony Lago and his Talbot-Lago Company in France, working in a developmental and managerial role, which, in turn, led to Chinetti partnering Louis Chiron in a Talbot-Lago T150C at the 1937 24-hour Le Mans race. It turned out to be a disappointing race for the pair as the car failed to finish. He suffered a similar fate in 1938, driving the same car, this time partnering Philippe Étancelin, and again, in 1939, partnered by Mathieson.

Chinetti's unplanned move to America was brought about by the onset of World War II. In May 1940, Chinetti sailed on the Conte di Savoia to America, where he lived out the next chapter of his life. Chinetti came to America with Dreyfus and René Le Bègue; they were headed to the Indianapolis 500 for American expatriate Lucy O'Reilly Schell, with a pair of Maseratis similar to the car Wilbur Shaw had used in 1939 to win his second Memorial Day classic. In 1939 Chinetti met Selim Lawrence Schell (Laury), an American with the idea of forming a racing team to maintain the costly driving activity of his wife Lucy, and his son Harry. Thanks to his considerable technical experience, Chinetti had been engaged as team manager of Lucy's Ecurie Bleue in France, and in 1940 had prepared the Maseratis for the Indianapolis race. He had argued against using the Talbot cars as they were not quick enough.

Unable to return to France because of the war, Chinetti remained in America after the Indianapolis 500 event. Had he attempted to return to France he would have been an enemy alien, and he had no wish to return to live in Italy. Whilst in America he helped in the war effort, working for Pratt & Whitney with the blessing of the US officials, and also working at J Inskip, tuning Rolls-Royce engines alongside Alfred Momo.

1

■ Luigi Chinetti driving the Ferrari 166 MM (0008 M) to an epic victory in the 1949 Le Mans race.

■ Lord Selsdon, Luigi Chinetti and his wife, Marion, look relaxed during victory celebrations at Le Mans.

During his early days in America he met and married Marion (18 April 1942), with whom he had a son, Luigi Jr. While living in New York he got to know the sports racing scene in the north-eastern United States intimately, through his association with ARCA (Automobile Racing Club of America) members.

In Italy, Enzo Ferrari had been producing machine tools during World War II. After the war he turned his attention to a potential new venture, building motor cars. The machine tool production equipment was old and outdated, and he could see that he would soon be uncompetitive against the companies, particularly in America, that had technically advanced machinery. The problem facing Ferrari in December 1946 was the state of the European economy. Ravaged by war, there were insufficient customers left in Europe to support the kind of automotive venture that Ferrari had in mind, leaving him with a dilemma.

In the early winter of 1946 Chinetti returned to visit France, only to find that his home and possessions had been lost in the conflict; it was during this trip that he and Enzo Ferrari made contact. Although they had met while practically teenagers, both had pursued separate and distinct careers in automobile racing. On Christmas Eve 1946 the two men met in Enzo's office at Modena, where Chinetti and Ferrari explored their ideas for the future. Ferrari explained that Gioacchino Colombo, who ostensibly still worked for Alfa Romeo, had come up with a design for a new V12 1500cc engine for a car to be called the 125. Seeing common ground, the idea of Ferrari producing cars in keeping with Chinetti's well-heeled friends' requirements evolved, which could generate momentum for Ferrari's production and generate cash for Chinetti. This meeting formed the basis of a long and successful venture for both parties, and in turn helped Chinetti finance the ambition he had to form his own racing team, which was to become the North American Racing Team. The first Ferrari Chinetti delivered in America was a 166 MM Barchetta (0002 M), sold to Tommy Lee, and delivered in the first quarter of 1949. The second was a 166 Corsa Spyder (016 I), sold to Briggs Cunningham in 1949, and delivered just in time for him to race the car at Bridgehampton on 11 June 1949.

Luigi Chinetti

Luigi Chinetti adjusts his goggles prior to the start of the 1949 Spa 24-hour race, while a mechanic refuels the car.

Chinetti's first business premises were briefly based on East 49th Street in 1948-49. Shortly after that, Chinetti took premises on 19th Street under the East Side Highway in New York, but the only indication to the uninitiated visitor that this was Ferrari headquarters in North America, was a small prancing horse decal pasted to a square of cardboard propped in the corner of a window.

Competition remained a priority in his life, and, driving in one of his customers' cars, Lord Peter Selsdon's Ferrari 166SC (016 I), he earned Ferrari's first significant international victory, a 12-hour event at Montlhéry in France on 12 September 1948. In November he went back to the banked track, and set three class E world speed records with the same car.

In 1949 Chinetti returned to Le Mans, this time with a Ferrari 166 MM (0008 M), owned and co-driven by Lord Selsdon. The unfortunate Lord Selsdon was overcome by food poisoning prior to the beginning of the race, and was unable to participate for any length of time in the event. Chinetti spent

Chinetti poses with his wife, Marion, and son, Luigi Jr, after winning the 1949 Spa 24-hour race with co-driver Jean Lucas.

Chinetti stands alongside his Ferrari 212 Inter (0171 EL) during the 1951 Carrera Panamericana, which he won with Piero Taruffi.

over 23 hours at the wheel of their 2-litre car, averaging a winning 82mph. The spell at the wheel would have taxed the fittest young driver, but Chinetti was 48 years old at the time, and this remarkable drive was followed by Chinetti's win in the 24-hour race at Spa two weeks later, partnered by Jean Lucas driving a Ferrari 166 MM (0010 M).

On the commercial front, Chinetti's showroom had moved again, this time to 444 West 55th Street. This was a building owned by the Fergus Motorcar Co, and Chinetti was based on the third and fourth floors, with cars brought up and down on a freight elevator.

Chinetti had petitioned to become a US citizen in 1947, and took the oath of allegiance on 6 March 1950.

Chinetti's racing activities continued into the early 1950s. He and Jean Lucas co-drove to another 12-hour victory at Montlhéry, with

New York Motor Show 1954. Chinetti bought the Ferrari Monoposto (0388) to race at Indianapolis in 1954, but the car did not start the event. Note the extended fuel tank on the left side of the car.

Luigi as riding mechanic, when Piero Taruffi won the 1951 Mexican Road Race (Carrera Panamericana) in a Ferrari 212 Inter Coupe, Ferrari's first major success in the Americas.

Enzo Ferrari had not wanted to enter the Carrera Panamericana but, aware of the potential of the American market, readily agreed to the Centro Deportivo Italiano team entering, giving Chinetti responsibility for the technical aspects of the preparation and maintenance of the two cars. The 2000-mile road race covered the length of Mexico, and was a gruelling and dangerous five-day affair. Chinetti, knowing that the softer compound European tyres would not last on the abrasive roads, approached BF Goodrich's Mexican subsidiary, Euzkati, to see what could be found in the way of a more durable tyre. The company came up with a compound more suited to the conditions, and by using these tyres Chinetti achieved a one-two overall victory for his cars. The following year he drove to a third-place finish, partnered by Jean Lucas in a Ferrari 340 Mexico, in the same gruelling, 2000-mile race.

In 1952 Luigi Chinetti played his part in helping Ferrari dispose of its now obsolete 4.5-litre 375 F1 cars, by first encouraging Ferrari to enter the Indianapolis 500 race, then managing to sell three of the five converted 375 F1 cars to American owners. The additional two cars were entered by Scuderia Ferrari.

Tragedy struck Chinetti's 1953 entry at Le Mans. Paired with Tom Cole, the Ferrari 340 MM had been running in third place in the race, but, in the 16th hour, Cole left the track at Maison-Blanche travelling at speed, and was fatally injured. Chinetti's luck also ran out for the 1953 Carrera Panamericana race, as he and Alfonso de Portago were non-finishers

when they ran out of time in one of the stages of the race.

Towards the end of 1953, various reports appeared in the American press that Ferrari was building a special car for Luigi Chinetti to enter the Indianapolis race in 1954. The car duly arrived in January 1954, and was put on display at the New York Motor Show. Bearing chassis number 0388, the car was a single-seat tub built on a special chassis, and though in some ways resembling the 1952 cars, the wheelbase was four inches shorter, and it had an enlarged fuel tank added to one side. Although *Car Life* magazine had sponsored the Indianapolis entry, on the week of the race the car arrived without the sponsorship, however. It was officially entered in the name of Marion Chinetti, but, without a regular driver, the Ferrari did not even get as far as official qualifying, and was withdrawn.

Luigi Chinetti

Bob Said sits behind the wheel of the 375 Monoposto that he drove at Daytona Beach.

anxious for the safety of Shakespeare entering the race. They need not have worried, as the big Ferrari managed to finish without incident in sixth place.

At over 50 years of age at this point, Chinetti decided to give up his role as a driver, and concentrate on his Ferrari car business interests. Now located at 780 11th Avenue and the corner of 54th Street on the west side of Manhattan, Luigi Chinetti Motors Inc was growing, with an ever-increasing client list for the road cars coming into America from the Ferrari factory.

The 1955 Daytona Beach NASCAR Annual Speed Week presented the opportunity for Luigi Chinetti to enter his 375 Monoposto (0388) for the timed runs along the beach. Bob Said was given the job of driving the car, and set a record of 174mph in one direction, and 170mph as an average in both directions. The following year Bill Holland was given an opportunity to drive the car at Daytona Beach, but he could not exceed 155mph due to the deteriorated state of the beach.

Chinetti's entrepreneurial nature was behind the idea of generating additional interest in

In 1954 Chinetti made his final attempt to repeat his feat of 1951 in the Carrera Panamericana, this time with John Shakespeare in his new Ferrari 375 MM. Shakespeare had ordered the car through Chinetti, who personally drove it from Modena to Genoa where it was put on a boat to Vera Cruz. Shakespeare was a member of the large fishing rod manufacturing family, and Chinetti had to deal with a number of worried people on the telephone,

1

A Bendix publicity photo, showing Chinetti working on a Bendix fuel pump. The photo was used by the company to promote its products.

Luigi Chinetti

Chinetti Sr and Jnr at Luigi Chinetti Motors. Chinetti Sr is standing by a 166 MM (0014 M), which had been made to look like a previous Le Mans winner, 0008. Chinetti Jr is standing alongside a new Ferrari 365 GTB.

Chinetti in a crowd at Le Mans.

the cars, with the best form of advertising he could think of, success on the track. That way the product spoke for itself, and selling the product was that much easier. It didn't take long for the American sports car enthusiasts to realise that the cars Chinetti was selling were closely linked to those winning races at venues such as Bridgehampton and Elkhart Lake. Into the 1960s, victories achieved by NART at international venues such as Sebring, Watkins Glen and Le Mans, served as the most potent advertising tool Ferrari could have. These victories were not public relation stunts put on by Chinetti, the cars did the talking. It was Luigi Chinetti who brought this fact to the attention of the American public, and the road cars sold. The money generated by sales of Ferraris was ploughed back into Chinetti's racing endeavours, and the perpetual cycle started over again.

In an article by Curt Friehs in around 1996 he wrote:

> Chinetti's life spanned more than nine decades. During those years, he meant many things to many people. When viewing such a significant life one can see many positive outcomes: an impressive career as a mechanic, driver and a manufacturer of cars as well as a successful entrepreneur. His impact however goes far beyond his accomplishments.

That one paragraph succinctly sums up who Luigi Chinetti was.

Stress begins to show as Chinetti does battle with the ACO at Le Mans in 1975.

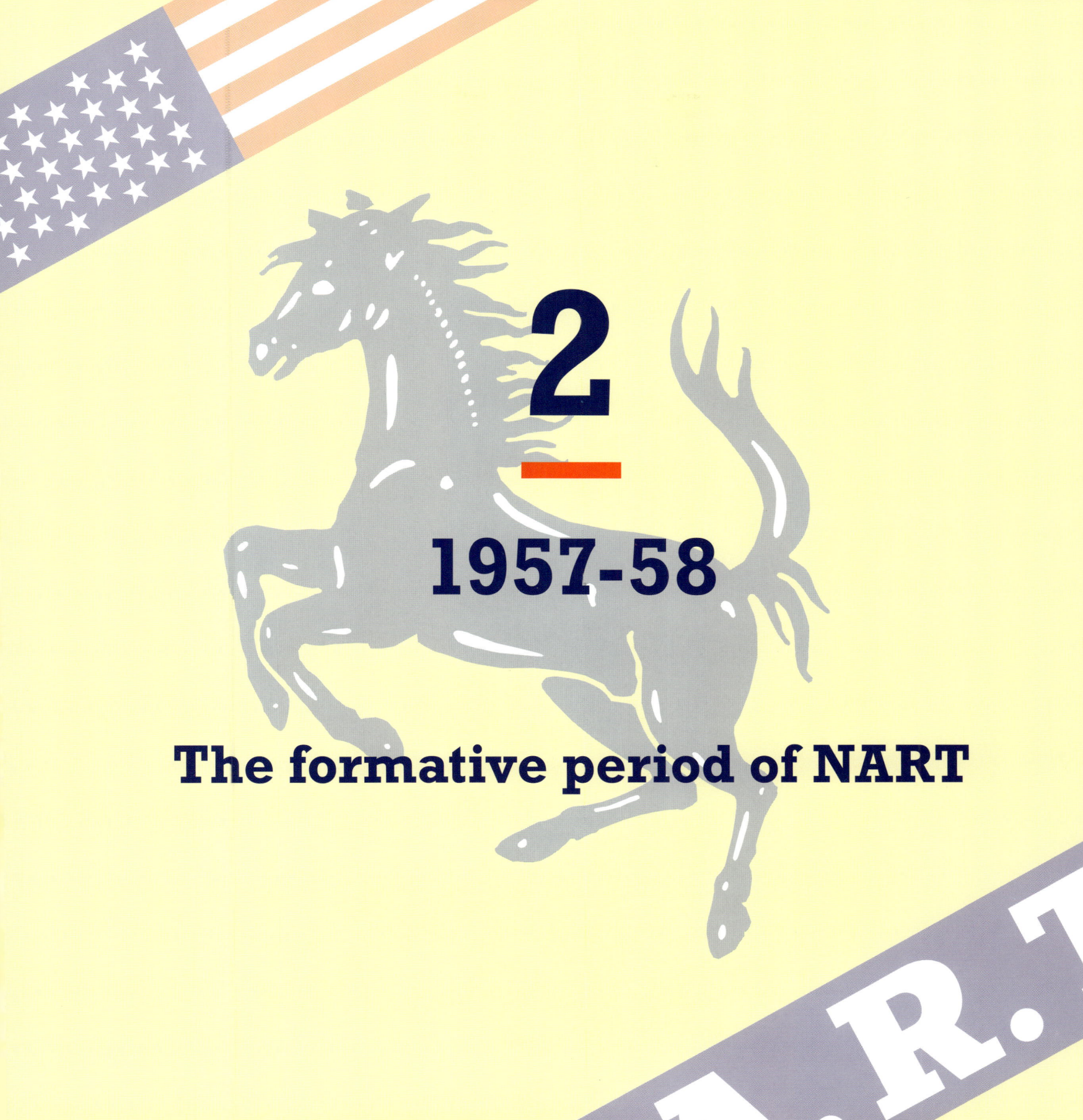

2
1957-58
The formative period of NART

2 | 1957-58

*When was the North American Racing Team officially formed? The question has been asked time and time again, but the answer has not yet been established beyond reasonable doubt, due to the fluid make-up of the organisation.*

Unfortunately, the few people who could have answered this question accurately are no longer alive – co-founders of the North American Racing Team, Luigi Chinetti Sr, George Arents, and Jan de Vroom.

Certain facts are known. NART came about as a confluence of wealthy individuals who wanted to obtain Ferraris to indulge their own egos on the race tracks of America, together with Luigi Chinetti's desire to have enough money to enter creditable drivers in endurance racing. George Arents, through his inherited tobacco empire, and Jan de Vroom, through dubiously acquired wealth, undoubtedly had the money and the enthusiasm to invest in sports cars, though, unfortunately, lacked real driving talent. However, for the cost of underwriting Chinetti's ambitions, they obtained a few of the latest Ferraris, and secured entries at major races such as Sebring and Le Mans, where they raced cars entered by Chinetti and then NART.

Chinetti's financial backers were certainly interesting characters. George Arents Jr was heir to the American Tobacco Company, and a stockholder in American Machine & Foundry. At one time he was married and had children, but in later life he developed a penchant for Ferraris and young boys. George lived in Florida in an impressive Coral Gables mansion with his handsome youthful lover, David Cunningham, a professional racing driver.

He purchased several cars from Chinetti, and paid to enter races along the east coast of America, sometimes with David Cunningham driving the car, promoting the newly-formed NART.

Jan de Vroom was born in Dutch Indonesia, and became a friend of Marquis George de Cuevas in Holland. George was born in Chile, met Margaret Strong in Paris and married her. Margaret Strong was the granddaughter of John Davidson Rockefeller, her mother being Bessie, the eldest of J D Rockefeller's five children. De Vroom was a frequent guest of the Marquis de Cuevas, and it soon became apparent that de Vroom was paying a disproportionate amount of attention to the Marquise.

When Margaret moved to America he followed, and as their friendship grew so did de Vroom's store of acquisitions. Through the misplaced generosity of the Marquise de Cuevas he soon owned an impressive sailing boat, and was able to purchase Ferraris from Chinetti.

De Vroom frequented the seedier sides of New York and Florida, and entertained Margaret with lurid stories of his dalliances with other men. Over the years he became more dependent on alcohol and drugs, and his life ended in an unseemly manner in 1975, when he was murdered in his apartment. He had his throat cut and was stabbed repeatedly (see The People v Greghegan, 66 AD 2d 279).

As Chinetti was not a part of that world, contact with Arents and de Vroom, as his financial backers, would have come through a third party, probably Margaret, Marquise de Cuevas.

The formative period of NART

During the meetings that the author had with Luigi Chinetti Jr, he remarked that "Chinetti Motors and the North American Racing Team were inextricably linked." Certainly there was a large degree of commonality between the two operations, as they shared facilities, manpower and the customer base. Financially it did not conform as a business entity with a licence, therefore did not report income or pay taxes. Indeed, all paperwork relating to the purchase of cars to be entered in races by NART was made out to Luigi Chinetti Motors Inc, and there is no evidence of internal transfers of vehicles or funds to NART. Similarly, all outgoings such as expenses or drivers' prize money, came from Luigi Chinetti Motors Inc. It may have been registered as a trademark with either New York State or the US government, but the registered trademark symbol fails to appear on any documentation.

Long before the formation of NART, Chinetti had been involved in procuring entries to the Le Mans 24-hour race for his clients. In 1951 he entered a 166 MM assigned to Mme Yvonne Simon and Ms Betty Haigh, and in 1952 entered a car for Simon and Vincent. In 1954 Chinetti entered a 375 MM for the celebrated Dominican playboy Porfirio Rubirosa and Italian nobleman Count Innocente Biaggio. The story goes that Count Biaggio's car spun out and bogged down at Tertre Rouge, he alighted from the car and, wearing a light grey alpaca suit, a silk shirt and a black bowtie, set about digging out the car. After an hour of effort he gave up, cleaned his hands, dusted off his trousers and shoes, replaced his hat and lit a cigarette.

Chinetti secured an entry at Sebring in 1955 for Harry Schell and Piero Taruffi to drive a 750 Monza, the car finishing the race in fifth place.

In 1956 the 375 Monoposto (0388) was hired to John Edgar for his leading driver, Carroll Shelby, to drive at three hillclimb events at Mount Washington, Giant's Despair and Breakneck. Shelby produced fastest time of day at each of the venues. Chinetti also leased a 500 TR (0614) to John Edgar, for Shelby to drive at Brynfan Tyddyn, and Shelby racked up another victory.

It was in 1957 when Luigi Chinetti became noticeably active in acquiring entries for clients in endurance road races. The Cuban Grand Prix, held in late February 1957, presented Chinetti with his golden opportunity to come to prominence. A full international field of drivers had been encouraged to attend the Grand Prix, no doubt attracted by the generous amount of prize money available. Whilst some of the cars arrived with their drivers, others were delivered from Italy, via New York, to Havana. The ship USS Independence departed from Genoa on 3 February with three new Ferrari 500 TRCs, two Gordinis and seven Maseratis, bound for New York. The ship was delayed as it approached New York after a report that a person had fallen overboard, and when it finally docked it was 30 minutes before midnight. The US east coast longshoremen's strike was due to start at midnight, so there was just enough time for the passengers and luggage to leave the ship, but no time for the cargo to be taken off, with the stevedores refusing to handle the cargo.

For the days leading up to 22 February the New York dock workers were promising to unload the cargo – and reneged each day despite negotiations. After ten days in port, the captain had no option but to sail back to Genoa, the cargo of cars still intact. With this situation threatening to lead to the cancellation of the

2 | 1957-58

Carroll Shelby won the main race at Brynfan Tyddyn in a Ferrari 500 TR.

Grand Prix in Cuba, the organisers contacted Luigi Chinetti to ascertain if anything could be done to find suitable replacement cars. Within 72 hours of the scheduled start to the event, Chinetti begged and borrowed his customers' cars, and had them transported by air freight to Havana. Cars were still arriving after the official practice sessions had begun, causing confusion for the officials trying to match available cars with an abundance of drivers. It appeared that any car emanating from the east coast of America had Chinetti's name as the entrant on the CSC listings, no matter who owned the car.

In reality, he had responsibility for six Ferraris: de Portago's 860 Monza for Castellotti; William Helburn's 500 TR for Gendebien; Howard Hively's 500 TR for Peter Collins; Chinetti's 375 Plus for Hively and Herman; John Kilborn's 121 LM for Jean Lucas; and de Portago's other 860 Monza. Chinetti arrived in Havana accompanied by six mechanics, one for each of the Ferraris that he was responsible for in the Grand Prix.

Chinetti's credibility was greatly enhanced by his success in providing the cars, and his actions would stand him in good stead with both race organisers and his customers in the near future.

The formative period of NART

Stirling Moss drove the 290 MM (0628) to victory in the Nassau Trophy race, held on the island of New Providence in the Bahamas.

For the Le Mans 24-hour race that year, he entered a Ferrari 290 MM (0616) to be driven by George Arents and Jan de Vroom. They appear to be the right combination of personnel to effect an entry under the NART banner, though no photographic evidence has come to light to suggest the presence of NART lettering or decals on the car. Interestingly the ACO (Automobile Club de l'Ouest) Liste des Concurrents Verifies lists the Arents/de Vroom entry as Ecurie North American R.T. It also verifies that places were allocated to the Ecurie North American R.T. for two Ford Thunderbirds, but these cars never appeared. It was probably pay-back time for Chinetti, giving Arents and de Vroom the opportunity to drive, while more likely candidates to drive the car were sitting in the wings. Chinetti's actions in giving de Vroom and Arents the drive, gives credence to the idea that, on paper, an agreement to form NART had already taken place between the main three players, by the time an application to race at Le Mans was submitted to the ACO. The Arents/de Vroom driver combination did surprisingly well, as they managed to work their way up to seventh place in the 16th hour after being 18th

2 | 1957-58

in the first hour, before being forced to retire the car with insurmountable brake problems. Two magazines refer to Ecurie North America, *Autosport* (June report) and *Auto Italiana* (April report), so the name was in the public domain at that point in time. Although not conclusive, it would appear by weight of evidence that Le Mans 1957 was indeed the first NART entry.

Uncertainty surrounds the origins of the name North American Racing Team. Stories vary and, with the passing of time, truth has become clouded. One story is that the name came about as a result of Chinetti driving down the road and seeing a North American Van Lines truck (as supposedly told by Chinetti in an interview), whereas another view is that the name came about as the result of a discussion around the kitchen table in Chinetti's New York house.

Equal uncertainty surrounded the entry of two cars at Nassau for the Bahamas Speed Weeks in 1957. Gene Greenspun had just purchased a Ferrari 315 S (0684) from Chinetti for a reported $32,000 and Jan de Vroom was present as a late entry in a Ferrari 290 MM (0628), a car that Chinetti had purchased from the factory in August 1957, and then sold to de Vroom later that month. It would appear from the Speed Week entries that de Vroom entered the car in his own name. However, as things transpired, Stirling Moss was without a car for the Nassau Trophy race, and Chinetti stepped in to broker a convoluted deal. He bought back the 290 MM from Jan de Vroom, and contrived a deal whereby he leased the car to the wealthy team owner Temple Buell, who, in turn, engaged Stirling Moss to drive it. Despite all the exchanges of names on paper, Chinetti's mechanics were looking after the Ferrari, as is evident from the story concerning the car driven by Gene Greenspun, a young gentleman driver who had a bank account greater than his talent at the wheel. Chinetti had encouraged Greenspun to attend the Speed Weeks by selling him a race package which included using Chinetti's mechanics.

A pit stop for tyres had been planned about mid-race, and Greenspun arrived in the pits at the appropriate time to be met by listless inactivity. No jacks were whisked under the car, and no mechanics swarmed over it either – Chinetti had used the tyres meant for Greenspun's car on Moss' car instead, a few laps earlier. When Greenspun asked why, Chinetti told him, "because Moss is winning and you aren't!" When the team eventually got around to looking at Greenspun's car, they discovered that the spare tyre was the incorrect size for the car, sent him out again while they found some correct tyres from a car in the car park, and eventually did the tyre change. The fiasco cost Greenspun some nine or ten places, finishing 15th overall.

Greenspun's car was never referred to as being officially entered by NART, although the presence of Luigi Chinetti and his mechanics looking after the car is beyond dispute. However, as entry to Nassau was part of the race package deal with Greenspun, technically Chinetti/NART should take the credit. It was also the ideal opportunity to advertise the fact that Chinetti was in the business of entering major races. Likewise, the 290 MM did not start out as a NART entry at Nassau, but as Chinetti leased the 290 MM to Temple Buell, again, technically, it should be referred to as a Chinetti/NART entry.

While some doubts remain as to the race entries in 1957, it is clearer who actually entered the Ferrari 250 GT TdF (0773 GT) in local east coast SCCA races in America during 1958. Driven by George Arents, the car turned up at Masters Field NAB, Florida, sporting a NART SOUTH decal, the first recorded sighting of a supposed NART entry in competition displaying a decal of any description.

However, doubt as to the authenticity of it being a true NART entry arises, as it was an SCCA event; because the SCCA was an organisation for amateur drivers, it did not pay for car entries into races. Under those circumstances it is doubtful that Chinetti would spend money on preparing and transporting a car for a local SCCA event held in Florida if there was no chance of a monetary return.

More likely was the scenario that Arents, as a resident in Florida, but as a partner within NART, chose to advertise the new racing team, even though he entered the car himself. If nothing else, it gave the foundling team visibility to the established Briggs Cunningham team, which was there in force with three Jaguar D-Types to support the races. Later in the season, Arents entered his car at several other venues on the east coast, displaying the same logo.

There can be no doubt that for the Cuban Grand Prix of 1958, the race entries were in the name of NART, being mentioned in print, with both *Road & Track* and *Motor Racing* referring to that acronym. Three cars came from the Chinetti operation, a Ferrari 335 S (0674) for Stirling Moss, a Ferrari 315 S (0656) for Wolfgang von Trips, and the Nassau Trophy winning Ferrari 290 MM (0628) for Ed Crawford, the latter car being a 'rent-a-drive' entry.

The whole affair was bizarre from start to finish. Politics clashed with sport, but neither emerged as the winner. Fangio was kidnapped by Castro rebels, the governing Batista regime insisted that the incident would not deter it and that the race should still take place. A bad accident involving Cifuentas ploughing into some spectators brought an early ending to the proceedings but, at the time of the accident, the leaders Gregory and Moss were unaware of the situation. Moss said "I was driving around and the next thing I knew there had been an accident and a temporary bridge had fallen down. Someone had produced an unofficial red flag and everybody slowed down. We came onto the start-finish straight with Gregory slightly ahead, and I could see the finish line coming up, so I put my foot down and went past him to take the win." When they stopped, Gregory wasn't too pleased, and said "Now listen, I was in the lead all the time," and Moss retorted "Well, yes, but not when we passed the finish line." They finally agreed that they would pool their winnings and split it. The large winner's trophy awarded to Moss was retained by Chinetti much to Moss' annoyance, as it was his car that crossed the line first.

Von Trips was classified as finishing fourth, while Ed Crawford was in eighth place, though in the confusion even those results are open to conjecture. What was not generally recognised was that the Ferrari 315 S von Trips was driving, actually belonged to Ed Martin, who was due to co-drive with von Trips in the race. Ed Martin had paid Chinetti $13,000 for the car, and had achieved a respectable qualifying time in the car at Havana to run under the NART banner.

It must have been around this time when Luigi Chinetti decided to have an insignia designed. He had ideas of using the black prancing horse used by Ferrari, and obtained Ferrari's permission to use it on a yellow background.

2 | 1957-58

Instead of having the Italian tricolour at the top, he had a dark blue stripe inserted with eight white stars on the blue background, and under the prancing horse was the name: North American Racing Team. Later this insignia was changed to incorporate the American flag across the top, with the initials N.A.R.T. replacing the words North American Racing Team under the prancing horse, as it was thought that the new design had a more immediate visual impact.

One month after the Cuban Grand Prix, the Sebring 12-hour race was run. There were two accepted NART entries to the race, though there should have been a third one. The Ferrari 250 TR (0720 TR) had been sold to James Johnson by Chinetti, and Johnson was promised an entry at Sebring as part of the deal. Through an unfortunate mix-up with the paperwork, his entry was relegated to the reserve category, and the car did not run. The two cars that did run were both race package-type entries, being prepared and maintained by Chinetti at the customers' expense. Neither of the cars' teams of drivers would have gone away disappointed, as the cars finished fifth and seventh overall, first and second in their GT Class. It is interesting to note that the car purported to belong to George Arents was driven by another team of drivers, while Arents joined with Reed and O'Dell to drive Reed's car 0893.

Wolfgang von Trips drove for NART in 1958, finishing fourth in the Cuban Grand Prix in a Ferrari 315 S belonging to Ed Martin, though entered by Luigi Chinetti.

The formative period of NART

The other significant event that happened at Sebring was that Chinetti allowed Dan Gurney four test laps in one of his cars. "I guess I got around all right," said Dan, "because Luigi arranged for me to drive for him at Le Mans with Bruce Kessler, which was an opportunity I'd been afraid to even dream about." Chinetti was widely acknowledged as having a keen eye when it came to spotting and developing driving talent. To him it didn't matter if a promising driver had money or not. If he had, he would have to pay Chinetti to run a NART entry, if not Chinetti would find someone else to foot the bill with a sponsorship deal.

While the racing aspect of Chinetti's business was busy, the retail side was expanding, and in April 1957 the company changed its name to Luigi Chinetti Motors Inc. The SCCA New England regional meeting, held at Thompson Raceway in June, was witness to the inclusion of a NART-owned car to be driven by Gaston Andrey. The Ferrari 335 S (0674) had been leased, provisionally, to Mike Garber, to see how it fared in the hands of Gaston Andrey, and if successful, would be leased for further appearances. Andrey handled the big car well and finished the race in second place behind Harry Carter, driving one of Briggs Cunningham's Jaguar D-Types.

Chinetti had shown a growing interest in the fortunes of two up-and-coming drivers from Mexico, Pedro and Ricardo Rodríguez. Don Pedro was keen that they were entered into the Le Mans race in June, and had approached Chinetti for a car and an entry. Chinetti put his business acumen into play, doing a deal with Don Pedro. Chinetti proposed to Don Pedro that he become an agent in Mexico, finding clients for Chinetti's cars among his rich friends. In return Don Pedro would receive a commission for each car sold, which would be applied to the cost of the race cars for Pedro and Ricardo. It was an arrangement that both parties were happy with. Ricardo had an acceptance letter from the FIA (Fédération Internationale de l'Automobile), stating that he could drive at Le Mans, but the ACO officials dismissed it, and refused to allow Ricardo to drive. It was only when Ricardo had been rejected by the ACO officials at the last moment that José Behra, Jean Behra's brother, was drafted into the NART Team.

The Le Mans 24-hour race had been eagerly anticipated, with NART entering a newly acquired 250 TR for Bruce Kessler and Dan Gurney, a 500 TR for Pedro Rodríguez and José Behra, together with a preparation and maintenance entry for Ed Martin and Fernand Tavano in a 250 TR (0730 TR), rebuilt at the factory in Italy after Chet Flynn's accident at Sebring. Chinetti had planned and submitted two other entries for the Le Mans race. One was for the Rodríguez brothers to drive an OSCA S750, but that was rejected on the grounds that in the organiser's eyes Ricardo was too young to race. The other entry was for Denise McCluggage, but that was also rejected. The head of the organising committee told Chinetti "This is an invitational race and we do not choose to invite women."

NART's new 250 TR was 0666, purchased by Chinetti after the Targa Florio, and rebuilt by the factory. He had anticipated it being ready for Le Mans but, to cover himself, Chinetti had entered another 250 TR (0756 TR), which he withdrew at the last moment when he knew 0666 was available.

The race proved a disaster for the 250 TR. During the evening of Saturday 21 June,

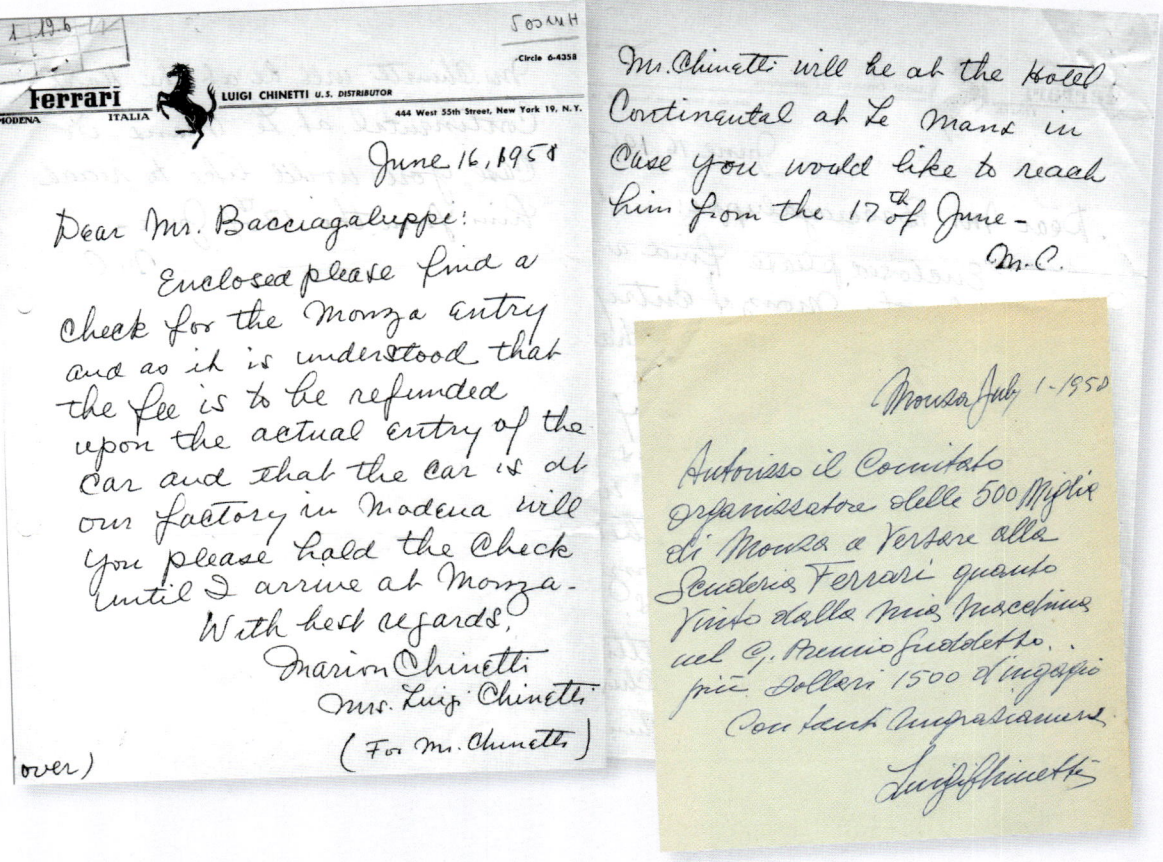

Accompanying letters sent by Marion Chinetti to Monza for the entry of 0388 into the Monza 500 races.

there was a heavy downpour of rain, causing numerous accidents. After six hours of racing, still with intermittent heavy showers, the Gurney/Kessler car, with Kessler at the wheel, had a tremendous collision with a D-Type Jaguar, the driver of which was killed. A fire broke out and although Kessler escaped, his injuries put him in hospital. The car had much of its bodywork burned off in the intense heat.

Dan Gurney, shocked by the accident, confirmed that Kessler could not avoid the crash that put the car out of the race. "But I got another crack at Europe, at Reims I shared a Ferrari with André Guelfi."

The two other NART entries fared no better, the Martin/Tavano 250 TR stopping just after midnight with a cracked cylinder liner which allowed the water to blow out, and the Rodríguez/Behra 500 TR covering 119 laps, before retiring with overheating problems.

The next race for NART involved something completely different for the team, an entry to participate in the 500 Miglia di Monza, held on the banked oval track at Monza. The race was intended as an exhibition event, allowing teams from the USAC National Championship to compete directly against teams from the Formula One World Championship based in

The formative period of NART

Harry Schell was hired to drive 0388 at Monza, his first drive for Chinetti.

Mechanics do a final check on Schell's car before the practice session commences.

2 | 1957-58

- *Harry Schell drives 0388 out onto the circuit for a practice session.*

- *Enzo Ferrari paid a rare visit to the Monza track to inspect Chinetti's entry in the race; the 375 Monoposto (0388).*

Europe. A $1500 cheque secured the entry, returnable upon the arrival of the car at Monza. NART's entry was the Ferrari 375 Monoposto (0388), which was originally intended to be entered for the 1954 Indianapolis 500, and was piloted by Harry Schell. Now fitted with a Type 335 Sport 4.1-litre engine, the car was never really competitive against more modern machinery on the oval banking, and was classified in 13th place after the three-heat race. Faulty magnetos slowed the car in practice, and it was the slowest but one qualifier for the race.

By the beginning of September, Bruce Kessler was back behind the wheel of a sports car. He had leased the ex-Portago Ferrari 860 Monza from NART to run in the USAC organised professional sports car race held at Lime Rock. He was second fastest in practice, earning a spot on the front row of the grid for the 100-lap race. However, while on lap 92 it started to rain quite heavily, and the Connecticut State police insisted that the race be stopped. George Constantine was declared the winner, with Bruce Kessler in second spot ahead of Alan Markelson.

On the same day as the professional race was being run at Lime Rock, the most prestigious SCCA event of the season, the Road America 500, was being run at Elkhart Lake. The track was one of the newer circuits, constructed to replace the old, flat airport circuits, disliked by many of the better drivers. For this race, Mike Garber again leased the Ferrari 335 S (0674) from NART, but this time for both Gus Andrey and Lance Reventlow to drive. Chinetti, however, had a stipulation that the car had to be entered under the NART banner. In return, Garber insisted that any earnings from the race would be his. Both men were hard negotiators. With this car Andréy and Reventlow had more than enough experience and power to deal with any other competition, which they duly did by

The formative period of NART

Gaston Andrey in the paddock at Road America in the Ferrari 335 S that he shared with Lance Reventlow.

Ferrari 335 S (0674), leased by Chinetti to Mike Garber for Gus Andrey and Lance Reventlow to drive at Road America. Lance Reventlow is at the wheel.

finishing in first place. In his first appearance at Road America, Andréy proved to be as capable as reputed, as he took control of the big Ferrari during his driving stint. Andréy and Reventlow completed the 125-lap race in six hours and 18 minutes.

One week later it was Bob Grossman who had an unexpected opportunity to shine at Bridgehampton. Chinetti's Ferrari 860 Monza had been safely returned by Bruce Kessler from Lime Rock, and was now due to appear at Bridgehampton with George Arents driving. However,

2 | 1957-58

Gaston Andrey sits at the wheel of the leased 335 S (0674), the car displaying an early NART decal.

38 | N.A.R.T.

The formative period of NART

Action from the race held at Elkhart Lake with Lance Reventlow driving the 335 S on its way to victory.

Arents was involved in an accident on the new Bridgehampton circuit in 1957, and refused to drive an open top car around Bridgehampton again. As a result Bob Grossman was drafted in to take his place. After failing to finish the first race he took third place in Race 6. Chinetti had a paper badge with his decal on it taped over the USAC decal, so as not to offend the SCCA officials, and to save Grossman from embarrassment.

Andréy's drive at Road America earned him another lease drive with Mike Garber at Watkins Glen in September driving the NART-owned 335 S, this time finishing the feature race in third spot behind the Cunningham Lister-Jaguars of Crawford and Hansgen.

Seven days later, the second USAC-sanctioned professional sports car race in Northeast America, took place at Watkins Glen. Advertised as an International Formule Libre race, it attracted a variety of cars other than sports cars to the event. With a purse of $6000 on offer, it was no surprise to see Dan Gurney and Bruce Kessler turn up with Chinetti's Ferrari

A concise history of the North American Racing Team 1957 to 1983

2 | 1957-58

The Lance Reventlow/Gaston Andrey Ferrari 335 S squeezes past a Ferrari 250 TR driven by Ed Martin at Road America.

The formative period of NART

290 MM and the 860 Monza. Joakim Bonnier won the race in a Maserati 250F, with Dan Gurney picking up $1000 for his second place finish and Bruce Kessler in the 860 Monza $800 for a third.

The 1958 season ended with the Bahamas Speed Weeks held in Nassau. Following the Le Mans race in June, Chinetti purchased the winning Ferrari, a 250 TR (0728 TR) on behalf of the Rodríguez family, with the stipulation that the car would be campaigned as a NART entry.

1958. Gus Andrey and Lance Reventlow won the race at Elkhart Lake in the Ferrari 335 S (0674) loaned by NART.

NART supplied the Rodríguez family with a 250 TR (0728 TR) which Pedro drove at Nassau, finishing second in the Nassau Trophy race. This would prove to be the first of many drives for Pedro under the NART banner.

The car was transported to Nassau for Pedro to drive in four of the races. He finished second in a preliminary race, fourth in the Governor's Trophy, second in the Ferrari race, and second in the Nassau Trophy. The other entry was Mike Garber's Ferrari 335 S, leased from NART for Gus Andréy to drive. After finishing fifth in a preliminary race, he failed to finish in both the Governor's Trophy and the Nassau Trophy.

Gil Geitner was also entered at Nassau with his 500 TRC, and it is most likely that his car was maintained by the NART pit crew, although there is no evidence to suggest that it was a NART entry.

An advert placed in trade magazines by Luigi Chinetti, extolling the race achievements of the 250 TR.

3
1959-61
Expanding horizons

3 | 1959-61

> The first race of the 1959 season where NART entries appeared was the 12-hour race at Sebring, held in March. The Ferrari 250 TR (0666) had been rebuilt by the factory yet again, having a new body and complete mechanical reconstruction, and was delivered to Chinetti in February 1959. Chinetti sold the car to Rod Carveth, but it was entered by NART at Sebring as part of the deal.

Two other cars were entered under the NART banner, a 250 TR (0722 TR), which was a reserve car used by Casner and Hunt in practice, and a 500 TR (0600 MDTR), which Casner, Hunt and Collins used in the race, finishing 13th after 180 laps. Chinetti felt that Hunt was not experienced enough to drive the 250 TR, so opted for the 500 TR instead. Chinetti also entered a 250 TR (0724 TR) for John Fulp. The car ran during practice, but did not start the race.

The Carveth/Geitner car ran consistently in the top ten places until late in the afternoon, when it spluttered to a halt about a mile beyond the pits, out of fuel. Geitner walked back to the pits, and announced he was too tired to continue, leaving Carveth to perform the heroic task of single-handedly pushing the 250 TR the remaining four miles around the circuit back to the pits.

Usually rain is never an issue at Sebring, but when it rains, it rains heavily, and on this occasion it poured. An hour later, as Carveth attempted to squeeze past a slower competitor, he collected a marker barrel full of water for his efforts. The front end of the car was quite badly damaged, and though the sheet metal could be hammered out enough to clear the wheels, the unfixable broken headlights resulted in the track official's refusal to allow the car to continue racing.

Three cars were entered by NART for the Le Mans 24-hour race in June. Carveth and Geitner were there after their race at the Nürburgring with the 250 TR (0666), and were joined by Pilette and Arents in a Ferrari 250 GT LWB (1461 GT). Luigi Chinetti had promised Bob Grossman 'something special' to replace his old 250 LWB California Spyder for Le Mans. It was another LWB California Spyder that cost Grossman $9000, but for that Chinetti entered the car under the NART banner. Grossman and Tavano drove the Ferrari 250 GT California (1451 GT) with a disguised Testa Rossa engine, having only three carburettors instead of six, something which was missed by officials during

Casner practised in the 250 TR (0722 TR) at Sebring, but decided to use the 500 TR (0600 TR) in the race, and finished in 13th place.

Expanding horizons

250 GT LWB California (1451 GT) finished in fifth position at Le Mans driven by Bob Grossman and Fernand Tavano.

Fernand Tavano during his driving stint in the 250 GT LWB California.

3 | 1959-61

■ *Rod Carveth and Gil Geitner had a 250 TR (0666), but the car failed to finish due to a shattered gearbox.*

■ *André Pilette and George Arents drove a 250 GT LWB (1461 GT) to a fourth place finish at Le Mans.*

■ *Bob Grossman and Fernand Tavano finished fifth in the Ferrari 250 GT LWB California in the 24-hour race at Le Mans.*

Expanding horizons

scrutineering. The last two of these managed to uphold Ferrari's reputation, as the factory-entered cars disappeared from the race one-by-one. The Pilette/Arents car finished fourth, covering 296 laps, followed home by Grossman and Tavano covering 294 laps. Carveth and Geitner were not as lucky, covering just 21 laps before retiring the 250 TR, when its gearbox shattered along the Mulsanne straight. A fourth car was submitted for entry in the race by NART, a 250 GT for Lance Reventlow to drive, but the car never attended.

A USAC professional race was run on 25 July at Lime Rock. Pedro Rodríguez had expressed a desire to drive in this race, and asked Chinetti to find him a suitable car. No 250 TRs were available and the 335 S (0764) was being sold to Connell, so Chinetti suggested a Maserati 300S. On race day there was one in the paddock that Rallye Motors had entered for Ed Fuchs, but he did not appear. Chinetti quickly arranged to rent the car for Pedro, saying that he would later buy it if Pedro liked it. On the basis of Chinetti's direct involvement, the entry has been included as a tentative one for Chinetti/NART.

Ferrari was well aware that its competition sports cars were becoming too complicated and expensive to run for privateers, so decided to develop a car with a smaller engine, a 2-litre V6; since May, Ferrari had been running their Dino V6 in international sports car races without any success. Frustrated by their failure, Ferrari sold a 196S model to Chinetti at a very competitive price ($9000) in November 1959. Chinetti did a deal with 'Papa' Rodríguez that involved NART entering the car in major races, and Rodríguez financing the running of the car.

The first outing for the car was at Nassau, for the annual Speed Week races. The car was

Pedro and Ricardo Rodríguez at the Bahamas Speed Weeks held on the island of New Providence.

Ricardo Rodriguez drove the Dino 196S (0776) to a second place finish in the Governor's Trophy preliminary race at Nassau. Pedro's younger brother was already making a name for himself.

3 | 1959-61

Ricardo gets out of the Dino 196S, while Pedro looks on quizzically.

driven by Ricardo Rodríguez, his first outing under the NART banner, while Pedro drove a Ferrari 250 TR (0766 TR) also entered by NART.

The Governor's Trophy preliminary race saw both cars safely through to the proper race, which was split into under- and over-2-litre cars. Ricardo drove to a second place finish in the under-2-litre race, the car's best result to date, while Pedro finished in third spot in the over-2-litre race with the 250 TR. What was to follow was not in the script. While moving the Dino 196S to the paddock, a ham-fisted mechanic shattered the gearbox, and with no spares available at Nassau, the Dino was side-lined for the remainder of the week. Ricardo took over the driving for the Ferrari race in Pedro's 250 TR, finishing second, and Pedro guided the car to 13th in the Nassau Trophy race.

The first race of the 1960 season attended by NART entailed a long journey to Cuba. The North American Racing Team entry originally intended to take two cars, but the Dino 196S was still unavailable because of ongoing work on the gearbox, following its unfortunate mishap at Nassau. The lone entry was the 250 TR for Pedro Rodríguez, while Ricardo was

Expanding horizons

driving a Porsche instead of the intended Dino 196S. Pedro drove well to take the 250 TR into a second place finish, albeit some distance behind the winning car, the Maserati T61 driven by Stirling Moss.

One month later the Sebring 12-hour race took place, but absent from the rank of cars were the Porsche and Ferrari factory teams, due to the conflicting commitments to various fuel companies. Sebring organisers had agreed that Amoco would sponsor the event, and have exclusive rights to supply their products to the competitors. However, Porsche were under contract to BP, and Ferrari to Shell. It was a stalemate which resulted in both Porsche and Ferrari factory teams withdrawing from the event.

For Ferrari it was a case of utilising the resources it already had in America to fill the

1960. The Rodríguez brothers drove the Dino 196S (0776) in the 12-hour race at Sebring.

A seventh place finish was attained by Arents and Kimberly driving the 250 GT SWB (1773 GT) at Sebring.

3 | 1959-61

The 250 GT SWB (1539 GT) was driven by Sturgis and D'Orey, finishing in sixth place.

Ginther and Daigh failed to finish the 12-hour race driving 250 TR 60 (0774 TR).

void. The valuable resource was Luigi Chinetti, who received a little more help than usual with his cars. Ferrari loaned him a 250 TR 59/60 (0774 TR) recently used in the Argentina GP, and Chinetti signed Ginther and Daigh to drive it. He had eight places allocated to him, five of which were officially filled, leaving three open.

There are photographs of a supposedly private entry sporting NART decals. This alone does not confirm its status as a NART entry, as some owners kept the decals on their car long after NART had anything to do with the car. This

Expanding horizons

- The Rodríguez brothers were given a Dino 196S (0776), but failed to complete the race. The car did not stand up to their hard-driving style.

- NART entered an OSCA S 750 for David Cunningham and John Fulp to drive at Sebring. They finished the 12-hour race in 23rd place.

- 1960. The Hugus/Reed Ferrari 250 GT SWB (1785) finished 4th at Sebring.

time it was different, as Gordon Pennington had purchased his 250 GT SWB (1539 GT) from Chinetti just prior to the Sebring event, and had arranged a race package with him to maintain and service the car at Sebring.

Two Porsche 718 RS-60 models filled the top spots after 12 hours of racing, to be followed by Nethercutt's 250 TR 59/60. Pete Lovely brought the car up to third spot from 12th, and could possibly have claimed second, but owner Jack Nethercutt, although a slower driver, insisted on taking the car to the finish himself. He was followed over the line by a group of five Ferrari GTs, led by the NART entries of Hugus and Pabst finishing in fourth, Sturgis and D'Orey in sixth, and Arents and Kimberly in seventh place.

The news was not so good for NART's 250 TR 59/60 (0774 TR), going out with a seized engine after being in second place for a while, the car covering 123 laps, and just as bleak for the Dino 196S driven by the Rodríguez brothers. At the start of the race it ran very strongly and was lying in fourth place, but it was the clutch that let them down after covering 126 laps.

Meanwhile, NART's OSCA S750 was performing well, and with Cunningham and Fulp at the wheel finished in 23rd spot.

The running cost of the Dino 196S owned by Rodríguez was mounting rapidly, but it was repaired in time for NART to send it to Italy to compete in the Targa Florio race in early May. It was to prove another expensive race for 'Papa' Rodríguez. In practice one of the boys put a sizable dent in the backend of the car, and in the race Ricardo bent both ends early on. Pedro then drove the car off the road into an olive grove, followed by a spectacular accident, rolling it over twice to land on its wheels; to his surprise it was still drivable. After making some crude panel repairs he returned it to the pits for Ricardo to take over the driving. Amazingly the

3 | 1959-61

Ricardo and Pedro Rodríguez drove the Dino 196S (0776) at the Nürburgring, but a broken valve meant that they failed to finish the race.

car finished in seventh place. The next stop for the Dino was back at Modena for repairs to its badly dented body.

The Ferrari competition department worked on the Dino 196S and managed to get it to the Nürburgring for the 1000km race on 22 May, the repair bill reported to amount to $6000. The car may have been repaired, but luck was still against the Rodríguez brothers as, after a strong challenge for the Class lead, the engine expired due to a broken valve after the car had completed 31 laps. Prior to retirement, only hasty action in the pit lane saved the car from being destroyed while it was being refuelled. The car had pitted just ahead of Scarlatti's Ferrari, but when refuelling his car, petrol ran onto a hot exhaust pipe with the result that fire broke out immediately. Within seconds, the front of the pit area was alight with running fuel, and the Rodríguez car had to be manhandled away to safety. The Nürburgring would be the final circuit where the Rodríguez brothers drove that car, though not the final time that NART would enter the Dino 196S (0776) in a race.

Back in America, NART's focus had been drawn to a less expensive formula car that was growing in popularity, the Formula Junior car. Chinetti had purchased two OSCAs, and it appears that several drivers were keen to try them out. The only downside to the new Formula Junior cars, was that they were becoming obsolete within weeks of being purchased, as

Expanding horizons

Following its initial appearance at Sebring, NART entered the OSCA S 750 at Le Mans. Bentley and Gordon successfully brought home the car in 18th place.

new improved models became available. Bob Rubin was heard to say "I never realised that I had just bought a car of the month."

Denise McCluggage had already established her credentials as being a more than competent driver, and was first to try one of Chinetti's OSCA FJs at the SCCA Cumberland National meeting held in May. In an outstanding drive she finished in second place, enhancing not only her reputation, but that of the OSCA as well. There were a few moments of uncertainty in the results when, at the end of the race, she was presented with a protest that she had all four wheels off the course at one stage, and should forfeit the race. She countered the protest, stating that she went off avoiding a car that had spun out in front of her. Her explanation was accepted and she retained her second place finish. At the same meeting NART had also arranged an entry for Ed Hugus with his 250 GT SWB (1785 GT), where he finished eighth in his race.

The OSCA Formula Junior car had another outing at the end of May, when Sy Kaback had

A concise history of the North American Racing Team 1957 to 1983

3 | 1959-61

Ricardo Rodríguez was a regular driver for NART, starting in 1959. His youth and limited experience belied his driving ability, and he gained prominence in the motoring world with his skill and bravery. His first victory for NART came at the Bahamas Speed Weeks in 1960.

Expanding horizons

a drive in the race held at Bridgehampton. The OSCA failed to finish in the race.

Three weeks later an OSCA FJ (thought to be 0003) was present at Roosevelt Raceway in the hands of Ricardo Rodríguez, for the running of the Vanderbilt Cup race, comprising two five-lap heats and the final race. C3-Rodríguez went in Heat One, narrowly missing out by a car's length to the winner Walt Hansgen. The final was of 50-lap duration, and Hansgen set off at a blistering pace, followed closely by Ricardo Rodríguez in the OSCA FJ. Hansgen was eventually forced out with a puncture, leaving Ricardo's OSCA in front of the chasing pack. He maintained the lead for about 20 minutes, but then he also had to retire with engine failure. The race was eventually won by Harry Carter driving a Stanguellini.

A month following the endurance race at the Nürburgring, the Le Mans 24-hour race took place. A last minute change in the factory driver pairings saw Pedro Rodríguez recruited to stand in for the injured Allison after his accident at Monaco, leaving Chinetti to decide who would

NART entered an OSCA Formula Junior for Ricardo Rodríguez at Roosevelt Raceway for the Vandebilt Cup race. After finishing second in the preliminary race, he failed to finish in the main race.

Ricardo Rodríguez and André Pilette secured a second place finish at Le Mans driving 250 TR (0766 TR).

A concise history of the North American Racing Team 1957 to 1983

3 | 1959-61

250 GT SWB (1759 GT) finished in seventh place at Le Mans, driven by Ed Hugus and Augie Pabst.

NART's 250 GT California (2015 GT), driven by Sturgus and Jo Schlesser, failed to finish at Le Mans.

partner Ricardo Rodríguez in the 250 TR (0766 TR) at Le Mans, in one of five entries by the North American Racing Team. The decision was to use André Pilette, a reliable driver who had partnered Arents for NART, to a fourth place finish at Le Mans the previous year. In addition NART would enter three cars in the GT category and an OSCA S750. Ferrari's overall supremacy was confirmed by having six out of the first seven cars to cross the line, including three cars entered by NART, in a race that started in the rain and finished in blazing sunshine. The

Expanding horizons

Rodríguez/Pilette car finished in second place, only four laps down on the winning Ferrari, the Arents/Connell 250 GT SWB was fifth, and the Hugus/Pabst 250 GT SWB seventh. The OSCA S750 driven by Bentley and Gordon finished in a commendable 18th place, while the Sturgis/Schlesser 250 GT SWB California covered 253 laps, before having to retire with engine failure while lying in 11th place.

The 250 GT SWB had been built to the order of Luigi Chinetti, and appears to have used the chassis of an intended 250 GT SWB

1960. John Fulp in action with the Ferrari 500TRC at Bridgehampton in the August meeting.

John Fulp drove NART's 500 TRC (0702 MDTR) at Bridgehampton in August. It was to become a habit for him to rent cars from Chinetti.

3 | 1959-61

OSCA S 750 (768) was rented by Fulp for the Bridgehampton races in August. The Le Mans race number has been taped over for the event.

competition Berlinetta, with an aluminium Spyder body fitted and the latest type 168B engine. Having been seconded to the Ferrari factory team from NART, Pedro found it particularly galling that he was out of the race in the second hour, due to a fuel miscalculation by the Ferrari team which left him stranded on the circuit.

The August meeting at Bridgehampton has traditionally been the Interclub Championship, a fun event held for the benefit of Boys Harbor, a charity home for wayward youngsters. 1960 saw NART enter three cars as a team. John Fulp used the NART OSCA S750, previously used at Le Mans by Bentley and Gordon, and a Ferrari 500 TRC (0702 MDTR), while George Arents was entered in a Ferrari class DM car, probably his 250 GT SWB (1931 GT). Lack of detail in both the entry list and the newspaper reports prevents positive identification. As neither driver appears in the brief results shown, it is assumed that they failed to make the top three places in their respective races.

The Road America 500 was run in September, and for this event two cars were entered by NART, one being a 250 TR59/60 model. When the world sports car championship had ended for 1960, the Ferrari factory decided to sell off the 250 TR59/60 De Dion version team cars, though it retained the IRS versions. One car (0774 TR) was purchased by Eleanor Von Neumann for Phil Hill to race on the west coast, while Chinetti purchased the other car (0770 TR). Wuesthoff/Pabst was entered as a 'rent-a-drive,' giving Chinetti the opportunity to assess the car, prior to putting the next part of his plan for it into operation. The car performed below expectations, partly due to the lack of time to adjust the gearing for the Road America track, finishing second to the Maserati T61 driven by Dave Causey and Luke Stear by 38 seconds. The other NART entry was a Ferrari 500 TR driven by David Cunningham, John Fulp and George Constantine, finishing in 15th spot.

Not overly concerned with the performance of the car at Road America, Chinetti went ahead with his idea to offer the 0770 TR to the Rodríguez family. Supposedly, it was to be sold to the Rodríguez family as part of a convoluted deal. Chinetti had commissioned the construction of a special 250 TR that would also be driven by Pedro or Ricardo at Nassau alongside the 0770 TR, with 'Papa' Rodríguez buying whichever of the two cars was the quickest. Part of the deal was that Chinetti would take the older 250 TR (0766 TR) in part exchange, as he already had a customer lined up for that car.

As promised, Chinetti's 250 TR 'special' (0746) arrived from Ferrari in time for the Bahamas Speed Weeks. The car turned out to be a re-creation of an original V6 Dino constructed in 1958. It had appeared at Silverstone that year, then was re-engineered to house a V12 engine, becoming a Testa Rossa. After appearing at the Nürburgring, it lay at the factory in an inoperative state for the next two years. When it appeared at Nassau it had a Fantuzzi built TR60 body, and was right-hand drive. Ricardo Rodríguez drove the car in the 102-mile Governor's Trophy race, scoring an easy but deserved win, while Pedro was less fortunate. Whilst battling for the lead on the first lap, Jeffords and Constantine collided, with Jeffords spinning and stopping in the middle of the track directly in the path of the fast approaching Pedro Rodríguez. Pedro had no chance to stop and smashed into the broadside Maserati, with the result that both drivers were out of the race.

In the main event, the Rodríguez brothers shared 0746. Knowing they would have to stop to refuel, Pedro set off at a blistering pace, trying to build up a lead to compensate for the refuelling stop. When it did occur they were powerless to stop Gurney's Lotus 19 taking the lead, and despite Ricardo's spirited attempt to catch him, had to settle for a second place finish. NART had also entered an OSCA S750 with Tom Fleming at the wheel, but the car failed to finish, going out on lap 38. Ricardo had also organised the final round of the Pan American Formula Junior race at Nassau. NART entered an OSCA FJ for Ricardo Rodríguez to

3 | 1959-61

Tom Fleming had rented NART's OSCA S 750 for the Bahamas Speed Weeks. The car failed to finish in the Nassau Trophy race.

Ricardo Rodríguez won the Governor's Trophy race at Nassau in 250 TR (0746 TR), and the car finished second in the Nassau Trophy.

Expanding horizons

Good friends and keen rivals, Ricardo Rodríguez and Stirling Moss pose for the camera.

drive, but he only lasted for three laps before having to retire the car.

1961 was a time of optimism for Luigi Chinetti. His friendship with Enzo Ferrari, together with his business acumen, resulted in him having access to a ready supply of ex-factory run competition cars from Ferrari, and enabling him to retain the better drivers. The first event of the season witnessed no less than seven NART entries accepted by the Sebring organisers for the annual 12-hour race.

The Rodríguez brothers were driving the 250 TR 'special,' and there were three Dino 246S models backing up the factory effort. In the GT category there was a 250 GT California and a 250 GT SWB, and in the small class sports cars an OSCA S1000.

3 | 1959-61

Ed Hugus (standing) and Alan Connell with their Ferrari, prior to the start of the 12-hour race at Sebring.

Hall and George Constantine drove Dino 246S (0784) at Sebring, finishing in seventh place.

It was the Rodríguez brothers who presented the strongest challenge to the Ferrari factory cars, so much so, that they led the race for long intervals throughout the 12 hours. With a two-lap lead, a malfunctioning generator cost them dearly, as the headlights dimmed. A 17 minute delay in the pits resulted in the car re-entering the race in third spot, too far behind the leader for even Ricardo Rodríguez to make up the distance. Jim Hall and George Constantine shared a high-tailed Dino 246S used in the Argentina GP in 1960, finishing seventh, while the Dino 196S of Helburn/Fulp/Hudson was 18th overall, winning its class

Expanding horizons

250 GT SWB (2455 GT) failed to finish the 12-hour Sebring race.

The 250 GT SWB (2455 GT) looking the worse for wear resulted in withdrawal from the race.

3 | 1959-61

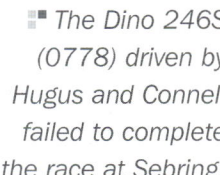
■ Pedro and Ricardo Rodríguez attained a 3rd place finish in the NART-entered Ferrari 250 TR 59/60 (0746) at Sebring.

■ The Dino 246S (0778) driven by Hugus and Connell failed to complete the race at Sebring.

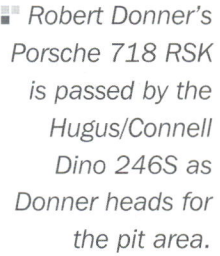
■ Robert Donner's Porsche 718 RSK is passed by the Hugus/Connell Dino 246S as Donner heads for the pit area.

despite numerous pit stops to sort out constant problems. The Hugus/Connell Dino 246S had to retire with gearbox failure, after covering less than 100 laps, as did the OSCA S1000 driven by Cunningham and Price. In the GT category the Pabst/Newman/Andréy/Publicker 250 GT SWB California finished second in class, but the 250 GT SWB (2455 GT) driven by Arents and Tavano failed to finish. The 250 GT SWB was a lightweight alloy-bodied car, and had been purchased from Chinetti by Colonel Price, with the idea that his son, Kent Price, would share the driving at Sebring. Chinetti thought about it and changed his mind, and the car was turned over to Arents and Tavano to drive. The car sustained body damage on the very first lap, and then, with the race less than half over, it succumbed to differential failure. That, Colonel Price, is what you get for $7200.

The Sebring result sheets show Andréy, Newman and Publicker as the drivers of Ferrari 250 GT SWB California (2015 GT), but neither Newman nor Publicker actually got to drive the car. Chinetti had told Pabst and Andréy to attend Sebring, but at the last moment were assigned to 2015 GT, leaving Publicker and Newman to watch from the pit wall. After the race, as a NART mechanic drove the car from the racing pits back to one of the old airport hangers, one of the rear axle components broke. Had the part failed five miles earlier, 2015 GT would have been among the non-finish cars in the 12-hour event.

At the Cumberland SCCA meeting in May, Sy Kaback rented an OSCA FJ from Chinetti, finishing in 11th place in his race.

For the race at the Nürburgring in late May the Ferrari factory loaned NART a 250 TRI 61

Expanding horizons

(0780 TR), and it was entered for the Rodríguez brothers to drive. The factory also supplied mechanics to prepare the car and perform pit stop duties. Chinetti's main hope was that they would perform better than at recent events, when the Ferrari pit crew looked shambolic. He had also spent some time advising the Rodríguez brothers on the tactics they should adopt in this gruelling race. It appeared to pay off as the car finished in second place despite a late scare, when the right front wheel broke entering the Karusel. Ricardo limped around to the pits where the wheel was changed, and he completed the final two laps to finish less than a minute behind the lead car, the Maserati T61 driven by Gregory and Casner.

The Rodríguez brothers were given the 250 TRI 60 (0780 TR) to compete in at the Nürburgring. The car finished in second place.

3 | 1959-61

The Moynett/Vidilles DB spins in the Esses at Le Mans in front of the Ferrari 250 GT SWB driven by Arents and Reed.

NART's 250 TRI 61 (0792 TR) makes its way through the Esses at Le Mans, driven by one of the Rodríguez brothers.

Le Mans 1961 was not a success for the North American Racing Team. Of the five entries, only one completed the 24-hour race. An explanation for the car that did finish is necessary, because of some unusual circumstances which surrounded its entry at Le Mans. The records show that Ferrari 250 GT SWB (2731 GT) finished in sixth place, though press reports are confused when it comes to ownership and entry of the car in the race.

Expanding horizons

- 250 GT SWB (2725 GT) driven by Arents and Reed failed to finish in the 24-hour race due to electrical trouble.

- Either Arents or Reed driving the 250 GT SWB (2725 GT) through the Esses.

- Grossman and Pilette drove 250 GT SWB (2731 GT) to a sixth place finish at Le Mans.

3 | 1959-61

Stirling Moss and Graham Hill were disappointed at having to retire their 250 GT SWB early on Sunday morning, with a broken radiator hose that caused the engine to overheat.

The facts are that 2731 GT raced in the colours of Equipe Nationale Belge, and was entered under its name. However, the car remained the property of Luigi Chinetti (NART), who nominated Bob Grossman to drive it and Belgian driver André Pilette to join him.

It was an example of cooperation between two major Ferrari representatives. For this race Chinetti only had two places allocated in the GT category, but had three cars available. On the other hand Swaters had a place free, but lacked a suitable car, thus the union came about. Technically it can be seen as a joint effort between the two teams, and as such has been included in this book.

None of the other cars fared as well, with the Rodríguez brothers going out after completing 305 laps in the 250 TRI 61 (0792 TR) loaned to NART by the Ferrari factory, with the factory pit staff in attendance. It was not a happy arrangement for Ferrari or Chinetti, as both wanted to deploy their own tactics for the race.

It could be said that Ferrari team manager, Tavoni, actually hindered the progress of work on the NART car, in favour of the works team. After 22 hours the end finally came for the car, when it rolled into the pits trailing oily smoke. A quick inspection revealed a hole in the side of the block, where a piston rod had exited.

The OSCA S1000 driven by Hugus and Cunningham went out with clutch trouble, after covering 125 laps, while the 250 GT SWB alloy-bodied car (2735 GT), driven by Moss and Graham Hill, retired with a broken radiator hose. The Arents/Reed 250 GT SWB alloy-bodied car (2725 GT) had electrical problems, which caused them to retire after just 76 laps. There may well have been some justice in this, as in practice Arents blew the engine in 2725 GT, a piston rod coming through the side of the block. The engine was craned out of the car and a spare 250 TR engine installed, and to make it legal the carburettors were changed. To cover its tracks it would appear that NART may well have restamped the block, since the car had been through scrutineering, and this number was noted on all the paperwork.

The disappointment of Le Mans had not dampened the enthusiasm of George Arents, so while the 250 GT SWB (2725 GT) was in Europe, the car (still with donor engine) was entered into the Pescara 4-hour race. Consistent, rather than exciting, progress culminated with the car finishing fourth overall, first in the GT category against some modest opposition.

The first Canadian Grand Prix for sports cars, held at Mosport in the autumn of 1961, gave Chinetti the opportunity to display his influence and authority, when it came to supplying top quality cars and drivers to attract public support for an event. British Empire Motor Club official George Moss was given the task of putting a field together for the Grand Prix, not an easy task considering the SCCA in America was still against its membership entering professional sports car races and receiving any appearance or prize money. Recalling Chinetti's success in getting together a group of cars in 1957 for the Cuban Grand Prix, George Moss arranged to visit Chinetti in New York to see if a deal could be struck for some Ferraris to appear at Mosport. The meeting was conducted in Chinetti's office at his modest premises. The introductions over, Chinetti got down to the crux of the matter, appearance money.

"How much will you pay?" was Chinetti's opening gambit. "How many cars can you bring?" was Moss' retort. "As many as you need," Chinetti responded. A figure of six was agreed upon, and for that amount Moss agreed to pay $7500 appearance money, $4000 up front, with the remainder in cash by midday on race day.

On the day Moss arrived with the money as agreed, and handed it to Chinetti, who promptly handed it back. "I trust you, take the money, give me a cheque," said Chinetti. A unique bond had been forged between Chinetti and Moss, one that would serve them both well over the forthcoming years.

A group of eight cars entered by NART arrived for practice at Mosport. Among them, the six Ferraris promised by Chinetti, including the Le Mans winning car (0794 TR) with modified bodywork, recently purchased by Chinetti for Pedro Rodríguez to drive. According to an unverified source, the car was purchased for $12,000. Ricardo had the Ferrari Dino 246S sporting a hybrid body, the tail having the 1961 shape, but the front having the single opening.

3 | 1959-61

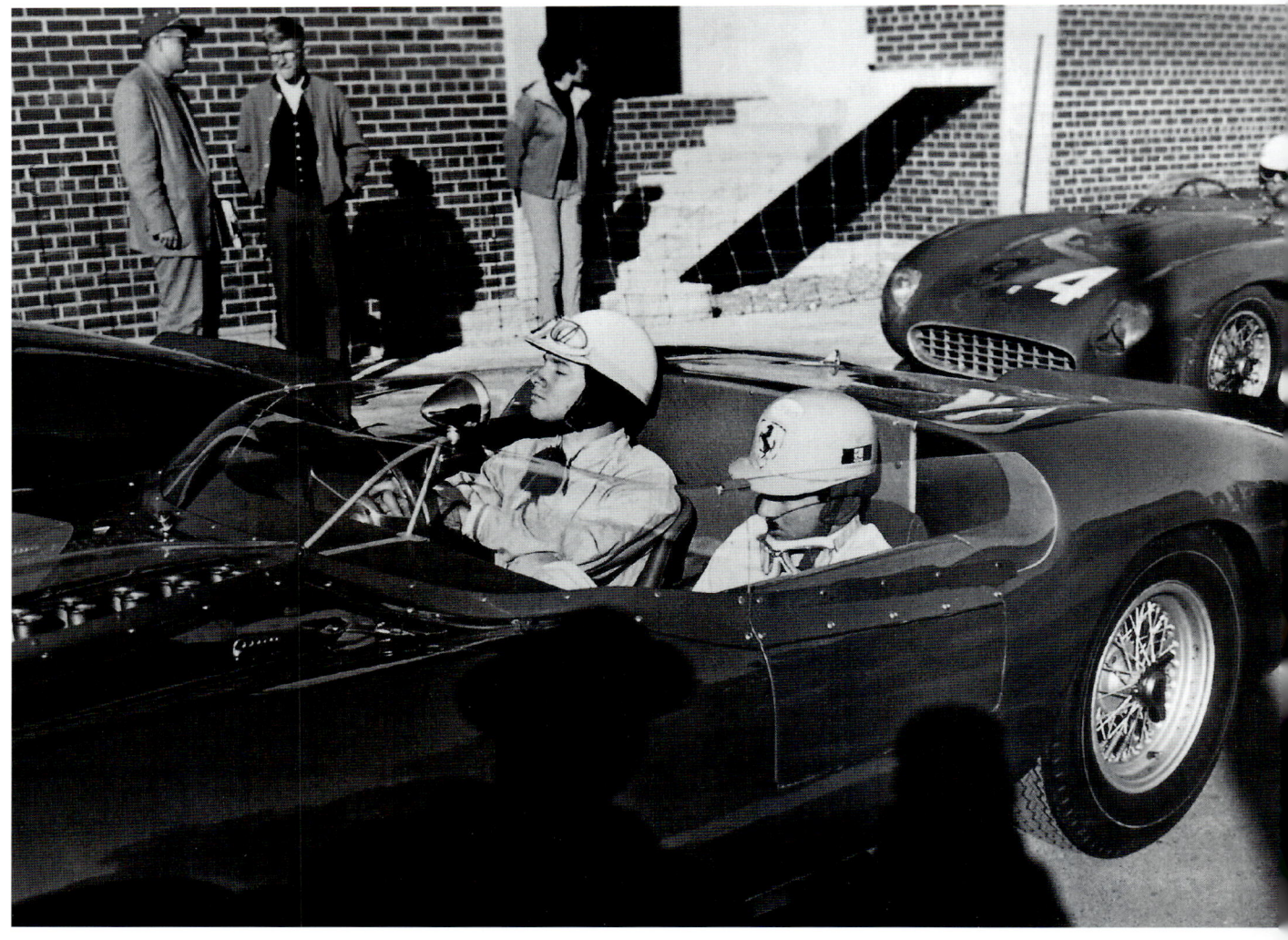

The Rodríguez brothers take a moment to relax at Mosport.

The Rodríguez brothers were a big enough attraction that the Canadian Automobile Sports Club's roll-bar rule was effectively waived, to allow them to race the Ferraris in the Grand Prix. The president of the CASC, Jim Gunn, had to agree that "the fact that neither of the Rodríguez brothers' heads reached the top of the back of the car, suggested that there was probably a roll-bar built in there somewhere." Constantine and Reed both had 250 TRs, while Fulp drove 0778, the Dino 246S that had failed to finish at Sebring earlier in the year. As an extra, Chinetti produced an OSCA S1000 for Toronto driver Fred Hayes, and an OSCA S2000 for Ray Heppenstall to drive. The sixth Ferrari was a 250 GT SWB for Bob Grossman to run in the production car race, where he piloted the car to an easy victory.

Ferrari did not have its own way in the main event, with three Lotus Monte Carlo models in the field. Initially Moss and Gendebien's Lotuses were dominating the race between them, with

Ryan's Lotus in third place, and Pedro Rodríguez trying to keep in touch. As the race progressed to the halfway stage, cars began dropping out. Ricardo Rodríguez's Dino blew the engine, Moss was in trouble, stuck in third gear, and Gendebien retired with the crown wheel and pinion having broken. This left Ryan in the lead, with Pedro Rodríguez remaining in second place until the end of the race. Constantine brought the 250 TR home in fourth place, with Reed's 250 TR in fifth, only to be disqualified for a pit infringement. Fulp finished sixth, while a spirited drive earned Fred Hayes a ninth place finish in the OSCA S1000.

Two weeks following the Mosport event, Ricardo Rodríguez was in California at the Riverside Raceway with the 250 TRI 61 (0794 TR). Although finishing in second place at Mosport, the 250 TRI61 had sounded rough, and at Riverside the consequences were plain to see, as Rodríguez failed to qualify the car for the Times GP. A consolation race had been arranged to sort out the back of the field for the Times GP, but the 250 TRI61 appeared to be suffering from differential, steering and breathing problems, and dropped out of the consolation race after only two laps.

The car was due to go to Laguna Seca the following weekend, but NART thought better of it, and had the car transported back to New York, so that it could be made ready for the Bahamas Speed Weeks at the beginning of December.

Towards the end of October, the Rodríguez brothers had been entered for the 1000km race at Montlhéry by NART in a field that had 11 other Ferrari 250 GT SWBs. Directly competing against them were three Aston Martins and seven Porsche models. Most of the race was dominated by the Ferraris, with a group of five of them, including the NART car, taking turns to lead the field. As the race approached its climax, Ricardo took the wheel at the final pit stop, with the car in second place some 45 seconds behind that of Mairesse. A puncture resulted in Mairesse making an unscheduled pit stop that cost him the race, as Ricardo passed him to regain his position at the head of the field, and take the chequered flag.

Chinetti had requested six places in the entry list for the Bahamas Speed Weeks, the first three submissions were for the Rodríguez brothers and John Fulp, the latter driving a Dino 246S (0778). It is unclear who the other three were, but it is likely that Allan Newman and George Constantine were two candidates for the places.

For the Governor's Trophy race, Rodríguez was in the 250 TRI 61 that had caused so many problems at Riverside, Fulp in the Dino 246S and Allen Newman was in his 250 GT SWB California. Ferraris dominated the race, with Pedro Rodríguez driving the 250 TRI 61, and easily capturing first place. Fulp finished in fourth place but Newman was forced to retire his car.

The main race of the week was the Nassau Trophy race, and five NART-entered cars were on the Le Mans-style start grid. Pedro Rodríguez was in the 250 TRI 61 again, while Ricardo was in the Dino 246S (0784), with Fulp alongside him in the other Dino 246S (0778). George Arents took over the driving duties in the 250 GT SWB California, and Constantine was driving his 250 TR59/60. Try as he might, Pedro Rodríguez could not keep up with race winner Dan Gurney's Lotus XIX, as Gurney made less stops to refuel. Rodríguez finished in third spot

Expanding horizons

▪▪ *Success for the Rodríguez brothers at Montlhéry where they piloted the 250 GT SWB 3005 GT to victory.*

▪▪ *The Rodríguez brothers do not appear to be enjoying the weather at Montlhéry.*

3 | 1959-61

◼ *Ricardo Rodríguez failed to finish in the Nassau Trophy race driving Dino 246S (0784).*

◼ *Stirling Moss and Graham Hill joined forces to drive a Ferrari 250 GT SWB at Le Mans in 1961. Moss first drove under the NART banner in 1958 at the Bahamas Speed Weeks, winning the Nassau Trophy race, whilst Le Mans 1961 was the first drive Graham Hill had for NART.*

◼ *Arents and Newman drove the 250 GT California at the Bahamas Speed Weeks, where Arents finished 26th in the Nassau Trophy race. Arents was not a fan of open-top cars.*

behind Roger Penske, while Constantine was sixth and Fulp eighth. Arents was down in 26th place, and freely admitted that he did not like the flexing of the car's body, making it, in his opinion, unsuitable for racing. The unfortunate Ricardo Rodríguez lost oil pressure in his Dino 246S, and was forced to retire after completing 25 laps of Oakes Field.

4
1962-64
NART diversifies

4 | 1962-64

 The classification of cars in endurance racing was introduced in 1962. The cars were categorised into two main sections: the Experimental class (called Prototype from 1963 onwards) and the GT class. These were then subdivided into other classes, depending on engine displacement.

In the GT category it was the largest of the displacement classes that Ferrari was interested in, and the factory made sure that 250 GT SWB and 250 GTOs were available for the private teams to use, so as to win the category for Ferrari.

Chinetti's busy race schedule for 1962 started with the Daytona 3-hour race held in February, with six cars entered in the event. NART had F1 World Driver Champion Phil Hill in a Dino 246 SP (0796), while Stirling Moss was in a special-bodied version of a 250 GT SWB (2643 GT) loaned to NART by UDT-Laystall. Hill shared his car with Ricardo Rodríguez, who also drove a 250 TRI 61 (0794), with Peter Ryan. John Fulp and Skip Hudson were in a Dino 246 SP (0784), Roberts in a 250 GT SWB (2725 GT), and Grossman and Thiem also in a 250 GT SWB (3005 GT). Hill's car (0796) was on loan from the Ferrari factory, and Chinetti was invoiced $5645 for the use of it. Chinetti's overall selection of cars reflected the fact that the major prize for car builders would be awarded to Grand Touring cars in 1962, not to the sports/racing cars as in the previous years.

The race began with a Le Mans type start, with the cars travelling in a counter-clockwise direction for the first time. Roger Penske's Cooper Monaco took an early lead followed by Phil Hill and Ricardo Rodríguez, that is, until Rodríguez blew a tyre on the 250 TRI 61. He limped back to the pits for a wheel change and to check for damage, losing a substantial amount of time. Hill's first fuel stop was poorly executed, and he had to stop again to have the fuel filler cap closed, costing him valuable time. Roberts also had a problematic pit stop, as the pit crew appeared overstretched.

Meanwhile, Moss had been driving smoothly in his 250 GT SWB, and was mixing it with the sports/racer class bringing his car up to fourth place. In the final part of the race, a struggle was witnessed between Ricardo Rodríguez (now in Hill's 246 SP from lap 45 onwards), and Jim Hall's Chaparral. The struggle went Ricardo's way as he took second place, and began chasing the lead car driven by Dan Gurney. Rodríguez did not immediately realise that Gurney had stopped just short of the finish line with a blown engine, about ten minutes from the end of the race. Try as he might, he fell just short of making up the distance, and, as the time elapsed, Gurney nudged the car over the finish line with the aid of the starter button. Moss did well to maintain his fourth position and win the Grand Touring class, the next GT car to finish being the 250 GT SWB driven by Roberts in 12th place. The 250 TRI 61 finished 15th after its long delay in the pits, and the Thiem/Grossman car finished in 18th spot.

It was a busy time for the NART pit personnel attending the Sebring 12-hour race, having nine cars to deal with. On paper the team had an abundance of machinery and drivers to compete for the Constructors' Championship event, and Chinetti decided to assign the Rodríguez brothers and the pairing of Moss and Ireland the task of being the 'hares' in

NART diversifies

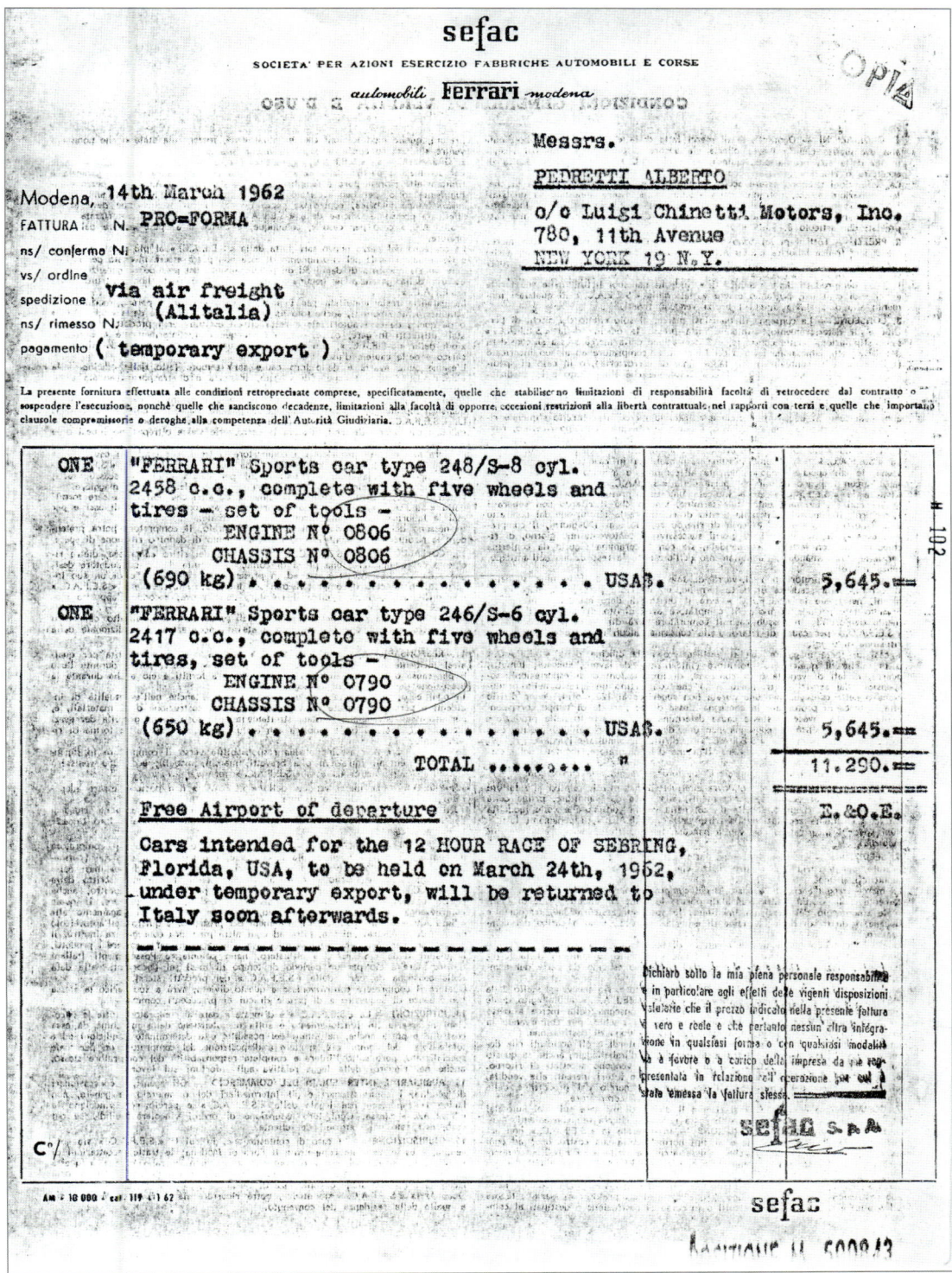

This pro-forma invoice was issued by Ferrari for the loan of two cars to NART for use in the Sebring 12-hour race.

an endeavour to split up the field. Backing these pairs were Ryan and Fulp in a Dino 248 SP, and Grossman and Connell in a Dino 246S. Moss and Ireland were originally going to drive the 248 SP, but after trying out their car decided to swap it for the 250 TRI 61, originally to be driven by Fulp and Ryan. The GT class would be contended by Phil Hill and Oliver Gendebien in a 250 GTO, together with two 250 GT SWB cars driven by Hayes/Haas/Dietrich and Hammill and Serena.

Two cars were on loan to the North American Racing Team: the Dino 248 SP (0806) and the Dino 246 SP (0790) now with 1962-style bodywork. They were shipped to America by the Ferrari factory for Chinetti to enter into the 12-hour race. For this privilege, Chinetti had to pay the factory $5645 for each car. As the 246 SP was being financed by Don Pedro Rodríguez for his two sons to drive, undoubtedly the charge for the loan of the car would have been passed on to him. Chinetti also purchased the 250 GTO (3387 GT) from the factory for $5500. It was not unusual for Chinetti to buy late-model hand-me-downs from the factory and, to a degree, had to trust that they were not recycled wrecks, carried weak engines or rewelded gearboxes. It was probable that money changed hands to ensure that it did not happen. To complete the NART entries, there were two OSCAs in attendance: an S1000 model for McCluggage and Eager, and a 1600 GT (007) for Publicker and Litchie.

The Le Mans-style start resulted in Innes Ireland taking the lead, and holding it for half an hour before the Rodríguez brothers' car took up the mantle. It stayed that way until the halfway stage of the race, when the engine of the V6 seized and the Ireland/Moss car went back into the lead. The Rodríguez brothers took over another NART car, the third place car of Grossman and Connell. They moved to second place after the controversial disqualification of the Ireland/Moss car and stayed there, four laps behind the leader, until the clutch failed in the ninth hour.

The Moss/Ireland disqualification came at the seven-hour thirty-minute mark, more than three hours after the infraction. The rule violation came just after the four-hour mark, when Ireland came in for new brake pads. "Can't drive the bloody thing without brakes you know," Innes said. However, during the stop an SCCA official broke the seal placed over the fuel filler cap, and the man on the fuel hose, seeing the open seal, dumped fuel into the tank. The rules only allowed refuelling at intervals of 20 laps or more. Everyone assumed that this stop occurred on schedule, and the tank was topped up. It then came to the officials' notice that the car had only completed 18 laps since its last stop for fuel. Lengthy heated discussions between Chinetti and the officials took place, and it took the officials over three hours to make their final decision, which was to disqualify Ireland and Moss, even though the infraction had in part been caused by the official's error. The only printable part of Stirling Moss' reaction was "NART were hopeless. They had nine cars in the race and didn't keep a lap chart. It seems quite unbelievable but this was so. Their pit organisation was a joke."

With the demise of the Rodríguez brothers, the Serenissima team 250 TR 61 inherited a considerable lead to take victory ahead of the Gendebien/Hill 250 GTO (which gained

Continued on page 83

NART diversifies

- Stirling Moss used all of his expertise to pilot the 250 GT SWB (2643 GT) to a fourth place finish at Sebring.

- Dino 246S (0784) was driven by Bob Grossman, Alan Connell and Pedro Rodríguez, but failed to finish at Sebring, having covered 168 laps.

- Hayes, Haas and Dietrich drove the 250 GT SWB (3327 GT) to a lowly 34th place finish in the 12-hour race after sustaining accident damage.

4 | 1962-64

Pedro Rodríguez drove the Dino 246 SP at Sebring with his brother Ricardo, but the car failed to finish.

The 3387 GT seen at speed during the 12-hour race where the GTO finished a creditable second.

NART diversifies

- Phil Hill and Oliver Gendebien sit on the pit wall and take a moment to reflect on the race ahead.

- Dino 246 SP (0806) was driven by Fulp and Ryan, finishing in 13th place following a number of delays.

- Innes Ireland sits in the 250 TRI 61 (0794 TR), which was later disqualified for a fuelling infraction. Innes was a hard driver, and played hard as well.

4 | 1962-64

Innes Ireland on track driving the 250 TRI 61 (0794 TR) at speed during the 12-hour race at Sebring.

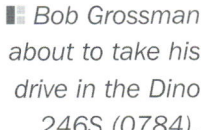 *Bob Grossman about to take his drive in the Dino 246S (0784).*

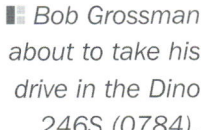 *Dino 246S (0784) sported extra driving lights, but these were not required as the car failed to finish the race in the ninth hour.*

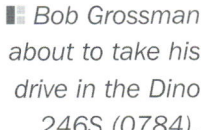 *The two Rodríguez brothers started the race in the Dino 246S (0790), but the car failed to make it to the finish due to a seized engine.*

NART diversifies

An MGA gives way to let the Hill/Gendebien 250 GTO through on its way to a second place finish.

Innes Ireland made a cameo appearance for NART at Sebring when driving with Stirling Moss. Their car was disqualified for a refuelling infraction.

Denise McCluggage was already an accomplished driver before having the loan of NART's OSCA FJ in 1960. She was one of only two drivers to compete in a 275 NART Spyder, co-driving with Pinkie Rollo at Sebring in 1967.

maximum Championship points), while Serena and Hammill finished a respectable fourth overall. Fulp's 248 SP ran out of fuel earlier in the race, and Fulp had to push the car back to the pits, losing a considerable amount of time. The car eventually finished in 13th place. Owing to a lubrication problem in practice, not too much time was spent on track, hence lack of data applicable to the fuel consumption of the Dino 248 SP. Both of the OSCA entries failed to finish, McCluggage being involved in an accident – scant reward for previously pushing the car back to the pits – when the car stopped on track through ignition trouble. Publicker's OSCA 1600 GT suffered from engine failure after covering 33 laps of the Sebring track.

For the SCCA National meeting held at Bridgehampton, Denise McCluggage had a rent-a-drive entry in an OSCA Formula Junior car, in which she managed a sixth-place finish in a field of 19 cars. The car would have been either 0003 or 0012 but no positive identification has been made.

An article in the *New York Times* suggested that Chinetti would have four Ferrari Grand Touring cars, one Testa Rossa and a 1.6-litre

4 | 1962-64

■ Fulp and Ryan's 250 TRI 61 beached at the Mulsanne bend after leaving the road. No amount of digging would free the car.

■ NART entered an OSCA 1600 GT for Arents and Hammill, but the car failed to last the distance.

■ The Arents/Hammill OSCA 1600 GT heads a Ferrari 250 GTO as it sweeps through the Esses.

NART diversifies

Grossman drove the 250 GTO and, along with Roberts, covered 2484 miles to finish in sixth place.

Grossman makes a pit stop in NART's 250 GTO (3387 GT).

OSCA entered into the Le Mans 24-hour race. As it happens, only three of those were on the grid: the 250 GTO driven by Grossman and Roberts, a 250 TRI 61 driven by Fulp and Ryan, and an OSCA 1600 GT for Arents, Hammill and Jose Behra. Hugus and Reed were mentioned, but their car was entered by William McKelvy. The 250 GTO (3387 GT) had just been sold to Grossman by Chinetti for $12,000, but he had agreed to prepare and maintain the car at Le Mans, for which Grossman had to pay an extra $1600 for 'costs.'

The only one of the three cars to finish was Grossman's 250 GTO, which, after a technical infringement, very nearly put them out of the race. Following a pit stop around lunch time on Sunday, the starter motor jammed. They rocked (or technically pushed) the car, but luckily it did not fire up. Finally, they managed to get it away on the starter, and the commissar took no further action against the team. The car finished sixth on distance, covering 3998km. The 250 TRI61, driven by Fulp and Ryan, retired in the 15th hour after being in 25th place. The car had left the track and ended up in the sand on the Mulsanne bend, a repeat of what had happened to the car in practice. Arents/Hammill/Behra's OSCA was performing well, being as high as 15th place, until gearbox failure caused the car to retire after covering 227 laps.

September was the time in North America for the running of the Bridgehampton and Mosport events. The Bridgehampton Double 400 took place on 15/16 September, with NART entering six cars. However, on the day there were only three cars in attendance. Pedro Rodríguez was given the 330 TRI LM to drive, Bob Grossman owned his 250 GTO but was entered under the NART banner, and although there was no class for small sports-racers, Chinetti brought along the OSCA S1000 for Denise McCluggage and Alan Eager to drive. Those entries that did not appear were the OSCA 1600 GT for Arents and Publicker in the first race, and a Dino for Charlie Hayes and an unspecified car for John Fulp, though probably a Dino.

The second race turned out to be an exhibition appearance for Pedro Rodríguez, as his 330 TRI LM effortlessly pulled away from the rest of the field to win the race two clear laps ahead of Bob Grossman in the 250 GTO. For a long spell of the race, Grossman had remained behind the other GTO, but put in a fine effort to gain second place when Hayes pitted to hand over to Ed Hugus. Denise McCluggage was found to be trying too hard, and flipped the OSCA on lap 42. Luckily she was unhurt, but co-driver Alan Eager never got to drive the car. For his efforts, Rodríguez picked up a trophy and cheque for $1000 and another $1300 for NART, while Grossman pocketed $1500 ($1000 for the class win, $500 for the overall position).

The meeting at Mosport happened one week after the Bridgehampton races. Pedro Rodríguez was again given the 330 TRI LM to drive. Ricardo was also meant to be there, but was unavailable due to illness. Persistent rain that fell during the support races finally stopped for the start of the 250-mile main event. Rodríguez started in eighth place on the grid and for the first few laps made little impression on the field. After ten laps he had moved up one place, but the track was beginning to dry out, giving better traction to the larger capacity cars. At one-third distance Rodríguez had moved up to fifth, and a flurry of activity for pit stops moved him further up the field. On lap 49 he pitted and refuelled in 90 seconds. Another ten laps saw him in third place, gaining steadily on Bradley in a Lotus XIX. On lap 93 Rodríguez overtook Bradley to take second place, but, with time running out, could do nothing to catch Masten Gregory in the leading Lotus XIX. Apart from the absence of Ricardo Rodríguez, there was an entry submitted for John Fulp, but he and his unspecified car did not turn up.

The final round of the Manufacturers' Championship took place at Montlhéry in October. Eight Ferrari 250 GTOs were on the start line, and amongst them was the NART entry (3987), Chinetti's recently purchased 250 GTO, for the Rodríguez brothers to drive. Pedro

NART diversifies

took up where he left off at Bridgehampton, and surged into the lead. By the time of the first pit stop, NART's lead was well ahead of the field, and the car progressed effortlessly through the race unchallenged. For the final three laps Ricardo was at the wheel, in which time he lapped the second place car, that of Surtees and Parkes, to take a comfortable victory.

During the 1950s and 1960s there were a number of deaths among racing drivers in all forms of motorsport. Safety measures were continually improving, both on the cars and at the tracks, but it was unfortunately true that barely a week went by without another death being announced in the motoring press. No death had a greater impact than when Ricardo Rodríguez was killed in a practice session for the Mexican Grand Prix in early November. His death was a great loss to motorsport in general, and had an immediate impact on those closest to him, both in terms of personal loss and for forthcoming race events.

The Puerto Rico Grand Prix was a new event, promoted by a group of enthusiasts headed by David Ash from America. He had arranged for a sports car Grand Prix and a number of support races to take place from 4-11 November at Caguas. While the races went ahead, several of the cars were withdrawn from the starting line-up, in respect to Ricardo Rodríguez. Scuderia SSS Republica di Venezia had already shipped two Ferraris to Puerto Rica, but the owner of the racing team, Count Giovanni Volpi di Misurata, instructed that his cars were not to run. As a result, they sat in the lobby of the Condado Beach Hotel for the duration of the weekend.

The North American Racing Team had also entered two cars. Phil Hill was to drive the Dino 268 SP (0798), and Pedro Rodríguez was to drive the Le Mans and Bridgehampton 400 winner 330 TRI LM (0808). Upon the news of Ricardo's death, Luigi Chinetti immediately withdrew the two cars from the event.

The final event of the year was the Bahamas Speed Weeks, held in Nassau during early December. Just prior to the event taking place, Chinetti purchased two more cars from the Ferrari factory, the Dino 268 SP (0798) together with a Dino 196 SP (0804) costing $9000, the latter being sold to John Fulp together with a

Lorenzo Bandini drove the Dino 268 SP (0798) for NART at the Bahamas Speed Weeks, finishing eighth in the Nassau Trophy race.

4 | 1962-64

Charlie Hayes drove the 250 GTO (3223 GT) at Nassau, finishing third in the Governor's Trophy race.

A side view of Gregory's 330 TRI at Nassau shows the prominent NART decal.

NART diversifies

John Fulp drives the Dino 196 SP to a fourth place finish in the Governor's Trophy race.

race entry to Nassau. There were five entries in all, the one for John Fulp, Masten Gregory driving the 330 TRI LM (0808) instead of Pedro Rodríguez, Bandini in the 268 SP (0798), Charlie Hayes in a 250 GTO (3223 GT), and an OSCA 1600 GT (007) for Tom Fleming.

Lorenzo Bandini's 250 GTO finished second in the Nassau Tourist Trophy race behind Mecom's 250 GTO, driven by Roger Penske, before being handed over to Hayes. Hayes then drove it to a third place finish in the Governor's Trophy race, and fifth place in the 252-mile Nassau Trophy. John Fulp finished in fourth place in the Governor's Trophy race, though failed to trouble the lap-scorers in the Nassau Trophy race, rolling into the pits at the end of the first lap with electrical problems which proved to be terminal for the car. Neither Gregory, whose car caught fire from a fuel leak, or Bandini, finished

American driver Phil Hill was one of Luigi Chinetti's prodigies, being recommended to Enzo Ferrari as a driver capable of winning a World Championship title for him. Hill started driving for NART in 1962, and drove regularly for Chinetti for the next two years, coming first at Daytona in 1964, co-driving with Pedro Rodríguez.

4 | 1962-64

Pedro Rodríguez was victorious in the Daytona 3-hour race driving a 250 GTO (4219 GT).

in the Governor's Trophy, the latter using it, as many did, as a warm-up for the Nassau Trophy. At Nassau, Gregory's repaired car finished in fourth place, Bandini was eighth, and Tom Fleming's OSCA 1600 GT failed to finish.

On a cold mid-February Saturday afternoon in 1963, cars lined up for the Daytona Challenge, a 250-mile race over the tri-oval course. The nature of the course caused obvious problems to the setup of the NART entry for 'Fireball' Roberts, as the car needed to run equally well on the high banks of the oval, and on the road course for the Daytona Continental three-hour race the next day. In the end they did as little as possible to the car for the Challenge race, in order to keep it competitive for the next day. Roberts drove a steady race, despite suspected fuel problems, to come home fourth against opposition that had set-ups specifically for the oval track.

For the Daytona Continental three-hour race, NART entered the same 250 GTO (3223 GT) for Roberts, and a second 250 GTO for Pedro Rodríguez. This second 250 GTO (4219 GT) had just been purchased from Ferrari, and then registered in the name of Mamie Reynolds, with the sole intention of her entering it at Daytona and Sebring. Ferrari supplied the car with the stipulation that it was attended to by Chinetti and driven by Pedro Rodríguez. Qualifying put Rodríguez in a good position on the grid, and during the opening session of the race, changed positions with Hudson's Cobra for the lead. With frequent pit stops and cars expiring around him, Rodríguez kept up the pressure, only temporarily losing the lead to Penske's 250 GTO while having a pit stop of his own. Rodríguez regained the lead on lap 50, and held on to win the event some 64 seconds ahead of Penske. But did he?

Controversy broke out after the race had finished, as it appears that Rodríguez and NART had contravened the pit stop regulations not once, but twice. In the drivers' meeting prior to the race, attended by members of the press as well as the drivers, a particular point was made

NART diversifies

about the number of people that could be over the pit wall during a pit stop. Firstly, the point was made that the driver must alight from the car during the refuelling process. Secondly, only the person who was refuelling the car, plus two other people working on the car, were allowed beyond the pit wall at any one time. If the driver helped to work on the car he would be counted as one of the two mechanics. If he did not work on the car he must go the other side of the wall.

During the first pit stop on the 45th lap, Pedro left the car and stood on the pit wall, not beyond it as the rule stated. The next infraction occurred during the closing minutes of the race, when Pedro pitted to take on a splash of fuel to get him to the end of the race. He remained in the car throughout the entire refuelling operation, claiming later that it was his understanding that as long as only one person was over the wall, the driver could remain in the car. This then accounted for the correct number of two persons that were allowed on the trackside of the wall to work on the car during a pit stop.

Even allowing for any language difficulties, the specific point made about getting out of the car during refuelling was quite clear, and would have been known by the NART pit crew. Any other time this infringement would have meant disqualification from the race, but the officials, in their wisdom, decided to inflict a 50-second time penalty on the driver. Considering that Rodríguez had finished 64 seconds ahead of Penske, the penalty meant absolutely nothing. Justice was not best served that day.

The Roberts/Cannon 250 GTO was placed 15th, but it was not a happy race for them. At the end of the Daytona Challenge race, Roberts had mentioned to Chinetti that the car had fluctuating fuel pressure. Evidently, the 250 GTO had been pushed into the corner of the garage that evening and ignored, or the problem was very elusive, because Roberts pitted on lap 29 for a driver changeover, reporting the same issue to Chinetti. Despite the problem, John Cannon managed to nurse the car through a record number of frustrating pit stops to finish in 15th place. The Goodyear Tire & Rubber Company sent Chinetti a $1000 voucher in appreciation of the winning car using its products.

After the Daytona race, Luigi Chinetti did an interview with *Car & Driver* magazine, and Daytona and Corvettes crept into the conversation. The magazine reported: "He thinks the Corvette is a very good car and a great bargain, but he's appalled by the bad show the cars and their crews put on at an important race meeting. He feels that the continual swapping of engines and over-preparation of the cars makes them look bad, and then to have 90% of the entry drop out with mechanical failures is even worse. He said 'Just once I'd like to set up a Corvette and have a man like Rodríguez drive it; we could show them how that car should run. It deserves to do better.'" Little did he realise that one day this ambition might be, in part, fulfilled.

The North American Racing Team garage at Sebring was a busy place the night prior to the 12-hour race. The race was the first to be run under the FIA's new Manufacturers' Championship rules. The changes made caused a great deal of havoc, not only for some of the Ferrari models but other manufacturers as well. The 250 GTOs came in for criticism by the officials about what constituted a legal door under the new rules.

4 | 1962-64

Graham Hill and Pedro Rodríguez piloted the 330 TRI (0808) to a third place finish at Sebring.

NART assisted Theodoli in obtaining tyres from Goodyear, and helping to prepare and look after the Sunbeam Harrington Alpine at Sebring.

John Fulp and Harry Heuer had the Dino 268 SP (0798) for the Sebring race, but the suspension failed and the car was withdrawn.

On the 250 GTO they were fitted with permanent Plexiglas windows, which the builders felt were actually part of the door. "Not so" ruled the FIA representative. "A door is a door and a window is a window." The result was an all-night session prior to practice, to rebuild the door up to the prescribed specification. This, however, made it almost impossible for the driver to see sideways out of the car, a potentially dangerous situation that could have resulted in an accident.

Among the six NART entries there were a couple of unusual cars. Admittedly not for the first time, an OSCA 1600 GT (007) appeared for Fleming/Baumann/Heppenstall to drive, but lurking in the corner of the garage was a Sunbeam Alpine with a Harrington body conversion. This car belonged to Fillipo Theodoli. He was a European account executive for the Gardner Advertising Agency, which handled Alitalia and Ferrari accounts. Theodoli was

NART diversifies

also a personal friend of Luigi Chinetti, so it appears that various racing parts were provided by NART for the car to race at Sebring, and it would be looked after and raced under the NART banner. NART also ordered tyres from the Goodyear Tire & Rubber Company for the Alpine, along with their own requirements for the Ferraris. Also in the garage were two 250 GTOs, Mamie Reynolds' car (4219 GT), this time to be driven by Bonnier and Cannon, and a 3223 GT to be driven by Grossman/Mayer/Thiem/Hayes. Alongside them was a Dino 268 SP (0798) for Fulp and Heuer, together with the 330 TRI LM for Pedro Rodríguez and Graham Hill. From photographs it would appear that the Ferrari 330 TRI LM bore an advertising slogan, something quite unusual in 1963.

Practice proved that once again the Ferraris were the cars to beat, with the NART contingent posting competitive lap times. The race had a Le Mans-style start, and surprisingly the first car to show was the NART-entered Sunbeam Alpine piloted by Bill Kneeland, Theodoli's co-driver. He didn't get beyond the length of the straightway though, before being swallowed up by the larger displacement cars; as he came through on the first lap it was Phil Hill in a Cobra, and moving up to him quickly, Pedro Rodríguez in the 330 TRI LM. Rodríguez took the lead on lap two, and he and Graham Hill held it from then until the ninth hour, apart from when the car had to pit for fuel and tyres. Wear and tear on the car began to show; first there were electrical problems that called for a change of headlights, then the tailpipe supports gave way and had to be fixed, costing the team two laps. A decision taken by Goodyear's Fred Gamble not to change the tyres when Pedro took over the car, could have cost them the race. Pedro was a harder driver than Graham Hill, and he wore out the right rear tyre which blew, demolishing the rear fender and creating an extra pit stop. With little time left, the gap could not be closed, so Hill and Rodríguez had to settle for third place behind the Ferraris of Surtees/Scarfiotti and Mairesse/Vacarella. For his services at Sebring, Graham Hill received a cheque from Chinetti for $700.

For once in an endurance race, the six NART entries all crossed the finish line. Bonnier and Cannon guided the 250 GTO to 13th place, with the other 250 GTO in 18th place. Theodoli's Sunbeam Alpine suffered from a leaking fuel filler, requiring the car to stop frequently, but finished in 33rd spot, one place ahead of the Fulp/Heuer Dino 268 SP that had suspension problems and spent a good deal of the time in the pits, while Fleming's OSCA finished the race in 40th place.

There were three NART entries for the Le Mans 24-hour race. The 250 GTO (4713 GT) had been purchased by Chinetti from the factory in early June, and was the only 250 GTO produced with the Pininfarina-designed 330 LM Berlinetta style body. Five days later Chinetti purchased a

Despite a bump and dynamo trouble, the 250 GTO (4713 GT) driven by Piper and Gregory finished sixth at Le Mans.

4 | 1962-64

NART's 330 TRI (0808) driven by Roger Penske and Pedro Rodríguez failed to finish, when the car left the road at Arnage.

Gurney and Hall went out of the 24-hour race in the ninth hour when the 330 LMB (4453 GT) sustained transmission damage.

Masten Gregory at the wheel of the 250 GTO (4713 GT) at Le Mans, driving to a sixth-place finish.

NART diversifies

330 LMB (4453 GT) for Mamie Reynolds, to be driven by Pedro Rodríguez, Dan Gurney and Jim Hall in the 24-hour race. Chinetti deposited two cheques with the factory, one for $13,017, the other for $8300. The third car entered was the well-used 330 TRI LM for Pedro Rodríguez and Roger Penske.

It did not turn out to be a successful trip back to Le Mans for the team, with the 330 TRI LM blowing up after 113 laps while Penske was driving. He lost control of the car, crashing off the road into a clump of trees, but luckily was unhurt. The same could not be said about the state of the car with its crumpled body. Rodríguez and Penske had been well up the leader board, and challenging for the lead earlier in the race. To make matters worse, the Gurney/Hall 330 LMB had been running well but using tyres at an alarming rate, when Hall experienced a loud thump as the driveshaft broke on lap 126. This just left the 250 GTO piloted by Gregory and Piper. They managed to guide the car to a sixth place finish, covering some 2608 miles at an average speed on 108.7mph.

It would appear that the sale of two cars to Mamie Reynolds also led to further developments between her and Chinetti Jr. On 29 July 1963 the Nevada State Journal printed the following report:

"Mamie Spears Reynolds twenty-year old millionairess granddaughter of the late Evalyn Walsh McLean, was married here Saturday to a handsome car salesman who sold her a racing car last February. Mamie is the sports-minded daughter of the late senator Robert R. Reynolds of North Carolina and the late Evalyn McLane Reynolds. Her grandmother, owner of the jinxed Hope diamond, was one of Washington's most renowned hostesses. Mamie inherited $10

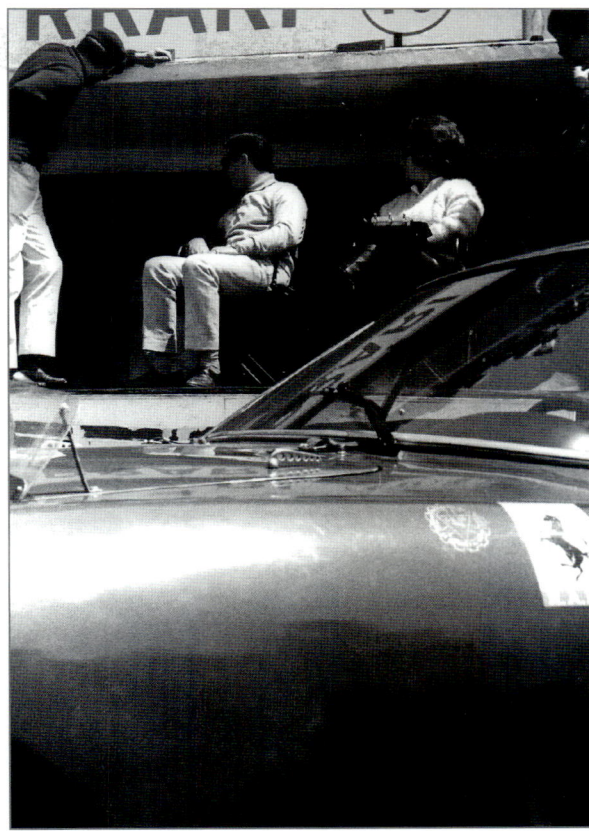

Pedro Rodríguez taking it easy in the Ferrari pit area, prior to the Le Mans 24-hour race.

million dollars when she was four and will inherit much more in 1968. Mamie raced her $10,000 Ferrari at Daytona Beach last February with Mexican driver Pedro Rodríguez at the wheel, and came in first. So Mamie bought several more sports cars from young Chinetti and raced them at Sebring and Le Mans under the banner of Chinetti's sponsored NART. Mamie and Luigi Jr attended the races together and their romance deepened. On April 12 they became engaged. Mamie will inherit the entire McLean estate, with the exception of the Hope diamond when she is twenty-five."

In August the 250 GTO used at Le Mans was entered into the Tourist Trophy race held at Goodwood, with Roger Penske at the wheel.

4 | 1962-64

■ The Gurney/Hall/Rodríguez Ferrari 330 LMB (4453 GT) sits in the pit area after retiring from the 24-hour race.

■ Dan Gurney first raced under the NART banner in 1958 at Le Mans, then followed with a race at Watkins Glen where he finished second and picked up $1000. He returned to drive for NART in 1963, driving at Le Mans and Bridgehampton.

■ Schlesser and Le Guezec failed to comply with the time limits on one stage of the Tour de France, and the 250 GTO (4713 GT) was eliminated.

NART diversifies

Roger Penske in pensive mood sits in the 250 GTO (4713 GT) at Goodwood.

Penske finished in sixth place in the Tourist Trophy race at Goodwood.

The car was competing against other standard-bodied GTOs and, over the relatively short-distance race on the tight Goodwood track, the difference showed. Penske finished in eighth place, completing 126 laps, four short of the winning 250 GTO driven by Graham Hill.

The 250 GTO (4713 GT) remained in Europe after the Goodwood event to take part in the Tour de France. Driven by Schlesser and Le Guezec on a rent-a-car basis, the car survived for only two stages before it was eliminated for being over the stipulated time limit for the second leg of the stage.

In America, mid-September heralded the Bridgehampton Double 500 races. The GT section championship was done and dusted, so Chinetti saw no point in entering a 250 GTO just to make up the numbers, especially as they had no suitable 250 GTO ready for the event. Dan Gurney was there in the 330 LMB, and could have been entered, but Chinetti rejected the idea, saving the car for the second of the races.

4 | 1962-64

Pedro Rodríguez inspects the Ferrari 250 P (0810) that he would drive to a second place finish in the Bridgehampton Double 500 race.

Pit stop for Pedro Rodríguez. A factory mechanic works at the front of the car, whilst Chinetti, in hat and long coat with his back to the camera, holds a new wheel for the car.

Not a man to miss an opportunity, Gurney drove a Shelby Cobra in the first race instead. Pedro Rodríguez was also there in the Le Mans-winning Ferrari 250 P, entered by NART, and in practice spent a considerable time messing about with gear ratios on the car. In a letter from Luigi Chinetti Jr to Enzo Ferrari, October 14 1963, it was stated that "Dan Gurney in the GT race refused to drive a GTO because of the lack of power to win overall."

The second of the Double 500 races began with a rolling start, in which the field thundered down Bridgehampton's 3300-ft straight, and plunged over a

NART diversifies

■ *Dan Gurney on his way to a third place finish, driving the 330 LMB (4453 GT) at Bridgehampton.*

■ *NART's 330 LMB (4453 GT) stands in the paddock at Bridgehampton.*

Gurney's car undergoing preparation for the Bridgehampton Double 500 race.

slope into a series of 100mph downhill right-handers. It was always going to be a battle between Hansgen's Cooper-Buick and the 250 P driven by Rodríguez. Sure enough, Hansgen led the first 47 laps, with Rodríguez in second place, some 50 seconds behind. Then Hansgen pitted, but due to a flat battery the car would not restart, delaying the pit stop another minute while a new battery was fitted. In the meantime Rodríguez had passed the pits, and was now leading by a lap.

It was then Rodríguez's turn to pit, and his stop was a complete disaster. In addition to oil and fuel, the 250 P needed two new tyres, and the pit stop took some three minutes. Rodríguez finally emerged from the pits, finding his car to be

4 | 1962-64

a minute and a half behind Hansgen. Meanwhile, Gurney was holding fourth spot in the 330 LMB, close behind the lightweight Corvette of Thompson, until the Corvette developed ignition problems and was forced to retire. This moved Gurney up into third place, where he stayed until the finish of the race. Both Rodríguez and Hansgen made one more pit stop, with Hansgen holding on to take the chequered flag some 30 seconds ahead of Rodríguez.

Two weeks later the cars turned up at Mosport. Rodríguez was there in the Ferrari 250 P but Gurney was missing. Instead, Bandini turned up with the Dino 268 SP (0798) to support a strong contingent of Ferraris from other teams.

Surtees grabbed pole position in his 250 P, with Rodríguez third on the grid. As the flag fell Rodríguez launched his car into the lead, but was soon engaged in a ferocious duel with Surtees, both of them pulling away from Graham Hill in third place, at a rate of two seconds a lap. Bandini was holding seventh spot in the Dino 268 SP. At the 25 lap mark, Surtees and Rodríguez had lapped all but six cars, both setting a new lap record in the process. Lap 31 saw Surtees pit with clutch problems, while Rodríguez continued on remorselessly. On lap 37 Bandini was unfortunate to lose a wheel, putting the Dino 268 SP out, while Rodríguez continued to complete the race, lapping all but Graham Hill and finishing in first place.

On 27th October there was a race at Virginia International Raceway, in which John Fulp entered the NART 250 P in a rent-a-drive deal with Chinetti. There was an unfortunate accident involving a Formula Junior driver in the same

Pedro and Rodríguez Sr watch the action in practice at Mosport.

NART diversifies

- *John Fulp drove the 250 P (0810) at VIR, but the race was stopped due to a fatal accident, and 'no result' was declared.*

- *John Fulp driving the Ferrari 250 P (0810) at Virginia International Raceway.*

- *Fulp attended the Bahamas Speed Weeks, and drove the Dino 268 SP (0798) to a fifth place finish in the Nassau Trophy race.*

- *Pedro Rodríguez drove the 250 P (0810) at Nassau, finishing in second place in both the Governor's Trophy and Nassau Trophy races.*

race as the 250 P, and the driver was killed. The officials decided to stop the race, and declared it void.

Just two NART entries turned up for the final races of the year, the Bahamas Speed Weeks. Pedro Rodríguez attended with the 250 P (0810), while John Fulp was there with the Dino 268 SP (0798). Surtees had an entry with NART but, due to an injury sustained in a race at Riverside in November, and mindful of his Formula One commitments to Ferrari with the South African Grand Prix coming up at the end of December, Surtees decided to withdraw from the Speed Weeks.

In the Governor's Trophy race, Pedro Rodríguez drove the 250 P into a second place finish, 73 seconds adrift of the winning car, Foyt's Scarab-Chevrolet. The race had a rolling start, but by the finish the attrition rate was high, a worrying development for the race organisers, who expected a full field for the main race at the end of the week. Fulp stayed out of trouble and brought the Dino 268SP across the finish line in fifth place.

The top order of finishers was repeated in the main event, the Nassau Trophy race, Foyt's Scarab holding off a late challenge by Rodríguez to take the main prize. In this race Fulp came across the finish line in 11th place overall, second in his class.

The 1964 season started at Daytona for NART, where there were two races on offer, the 252-mile Daytona Continental for prototypes and sports cars on Saturday, and the much longer 2000km for Grand Touring cars on Sunday.

NART entered Pedro Rodríguez into the Continental Cup, driving a Ferrari 250 LM. After coming fifth fastest in practice, Rodríguez failed

4 | 1962-64

Pedro Rodríguez and Phil Hill claimed victory in the Daytona 2000km race driving a 250 GTO (5571 GT).

to trouble the front-runners from the moving pace lap. It soon became apparent that the oil was leaking out of the engine at a rapid rate and, to add to Rodríguez's woes, the petrol tank came loose, rupturing the filler tube neck. Pedro managed to get the car back to the pits and immediately exited the car. His race was run for the day.

Rodríguez and Phil Hill turned to a Ferrari 250 GTO (5571 GT) for the 2000km race, with Grossman and Hansgen in the older NART 250 GTO (4713 GT). In the early part of the race, Holbert's Shelby Cobra eased away from the Rodríguez/Hill GTO, the Ferrari taking the lead when the Cobra made the first pit stop. Around half way through the race, Rodríguez's car sustained a puncture, the flying rubber doing damage to the left front wing and headlight.

He nursed the car back to the pits where the wing was levered out, a new wheel and tyre fitted, and a replacement for the headlight rigged up. This unforeseen damage had put the car back to fourth place at the halfway stage of the race, but in the second half of the race the Shelby Cobras fell away, leaving the Piper/Bianchi Ferrari between the Rodríguez/Hill car and victory. A generator failure on the Piper/Bianchi car cost them the victory in the later stages of the event, and they had to content themselves with second place behind Rodríguez and Hill, who managed to circulate with just enough light to give them adequate visibility. Bob Grossman and Walt Hansgen rounded off a good weekend for NART, by driving their 330 LMB-bodied 250 GTO into third place.

NART diversifies

John Fulp drove with Pedro Rodríguez at Sebring, but the 330 P (0810), now with a larger engine, failed to finish.

The next appearance for the NART-entered 250 LM (5149) was at the USRRC event at Augusta. John Fulp made a rent-a-drive appearance at the event. He qualified in fifth place and managed to finish eighth having covered 49 laps, three short of Dave MacDonald's winning car, a Cooper King Cobra-Ford.

The 12-hour race at Sebring was held in late March. While the race turned out to be a good one for Ferrari, for once it was not the NART-entered cars that were to the fore. Chinetti put four cars in the race, the Daytona-winning 250 GTO (5571 GT), as well as the other GTO from Daytona (4713 GT), a 250 LM and a 330 P. The highest-place car was the 250 GTO, driven by Piper, Gammino and Rodríguez (later in the race) finishing in seventh place behind three factory-entered Ferraris and three Shelby Cobras. The exceptional performance of the Shelby Cobra had been expected for a long time, and this came to fruition at Sebring. Ferrari had no answer in the GT category, even with Rodríguez drafted in to help Piper and Gammino. Thompson and Grossman completed 186 laps to finish in 15th place, while the Sebring debut for the 250 LM ended after four hours when the Kolb/O'Brien car caught fire. The Rodríguez/Fulp 330 P ended up stranded on the far side of the circuit from the pits, after the gearbox broke, hence Pedro Rodriguez gaining the chance to drive in the 250 GTO later in the race.

NART came to Le Mans for the 24-hour race more in hope than expectation. The Ferrari works team had ensured that it kept the more competitive cars, which meant the private teams had to make do with what was left over. NART entered the old 330 P (0810) for Rodríguez and Hudson, while Piper and Rindt were given a new 250 LM. Hugus and Rosinski ended up with a 250 GTO, as did Grossman and Tavano, their car being a rent-a-drive entered in Tavano's name. It was disappointment all round, as first the Piper/Rindt 250 LM retired with a broken oil seal on the first lap, and, after being third fastest in practice, the Rodríguez/Hudson car went out after 58 laps when the driveshaft snapped. Hugus battled on for 110 laps before a shattered gearbox put an end to

4 | 1962-64

■ Charlie Kolb and Tom O'Brien's 250 LM (5149) on the start line at Sebring.

■ Tom O'Brien at the wheel of the Ferrari 250 LM, minus decals, prior to the Sebring 12-hour race.

his race leaving just the Tavano/Grossman car to try and salvage something. To have kept it running was some sort of success, and that they finished in ninth place covering 315 laps was quite an achievement.

Early August heralded the running of the Reims 12-hour race. Chinetti made three entries to the race, two 250 GTOs and a 250 LM to join with the other privately entered Ferraris. It was noticeable that there were no factory entries and no P cars present to stave off the challenge from Ford. Surtees and Bandini were piloting the 250 LM, while the 250 GTOs went to the pairing of Rodríguez and Vaccarella, and Grossman and Hudson.

The Surtees/Bandini 250 LM claimed pole position ahead of two Ford GT40s, with the Hill/Bonnier 250 LM in fourth place. The race opened with a sustained three-way struggle between the rival 250 LMs of Graham Hill and Surtees and Ginther's Ford GT40. Nobody was sure which order they would be in as they passed the pits, lap after lap. The two NART 250 GTOs were well off the leaders' pace, and having a

Continued on page 110

NART diversifies

A concise history of the North American Racing Team 1957 to 1983

4 | 1962-64

Grossman's 250 GTO (4713 GT) chases down an ISO-Chevrolet driven by Hugus.

NART's 330 P (0810) at Sebring prior to having white stripe decals added to the car's livery of the car.

NART diversifies

The Tavano/Grossman 250 GTO ran well enough to record a ninth-place finish; the only NART entry to complete the 24-hour race.

Pedro Rodríguez's 330 P (0810) failed to finish at Le Mans due to a cracked cylinder head.

The 250 GTO (5571 GT) was driven by Hugus and Rosinsky, but failed to finish due to a broken transmission.

NART diversifies

■ Pedro Rodríguez in the 330 P on the infield at Le Mans.

■ The 250 GTO (5573 GT) appeared at Le Mans, with Grossman at the wheel.

■ Piper and Rindt drove the 250 LM (5909), but retired with a broken oil filter seal.

■ The Hugus/Rosinsky 250 GTO in the pits at Le Mans prior to the start.

The Piper/Rindt 250 LM parked in the paddock at Le Mans.

A concise history of the North American Racing Team 1957 to 1983 — 109

4 | 1962-64

Rodríguez and Vaccarella could finish no higher than 11th in the 12-hour race at Reims, driving the 250 GTO (5571 GT).

race of their own with the other competitors, as, one-by-one, the Ford GT40s were retiring, and by lap 200 the threat to the Ferraris had vanished. On lap 218 the Grossman/Hudson 250 GTO went out with a blown engine but, at the front, the two 250 LMs were still trading places.

In the end it was Hill who triumphed as, with ten minutes of the race remaining, Surtees limped into the pits with a flat tyre. A quick wheel change got Surtees back on track but there was insufficient time to catch Hill. The Rodríguez/Vaccarella car suffered niggling problems throughout the race, visiting the pits frequently, and as a consequence finished down in 11th place.

The Tourist Trophy race was held at Goodwood on 24 August. One NART entry turned up, the 250 GTO (5573 GT), to be driven by John Surtees. Not too much of the car was seen as, early in the race, Innes Ireland in the Maranello Concessionaires 250 GTO spun in front of Surtees. Surtees had to take avoiding action, hitting another car before rolling onto a bank and out of the race.

A top field of contenders turned up for the official opening of the Mont Tremblant-St Jovite circuit in September. Among their number,

NART diversifies

NART had entered Pedro Rodríguez to drive a Ferrari 275 P (0812). After claiming pole position, Rodríguez led for 57 of the 63 laps in the 100-mile race, crossing the finish line some 13 seconds ahead of second place Ludwig Heimrath driving a Cooper-Ford. For his efforts, Rodríguez won $1275 out of a total purse of $5100. A few days after the race Chinetti wrote him a cheque for $1515, that would have covered prize money and expenses.

The Bridgehampton Double 500 race was the opportunity for Chinetti to enter cars into both sections of the race. However, he concentrated his efforts on the sports-racers and prototype section, entering three cars. Rodríguez had the 275 P, Fulp a 330 P, while the third car went to Ludovico Scarfiotti, who was flown in by Chinetti to race the car. For this race, Chinetti chose to use Goodyear tyres on his cars, a theme that continued for the remainder of 1964.

During practice both Scarfiotti and Rodríguez broke the lap record, with Scarfiotti gaining pole position ahead of Hansgen, and Rodríguez in fourth place on the grid. Walt Hansgen set a blistering pace in the Scarab-Chevrolet, leaving the rest of the field trailing in his wake. By one third race distance, he had lapped everyone up to third place in the field, but seeing that Rodríguez and Sherman Decker were fighting over the second spot, decided to stay behind them, and not risk being shunted off the track. Rodríguez eventually got the better of Decker, finishing strongly in second spot ahead of Bob Grossman in William McKelvy's Ferrari 250 LM. John

Rodríguez Sr and Chinetti Sr oversee the preparation of the 275 P, during practice for the Bridgehampton Double 500.

Ludovico Scarfiotti at the Bridgehampton Double 500 in a 330 P (0824).

A concise history of the North American Racing Team 1957 to 1983

4 | 1962-64

A pit stop for John Fulp in the Bridgehampton Double 500 in which he finished in fifth place.

Pedro Rodríguez in a 275 P (0814) being chased by McClellan in a Dino 196S (not a NART entry despite the decals). Rodríguez finished in second place. (Courtesy Dave Nicholas)

NART diversifies

Ludovico Scarfiotti in the 330 P (0824) at Bridgehampton. He failed to complete the race.

John Fulp in action at Bridgehampton in the 330 P (0820).

Fulp finished in fifth place, three laps down on the winning car, while Scarfiotti covered 105 laps before being forced to retire the 330 P with engine failure, just five laps from the end. The engine blew in a cloud of white smoke as he crossed the start/finish line, and laid down a trail of oil halfway around the track. Early in October, the Goodyear Tire & Rubber Company sent Chinetti a voucher for $250 to cover Rodríguez's second place finish at Bridgehampton. It would shortly be followed by one for $500 to cover Pedro's win at Mosport.

One week had elapsed between the end of the Bridgehampton Double 500 and the start of the race at Mosport. The NART entourage travelled north with three cars: 330 Ps for Rodríguez and Scarfiotti, and the 275 P for Walt Hansgen, who had accepted an invitation to drive the car that Rodríguez had driven at Bridgehampton, as the Mecom team had travelled back to Texas to prepare for the West Coast pro series.

Qualifying put Rodríguez seventh and Scarfiotti eighth on the grid, with Hansgen near the back. From a rolling start, Rodríguez and Scarfiotti moved up the field, and by the end of the first lap were fourth and fifth. No such luck for Hansgen who experienced overheating with the 275 P, and pitted at the end of the opening lap. A flurry of activity on the car appeared to work, and Hansgen re-entered the race in last place. At quarter distance, Bruce McLaren held a 15 second lead over Rodríguez, with Scarfiotti a further 15 seconds back in third.

Half distance saw the same leader board, but now with Hansgen up into eighth place and continuing to make up ground on the cars ahead of him. 26 laps from the end, McLaren drove into the pits with the linkage to one carburettor adrift. Repairs cost him four laps, enabling Rodríguez and the chasing Scarfiotti to pull out a commanding lead. Despite a pit stop for the two lead Ferraris, they maintained their lead over McLaren, with Hansgen capping a fine drive to finish in fourth place.

October of 1964 saw the North American Racing Team rise to prominence on the world stage, in a most unprecedented manner. The venue was Watkins Glen and the occasion was the United States Grand Prix. The chance of receiving this extra publicity was not planned, but all down to chance.

In mid 1963, Ferrari had begun work on developing a sports car to succeed the 250 GTO. Ferrari looked to the 250 P, deciding to build a closed top version called the 250 Le Mans Berlinetta. In April 1964, the factory requested homologation, but the request was not looked at by the FIA until July. On reviewing the request, the FIA decided not to homologate the 250 LM as a Grand Touring car, the rejection seemingly spilling over from the trouble over homologating the 250 GTO, when the FIA had the wool pulled over its eyes by Ferrari. They had got away with that on a technicality, despite protests from Carroll Shelby, but this time it was different. The 250 LM did not look like a modified 250 GT or GTO, and the FIA could not see Ferrari building the requisite 100 cars. This restricted the 250 LM to the Prototype class, for which Ferrari already had quicker cars.

The backlash to the FIA's decision was about to take place. In a fit of rage, Ferrari vented his spleen on the Italian press and the AC d'Italia. He handed in his FIA competitor's licence and issued a warning that his cars would never race in Italian colours again.

NART diversifies

The paperwork trail relating to 275 P (0814), from the Ferrari factory to Luigi Chinetti.

A concise history of the North American Racing Team 1957 to 1983

4 | 1962-64

As a result of what other people considered purely an Italian outpouring of emotion, when it came to the United States Grand Prix at Watkins Glen, Enzo Ferrari stunned everyone. His Grand Prix cars turned up in the blue and white livery of the United States, and were entered by Luigi Chinetti's North American Racing Team. Running the Ferrari team in America, in his name and American livery, was a worthy testimonial to the man who was putting Ferrari on the American map. Despite his anger at the FIA, Enzo Ferrari was more than aware that he had the opportunity of having a world championship driver by the end of the season so, understandably, did not boycott the races.

Four Ferraris were in attendance at Watkins Glen: two V8s, an old V6, and a new flat-12. Surtees was not particularly pleased with the performance of any of them, all seemingly slower than the V6 he had driven the previous year, but he finally settled on one of the V8 cars, and left Bandini to run the flat-12 model. Qualifying put Surtees on the front row of the grid, next to Jim Clark's Lotus-Climax, with Bandini in seventh place.

Surtees led for a few laps, in close company with Clark and Graham Hill, but Clark's Lotus was suffering from fuel-injection problems, and dropped out of contention, leaving Hill and Surtees to battle it out for

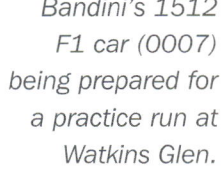

Bandini's 1512 F1 car (0007) being prepared for a practice run at Watkins Glen.

NART diversifies

Watkins Glen was the venue of the 1964 US Grand Prix. Surtees rides in a 158 F1 car (0005), painted in NART colours and entered by Chinetti Sr on behalf of the Ferrari factory.

The line-up for the start of the US Grand Prix at Watkins Glen; Surtees on the front row of the grid.

4 | 1962-64

Lorenzo Bandini makes his way round Watkins Glen, but failed to finish the race.

the win. Near the completion of the race, a spin put Surtees behind Graham Hill's BRM, and Surtees had to settle for a second place finish. Bandini was not as fortunate, having to retire the flat-12, one bank of exhausts smoking badly, with electrical problems.

The biggest non-FIA event in Europe was the 1000 km de Paris, held at the Montlhéry circuit in October. Although the race was won by the Ferrari 330 P sports prototype of Graham Hill and Jo Bonnier, the NART entered 250 GTO of Pedro Rodríguez and Jo Schlesser finished second overall, and won the GT category against stiff opposition from a pair of lightweight Jaguar E-types. Once again Goodyear was forthcoming, with award money to the sum of $500 for, as they put it, "an event in which we too shared in your glory."

The final round of the Formula One Grand Prix season was held in Mexico City, with three drivers still having a chance of claiming the driver's championship: Surtees, Hill and Clark. The four North American Racing Team Ferrari's present at Watkins Glen turned up, but this time with an extra driver, Pedro Rodríguez, for his home Grand Prix. Once again Surtees opted to use the 158 V8, Bandini the flat-12 1512, and Rodríguez was given the V6 Dino 156 model.

Surtees started on the second row of the grid but had a poor start, letting Clark and Hill get away from him. Aiding Surtees' effort to catch up, Rodriguez pulled to one side, allowing

NART diversifies

Surtees to gain one position, then Surtees gradually caught and passed Brabham. In front of Surtees, Bandini and Hill were having a tussle that would end in contact, with Hill against a barrier and breaking a tailpipe. A visit to the pits cost Hill both a lap and the chance of taking the Drivers' Championship. Surtees tucked in behind Bandini and commenced his chase of Clark, some 45 seconds ahead of both Bandini and Surtees, with Gurney a further 15 seconds behind Surtees.

It was not to be Clark's day either, as on lap 63 the oil pressure in the Lotus read zero, and the car came to a spluttering stop in the pits. The Ferrari team quickly assessed the situation and frantically signalled Bandini to let Surtees by. Being a true team member, he did that on the final lap, gifting Surtees second place in the race behind Gurney and, importantly, allowing Surtees to take the World Drivers' Championship for 1964. Luigi Chinetti could be proud of having played a small but important part in having helped Ferrari take this prize.

For the end of season races in Nassau, Chinetti entered two cars: the Ferrari 330 P (0820), and a 250 GTO (5571 GT) for Pedro Rodríguez to drive. The 250 GTO was entered in the opening race for GT cars and Pedro finished

Bandini put up a spirited display at Mexico City to finish third in the Mexico F1 Grand Prix in a Ferrari F1 1512.

Lorenzo Bandini primarily drove for the Ferrari factory team but, when the F1 cars were entered under the NART banner, Bandini continued to drive the car, also appearing at Nassau with a Ferrari 250 GTO entered by NART.

4 | 1962-64

Pedro Rodríguez drove a 330 P (0820) at Nassau, finishing third in the Nassau Trophy race.

John Fulp, a regular driver of NART-entered cars.

in seventh place. The Nassau Tourist Trophy followed, and Rodríguez was challenging the leaders when he was forced into the pits to replace a wheel, as the spokes were breaking up. He came back out, but could do no better than sixth place; third in the GT class.

Rodríguez swapped to the 330 P for the Governor's Trophy race, finishing in fourth place, and drove the car again in the Nassau Trophy race, finishing in third spot, two laps down on the winning car, the Chaparral, originally driven by Hap Sharp but taken over by Roger Penske. In a surprise move, Phil Hill took the wheel of the NART 250 GTO, after his original Ford entry, a Ford GT-40, expired very early in the week. Despite having trouble with the windscreen wipers, which failed to clear a film of oil, he finished in 11th place, claiming victory in the 11/12GT class.

It is unclear what prize money or appearance money was paid; however, Rodríguez did receive a cheque from Chinetti for $415 to cover travel expenses for the event.

John Surtees was offered a NART drive at Nassau by Chinetti, but due to the bad feelings between the race organiser, Sherman Crise, and Surtees the previous year, Surtees later declined the offer.

5
1965
Le Mans success for NART

5 | 1965

> Throughout the three decades that NART entered cars into races in America and Europe, 1965 is the most complicated to report upon. It is not the number of cars involved that raises issues, more the politics of the sport interfering with the normal procedures of the team that makes it complicated.

As a result, there are doubts as to the validity of certain aspects of the written history of this year, with serious questions revolving around the races held at Sebring and Le Mans.

The first major race of the season at Daytona confirmed two things. First, that Ferrari had serious competition from Ford, which was throwing a large amount of money at its sports racing programme, under the direction of Carroll Shelby, and second, Ferrari was in for a miserable time if it did not do something about its tyre supplier, as the Dunlop Rubber Company tyres were proving not to be up to the job. NART entered three cars, a new 330 P2 for Surtees and Rodríguez, a 330 P for Hansgen and Piper, and a 275 P for Fulp and Hugus.

Luck was not on NART's side as, after impressing in qualifying, all three cars disappeared from the score charts early in the race. First to go was Walt Hansgen, when he hit some debris on the track, sustained a puncture in the left rear tyre, and gave the spectators a demonstration on how to handle a seemingly uncontrollable car at speed. Although the car made it back on track after losing some 20 laps, it eventually had to be retired because of the suspension damage inflicted on the car.

Next to go was the Surtees/Rodríguez car. First Rodríguez had a tyre blow off, smashing the car's battery. Rodríguez ran back to the pits to collect another battery, refitted it, and made it back to the pits for a set of new tyres. Surtees took over the driving but, shortly afterwards, another rear tyre failure caused suspension damage and the car was retired. Finally, the 275 P, now seemingly driven by every available Ferrari driver, retired with damaged transmission after covering 129 laps. David Piper, who had driven with Walt Hansgen, received a cheque for $500 from Luigi Chinetti later in the month, as did Pedro Rodríguez, either as appearance or prize money.

In the lead-up to the annual Sebring 12-hour race, speculation and confusion reigned between race organiser Alec Ulmann, and Enzo Ferrari. Ulmann had taken the decision to introduce a special sports car class for this year's race, but this was a class for non-Appendix J Sports-Racers, and Enzo Ferrari objected strongly to its introduction. In Enzo's reckoning, Sebring was officially a race for GT Prototype cars. Ferrari knew the value of an outright win, regardless of the fact that championship points only went to the GT cars, but also realised there was nothing at the factory that could compete against the larger American-engined cars. Ulmann's ulterior motive was plain to see. His aim was to increase the revenue at Sebring, and to get the American public excited enough to attend, in anticipation of watching an American victory at one of their prime races. With a total purse of $40,000 on offer, Ulmann was confident his plan would succeed.

At first, Enzo Ferrari threatened to boycott the race, thinking that Ulmann would change his mind, but Ulmann did

Le Mans success for NART

Bob Grossman driving the 330 P (0810) at Sebring. The car covered 143 laps before retiring.

Graham Hill and Pedro Rodríguez drove the 330 P (0820) for 133 laps before the car was withdrawn.

Bad weather did nothing to enhance the performance of the cars at Sebring.

not respond to this threat. Ferrari tried a different approach, setting up negotiations between the two parties to discuss an increase in appearance and prize money for the GT Prototype class, but again, the organisers were unwilling to change the existing rates. At this point Ferrari had reportedly agreed with Ulmann to attend, albeit reluctantly, then later denied he had done anything of the sort, causing extra friction between the two parties. The result of the disagreement was an announcement that not only the Ferrari factory team, but also both NART and Maranello Concessionaires would boycott the race. Consequently, the official programme showed no SEFAC (Societa Esercizio Fabbriche Automobilistiche & Corse SpA), Maranello Concessionaires and NART entries for the race.

Despite the 'boycott,' eight Maranello products turned up at Sebring, six of which were entered under the banner of the Ferrari Owners Racing Association. This group was supposedly composed of loyal Ferrari owners determined to uphold the name of the marque. Accompanying them was a clutch of mechanics clothed in Italia Army brown coveralls, none of whom could speak a word of English, employed to look after the array of assorted brightly-coloured cars. Although announced by Ferrari that NART would have nothing to do with the proceedings, it would have, in reality, already submitted its entries to the organisers prior to the confrontation between Ferrari and Ulmann, and would have had race slots confirmed.

That being the case it would most probably mean that at least three of the cars entered would have originally been NART entries, but on paper, changed to private entries so as to conform to the 'boycott.' The cars driven by Grossman and Hugus were already in the hands of Chinetti, and would be entered by him again later in the season,

5 | 1965

Grossman/Hudson's Ferrari 330P (0810) leads Graham Hill's similar car, two hours in the race at Sebring.

The Fulp/Kolb Ferrari 330P (0822) failed to complete the 12-hour race, running for just 104 laps.

The Hugus/O'Brien/Hayes Ferrari 330P managed a 12th place finish at Sebring.

while 0822 had only recently arrived in America and had been delivered to Chinetti prior to the Sebring race.

The best performance of these three cars was put up by the Ferrari 275 P finishing 12th overall, despite heat problems for the drivers. The 330 P driven by Fulp and Kolb went out after 104 laps with a broken gearbox, while Grossman's 330 P covered 143 laps before differential problems put paid to any further involvement in the race. It is pertinent to mention that a number of the Ferraris, as 'private entries' ran with either Goodyear or Firestone tyres rather than Dunlop, as run on official factory entries.

Unsubstantiated claims and speculation have thrown into doubt exactly which chassis numbers were driven by which drivers, the ones shown are to the best of the author's knowledge.

To add to the complexity of the situation, a week after the race a number of cheques were raised by Luigi Chinetti, as payment to some of the drivers that took part in the race. Pedro Rodríguez had payment for his appearance at Daytona and Sebring, and Maglioli, Baghetti and Graham Hill received cheques related to their time at Sebring. It is interesting to note that none of those drivers were driving the three aforementioned cars, but were in cars that one can only imagine were originally intended to be factory entries. At the end of the day, it could be that the only thing missing at Sebring were the names of SEFAC, Maranello and NART on a piece of paper.

Just once in a while dreams can come true. This was the time for Luigi Chinetti's dream to come true. Can you imagine...

The venue was Le Mans for the 24-hour race, and this year Ford had brought with them a very

Le Mans success for NART

strong team of cars and drivers, determined to break Ferrari's stranglehold on this race.

The North American Racing Team had just two cars entered to give support to the factory team. They were put into the capable hands of John Baus, who worked as liaison between the different race organisers and NART. Le Mans scrutineering became so complex that NART entrusted the inspection of its cars to John Baus, whose experience in dealing with the Le Mans bureaucracy went back 20 years to the time when he carried out the same function for the Cunningham team. John Baus also played a part in getting Jochen Rindt into a Ferrari in 1964. Fred Gamble, who was Manager of Field Operations for Goodyear Tire & Rubber Company at that time, had recommended Rindt as an up-and-coming driver to Chinetti. Accordingly, he brought Rindt to be interviewed by NART's John Baus, who told Chinetti that he would be able to do a good job for NART. With just one week to go before the race at Le Mans, BP fuel agreed that Rindt, who was contracted to BP, could race with NART (who was contracted to

Le Mans was the scene of a fantastic, if unexpected, victory for the NART-entered 250 LM (5893) driven by Gregory, Rindt, and possibly Hugus.

5 | 1965

Rodríguez driving the 365 P2 at speed around the le Mans circuit.

The winning 250 LM of Rindt and Gregory follows Bandini's 275 P2 closed-version, with Kolb's Alfa TZ behind them.

Shell fuel). It all tied in neatly for what was about to transpire at Le Mans.

Rodríguez and Vaccarella had been entered in the 365 P2 (0838), while Rindt and Gregory were in a 250 LM (5893), much to the displeasure of Rindt who expected to be in the larger 365 P2. According to Bob Grossman "Initially I was due to drive the 250 LM (5893), but due to a misinterpretation of my actions by Luigi Chinetti, he refused to let

Le Mans success for NART

me drive." At the time, Chinetti Jr was married to heiress Mamie Reynolds. Their marriage had broken up by the time Le Mans was run, and he was ignoring Mamie. Consequently, she befriended Bob Grossman, and Chinetti Sr thought that it was Grossman who had broken up the marriage. Hence, Chinetti Sr did not allow Grossman to drive for him at Le Mans, but put Rindt into the car instead. (It would only be a matter of three months before Luigi Jr and Mamie were divorced, only for Mamie to remarry the same day, 14 September, to Joe Gregory from Louisville.)

It was significant that Chinetti had chosen to use Goodyear tyres on the 250 LM for the first time, instead of the usual Dunlop tyres, although Goodyear tyres had been used on NART-entered P cars and 250 GTOs in 1964. Ferrari's overall strategy was to use one or two cars as 'hares' to try and break the Ford GTs and Shelby Cobras, but Chinetti was not buying into this plan, having a more conservative 'wait and see' strategy of his own.

As the race commenced, the 7-litre Fords took an early lead over the first few laps, with Surtees, Bondurant and Rindt trying to stay in touch. So rapid were the Fords, that by lap nine Bruce McLaren's Ford had lapped one of the Ferraris, and only 16 starters were still on the same lap as each other. Thus, Ferrari's strategy had dissolved, barely after the race had settled down. One hour's hard motoring signalled the beginning of the scheduled pit stops, and McLaren's Ford dropped down to ninth place. The second hour saw the demise of Bondurant's Ford, and, from thereon in, started a trend which saw the other Ford challengers retire one-by-one, leaving the way open for another Ferrari victory.

By nine o'clock, Rodríguez had moved the NART 365 P2 up to sixth place, having had a condenser changed on the car, and at 11 o'clock had progressed up to fourth. The Gregory/Rindt car came into the pits to have all four wheels changed and brake pads replaced, after being driven hard by Rindt. Still feeling resentful for not being given a drive in the 365 P2, he was determined to drive the 250 LM to the limit, then if the car broke he could leave early, but was surprised how resilient the car was to being mistreated.

Retirements in the first 12 hours diminished the field to 27 cars and, as it was night-time, things around the pits were quieter than usual. Gregory, who suffered from poor night vision, had just taken over to do his early morning driving spell but, it is surmised by some people, immediately pulled back into the pits and commented to Ed Hugus that he could not see well enough in the semi-darkness, and wondered if he could take over until it became a little lighter. Ed Hugus was the official reserve driver, and it is said, took over Gregory's driving duties for about 50 minutes, until the light improved enough for Gregory to resume his spell at the wheel. According to Ed Hugus, this driver swap went unnoticed by the few members of the pit crew who may have been there, or any of the Le Mans officials.

At 6am the Dumay/Gosselin Ferrari had covered 203 laps, but was being chased by the NART car driven by Gregory and Rindt.

By 9.30am Ferrari was assured of victory, but it was uncertain which one would cross the finish line first. The Rodríguez/Vaccarella NART 365 P2 entry was in trouble with clutch problems, and remained in the pits for an hour, and Surtees' car was wheeled away with a

5 | 1965

broken gearbox. With four hours to go, the leading Ferrari of Dumay blew a tyre on the Mulsanne straight, and limped into the pits with a collapsed wheel and damaged bodywork. The repair took such a long time that it allowed the Gregory/Rindt car to take the lead, and the Belgians could do nothing about it, coming out of the pits five laps down on the leader. The NART 250 LM continued on its way to victory, amid scenes of jubilation in the NART pits, giving Luigi Chinetti his first Le Mans win as a team owner to go with the three victories he already had as a driver. The 365 P2, driven by Rodríguez and Vaccarella, managed to overcome its difficulties, and went on to finish in seventh place having covered 230 laps.

For their efforts the drivers would be entitled to a share of the appearance and prize money which went to the entrants of the cars. Payments made by Chinetti, and seen by the author, would doubtless not cover the entire payments made, however,

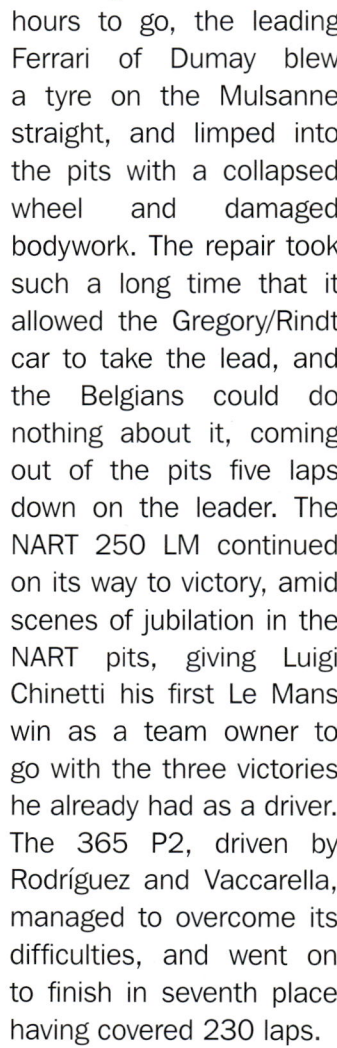

Rodríguez and Vaccarella drove a 365 P2 (0838) to a seventh place finish at Le Mans.

Le Mans success for NART

■ *Masten Gregory was one of the drivers in the winning Ferrari at Le Mans in 1965. His first race for NART was in 1964 at Nassau.*

■ *Nino Vaccarella was primarily a Ferrari factory driver, but was used by NART on the rare occasions he was not in a factory car.*

the author has seen the following cheques: Rindt received a cheque for $602, and Gregory two cheques totalling $674. Vaccarella had two cheques totalling $350, while Pedro Rodríguez had $1000 for piloting the 365 P2. Nothing was seen written out for Ed Hugus.

In the years since that famous victory, there has been much speculation surrounding the drivers, or one particular driver, of the winning Ferrari 250 LM. The official records show that Masten Gregory and Jochen Rindt as the drivers, but fail to mention Ed Hugus, the officially nominated third driver of the car.

The author approached Ed Hugus to verify that he drove the car, to which he gave an unequivocal 'yes.'

❝ I only made a short – less than one hour – relief of Masten in the early am. He came in unexpected – could not see OK in some fog. Since I was the relief driver, out I went for bal (balance) of tour. As I remember, the only people in the pits at that time were John Baus, myself and a mechanic or two – I do not remember sitting down more than a few minutes for the whole 24 hours. ❞

Extract from letter, 27 November 2000.

❝ As to the '65 Le Mans – it was 35 years ago now and I no longer care what anything shows – I have my memories and that is enough. Jacques Loest, then head of ACO told John Baus, my European manager, he would correct the ACO records in the late 60s – but I guess he never got round to it. 99

Extract from letter, 1 December 2000.

Unfortunately, the people who could confirm Ed's statements are all dead (Rindt, Gregory, Baus and Luigi Chinetti), and Chinetti Jr is very non-committal, saying he was at Le Mans but doesn't recall paying much attention to the car during that period. Lacking such independent corroboration, the author has approached a number of people acquainted with Ed Hugus, and the consensus was that he was an honest and humble man. Why should he not be telling the truth? While he had nothing material to gain from his achievement, it did not matter to him, but if he was perpetuating a lie, he would stand to lose his reputation, dignity and self-respect.

It could be that the whole affair was deliberately hushed-up by NART, due to the Le Mans ruling that once a reserve driver had been used, the substituted driver was not allowed to drive the car again. As Gregory did drive again, the car would have been disqualified had the officials been aware of Hugus driving the car.

The author's heart says that it would have been possible for Ed Hugus to have driven the car at around 5.16am but, without verification from a second person, the 'fact' can only remain speculative. Around 5.20am is the crucial point at which Ed Hugus claims to have driven the car. If there had been patchy fog at Le Mans it would have formed at around this time, not necessarily around the pit area, but more in the open countryside; also, at this time, fewer people would have been around the pit area to witness events. When Gregory took over the car and went out at 5.16am he may well have encountered some fog patches that would have unnerved him.

However, the head says otherwise, as certain facts are available that would suggest it to be a less likely scenario. Between midnight and 5.00am the car was recording very quick lap times, leaving no allowance for pit stops, or indeed for a less skilful driver to be in the car. These quick lap times continued for another hour beyond 5.00am. According to the official reports from *Journal des 24 heures*, Gregory stopped at 1.56am, with Rindt leaving the pits at 1.59am, which rules out Hugus driving at that time of day. Later, Rindt stopped at 5.14am, with Gregory leaving at 5.16am. The question remains, did Gregory pit soon after so that Hugus could drive?

In the author's opinion there is little clear evidence to suggest that Hugus drove the 250 LM at Le Mans, and if he did, his contribution was unable to be recognised due to the infraction of the rules.

The victory at Le Mans for Chinetti also happened to be a big win for the Goodyear Tire & Rubber Company, since this was the first time a car fitted with Goodyear tyres finished first overall in the prestigious endurance race.

The Reims 12-hour race failed to attract any factory teams, though a number of interesting cars, mainly Ferraris, turned up in the hands of privateers. NART employed the services of Rodríguez and Guichet for their entry, a 365 P2 (0838). After making a strong start and taking the lead, the car developed clutch trouble, dropping down the order from third to 15th place during the night. A 20-minute stop to change the clutch solved the problem and, as dawn broke, they were chasing down the

Le Mans success for NART

■ The winning car at the Reims 12-hour race was the 365 P2, driven by Rodríguez and Guichet.

■ The 365 P2 (0838) on its way to victory at Reims.

■ Shortly after the Reims event, 0838 was returned to the Ferrari factory, where changes to the bodywork were made in preparation for the North American races at Mosport and Bridgehampton.

5 | 1965

The 365 P2 (0838) driven by Rodríguez finished the race at Bridgehampton in second position.

Andretti drove the 275 P2 (0814) at Bridgehampton but retired with gearbox trouble.

Pedro Rodríguez leads the field on the first lap of the race at Bridgehampton.

leading Ferraris. With 90 minutes to go, the NART 365 P2 took the lead and provided Luigi Chinetti with his second victory in two races. A second car entered by NART shows on the entry list, a 250 LM for Nino Vaccarella to drive, but the car failed to appear. For his efforts Guichet had to wait until February 1966 to be rewarded by Chinetti.

The 200km race at Zeltweg was another low key, non-championship race, but was the home venue for Rindt. He took charge of a 250 LM, which had just been rebuilt by the factory after being involved in an accident in late August 1964. It is unclear if Chinetti bought the vehicle from the factory, and entered Rindt to use it at Zeltweg before being shipped to America, but it appears to be the most likely scenario, as the car was then sold by Chinetti to Arthur Swanson, who lived in Connecticut.

Three NART-entered cars appeared for the Bridgehampton Double 500 race in September. Rodríguez was driving the familiar 365 P2 (0838), and Andretti was in a 275 P2 (0814), while Arents and Hutchins were in the newly acquired 275 GTB/C (6885 GT). NART had bought the car from Ecurie Francorchamps after the Le Mans race. For Andretti, it was his first race in a Ferrari, and during practice he was finding out the idiosyncrasies of the 275 P. The Ferrari pits were busy with Rodríguez and Andretti making frequent stops; the NART crew were complaining of tyre problems on Pedro's car, and Andretti's machine didn't exhibit the most desirable handling characteristics either. Andretti's 275 P was in and out of the pits to clean sand out of the Weber carburettors, as the result of a few off-course excursions. The pit crew worked frantically and, to outsiders

Le Mans success for NART

watching the proceedings, must have looked akin to a Chinese fire drill.

The field of 24 starters set off from a rolling start, with Rodríguez taking the lead from his second row grid spot, followed by Hansgen and Sharp. After 30 minutes Hansgen had retired, Sharp had taken the lead, and Rodríguez was following in second spot. About this time, Andretti, who was in the middle of the pack, retired the 275 P, having no oil in the gearbox. Rodríguez maintained his second place, finishing some two laps down on the race winner, Hap Sharp in his Chaparral. After the race, Andretti was asked how he had enjoyed his first competitive drive in a Ferrari: "I woulda liked it a lot better if it'd lasted longer," he growled back. The Arents/Hutchins 275 GTB/C proved to be no competition to the Shelby Cobras in the GT category, finishing 11th overall and fourth in class, following a spectacular spin.

Pedro Rodríguez turned up at Mosport one week after the Bridgehampton race, determined to maintain his good form in the NART-entered 365 P2. After qualifying fourth on the grid, he was never quite on the pace, duelling with Charlie Hayes for most of the race. He eventually managed to get the better of Hayes to achieve a third place finish, five laps adrift on the winning Chaparral driven by Jim Hall, who just managed to beat Bruce McLaren over the finish line by one-fifth of a second. For his weekend efforts Rodríguez received a cheque for $1450 from Luigi Chinetti.

Whereas in 1964 at Watkins Glen, all of the Ferrari F1 cars were painted blue and white for the US Grand Prix, this year Bandini's car was an official Ferrari entry, but the cars for Pedro Rodríguez and Bob Bondurant (standing in for the injured John Surtees) had blue and white stripes painted over the red cars. The two cars were entered under the banner of the North American Racing Team, and had either been loaned by the factory or rented by Chinetti. Unlike the other F1 cars, the Ferraris were not garaged at the track, but at the Chevrolet dealers' premises in Watkins Glen. They were supposed to be transported out to the circuit by trailer, but when no trailers showed up it was decided they would have to be driven there. One can imagine the sight and sound of the cars being driven on public roads up to the track! Bondurant had been given the V8 model and Rodríguez a flat-12 1512 model.

Watkins Glen 1965 saw the return of NART-entered F1 cars for Pedro Rodríguez and Bob Bondurant.

Pedro Rodríguez on his way to a fifth place finish in the US Grand Prix in the 1512 F1 car (0007).

5 | 1965

Charlie Kolb drove 275 GTB/C (6885 GT) to victory in the Nassau Tourist Trophy during the Bahamas Speed Weeks.

After starting 15th on the grid, Rodríguez drove a solid race finishing in fifth place, while Bondurant started 14th and finished ninth, not through any fault of the car which performed well, but due to Bondurant having trouble with his goggles, which kept slipping off his face after the strap stretched in the rain.

Three weeks later the Mexican Grand Prix took place, and NART arranged for Pedro Rodríguez to enter his home Grand Prix in a 1512 model and, because it was a private entry, allowed Pedro to try Firestone's latest semi-slick tyres. Unfortunately, before any meaningful evaluation could be made, Pedro crashed the car and was allowed to compete in Scarfiotti's factory car. Off the pace, Pedro finished in seventh place after managing to collide with Bandini's Ferrari in the hairpin bend.

The final entry of the year for the Ferrari 275 GTB/C (6885 GT) that appeared at Bridgehampton in September, was at the Bahamas Speed Weeks. It was provided by NART for Charlie Kolb and Al Durham to drive. The car had four outings, being driven to victory twice by Charlie Kolb in the Nassau Tourist Trophy preliminary race and the Nassau Tourist Trophy, then by Al Durham who finished 11th in the Governor's Trophy but failed to finish in the Nassau Trophy race.

The retail side of the business was flourishing, as the NART team gained publicity, and Chinetti decided to move his main premises to 600 West Putnam Avenue, Greenwich. The business continued to expand and, in the early 1970s, Chinetti also had a New York City showroom at 1100 Second Ave at 56th Street.

1966-69

> 1966 was a time of turmoil for Ferrari. Italy was hit by seemingly endless strikes in the manufacturing sector, and the company's strength had been sapped, as it struggled to manufacture its production cars, the lifeblood of its racing operation.

Accordingly, development of new prototypes was limited, and those that were produced would only be used in the factory team. That meant that the private teams would, in the main, have to make do with what they already had.

February signalled the start of another season for the North American Racing Team. Its first race was at Daytona for the 24-hour race, with part of it run in sub-zero temperatures. Chinetti entered three Ferraris under the NART banner, two of which had been used by the team in 1965. The latest addition to the team was the 250 LM (5901), which had been ordered by Chinetti in November 1965, and shipped to America aboard the Maria Costa. Rodríguez and Andretti were paired in the refurbished 365 P2 (0838), with Rindt and Bondurant in the 250 LM (5893), while Wester, Hawkins and Follmer had the new 250 LM. There was no official Ferrari factory representation at Daytona, the factory deciding that the Daytona banking was not really suitable for the set-up of its cars, which would perform far better on the European tracks in their bid to win the FIA Prototype championship.

It was left to NART and other privateers to salvage what they could from the race, and to that end NART played its part. Ford had bought a strong team of cars to Daytona, and for them it paid off, finishing 1-2-3 overall, with the NART-entered 365 P2 in fourth place. The car suffered with rear brake problems, and the brake pads had to be changed a couple of times. The rear springs also weakened, resulting in some imaginative redesigning of the rear wings, so as to keep the bodywork from rubbing on the tyres. Despite these problems, the car finished just 14 laps behind the winning car. The Rindt/Bondurant 250 LM finished in ninth place, having covered 591 laps, but the other 250 LM (5901) went out after 428 laps with a defective generator. Bondurant received a cheque from Chinetti for $896, though had to wait until May before he received it.

Only one car was entered by NART for the Sebring 12-hour race. Rodríguez and Andretti were again paired to drive the 365 P2/3. After qualifying ninth fastest, the car was in third place when it was involved in a tragic accident that would eliminate it. The accident took place in the 11th hour of the race, when, coming down the short warehouse straight, Andretti missed a gearshift in the Ferrari, and instead of changing from fourth to third, selected first gear. The Ferrari went spinning across the track and was hit by Don Wester's Porsche Carrera 6. Both cars left the track, Andretti's Ferrari coming to rest against a spectator fence, fortunately without injury to anyone. However, Don Wester was less fortunate, his Porsche veered off to the left, striking and fatally injuring four people who were watching from an unfenced, non-designated spectator area. Wester was trapped in the car for several minutes before being freed, and hospitalised suffering from a broken ankle, cuts and shock.

Andretti was able to drive the Ferrari back to the pits, where the damage was assessed and the car was deemed

A series of disappointments

The 365 P2 (0838) driven by Rodríguez and Andretti finished in fourth place at Daytona.

Rindt and Bondurant's 250 LM (5893) finished ninth at Daytona.

The 250 LM (5901) failed to finish at Daytona due to electrical faults.

6 | 1966-69

NART entered 330 P2 (0838) for the Sebring 12-hour race, driven by Pedro Rodríguez and Mario Andretti, but the car failed to finish.

to be drivable after straightening some bodywork. On starting the car up again it broke into flames, and the team had no option but to retire the car, having covered 188 laps. Though not apparent at the time the accident would have repercussions for NART in the future. For their efforts at Daytona and Sebring, both Rodríguez and Andretti received a cheque from Chinetti for the sum of $1000. The 365 P2 was sent back to Italy for a radical rebuild, with the Le Mans 24-hour race in mind.

NART entered a Dino 206S for the Monza 1000km race, but Bondurant had an accident during the practice session, and the car was badly damaged enough for it to not make the start grid.

Chinetti Jr took 275 P (0814) to Watkins Glen for the two-day SCCA meeting, in which he came first in the preliminary race on Saturday, and second in the main race held on Sunday.

The Prototype World Championship was in full swing in Europe, Chinetti avoiding the round at Spa and the Targa Florio, but entering A Dino 206S in the round to be run at the Nürburgring. Of the three Dinos entered, only the factory car had a twin-plug fuel-injected unit, the NART car having a single ignition carburettor type unit, as did the Piper/Attwood entry. The Ferrari factory had made a token gesture to the entry list, by sending a 330 P3 for Surtees to drive, as well as the Dino 206S for Scarfiotti/Bandini, but beyond that it was down to the privateers to

A series of disappointments

uphold the honour of Ferrari. The small Dinos held up extremely well against much stronger opposition, the factory entry finishing second to the Chaparral driven by Phil Hill and Jo Bonnier, with the less powerful Dino 206S of NART drivers Rodríguez and Ginther finishing in third spot, on the same lap as the winning car. Doubtless, the fickle weather at the Nürburgring helped the smaller cars keep pace with the Chaparral, with

Rodríguez and Ginther piloted the Dino 206S (008) to a third place finish at the Nürburgring.

Richie Ginther in conversation with Henry Manney, while the NART crew works on the Dino 206S at the Nürburgring.

6 | 1966-69

The Dino 206S makes its way round the German countryside, finishing third overall, driven by Pedro Rodríguez and Richie Ginther.

140 | N.A.R.T.

A series of disappointments

heavy rain descending three-quarters of the way through the race. A cheque for $2250 was made out to Ginther for his contribution at Nürburgring and Le Mans, and Rodríguez pocketed the same amount.

The Ferrari Dino 268 SP 0798 was rented to Bob Hutchins, for a series of SCCA events held in the first half of 1966. He appeared at Vineland in April, finishing fifth overall, and followed up with races at Virginia International Raceway and Cumberland, finishing eighth at the latter venue.

Late in 1965, Chinetti had ordered from the factory a 275 GTB, which arrived in January 1966. Chassis number 9057 was retained by Chinetti and rented to Bob Hutchins in mid-1966 appearing at Vineland in June for the SCCA National races.

What comes next is believable, though unsubstantiated in its detail. In an interview with Rick Anderson he told me,

> In June there was a race held at St Jovite in Canada. This was the venue of a Canadian rally the previous year, and Chinetti Jr had decided to enter with a Ferrari. Upon early arrival he gets drunk and does a burn-out across the local mayor's lawn. Consequently the mayor is not best pleased and has Chinetti Jr thrown out of the rally. The next year Chinetti Jr trailered the Ferrari 275 P (0814) up to St Jovite for the race. In the race he crashes into an Elva Mk VIII-BMW driven by Tom Ashwell. Well, well, guess what old Tom Ashwell is when he is not driving his Elva; he's the local mayor.

Ritchie Ginther made just one appearance for NART in 1966, when he drove with Pedro Rodríguez at the Nürburgring, finishing in third place.

Luigi Chinetti Jr sustained damage to the 275 P in an accident at St Jovite, this resulted in the fire that destroyed 0814.

Luigi Chinetti Motors Inc was the American distributor for ASA. This is an example of an advert for Ferrari and ASA cars placed by Luigi Chinetti Motors Inc.

The 275 GTB/C (9015 GT) experienced clutch trouble and failed to finish at Le Mans.

That must have been some reunion! Chinetti Jr's car sustained substantial damage including fire damage, so it was a case of taking just the remnants back home to face his father. It was unfortunate for Chinetti Jr that all the fire equipment was on the far side of the track, dealing with another car that was on fire at the same time as this incident.

Luigi Chinetti came up with a diverse mix of cars for the Le Mans 24-hour race. The car that grabbed everyone's attention was the 365 P2, which had been delivered direct from the factory to Le Mans. Hardly recognisable as the damaged and burnt 0838 from the Sebring race, the car now looked resplendent, with a new body built by Drogo, which incorporated a long tail and a roof. It was one of five various Ferraris entered by Chinetti, together with, for the first time, an ASA RB613.

A series of disappointments

NART's mechanics prepare the Dino 206S (008) prior to the Le Mans 24-hour race.

6 | 1966-69

NART brought an ASA to Le Mans, but it did not finish due to an accident on lap 50.

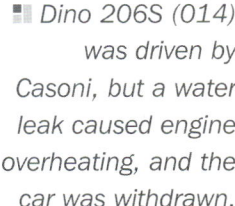 *Dino 206S (014) was driven by Casoni, but a water leak caused engine overheating, and the car was withdrawn.*

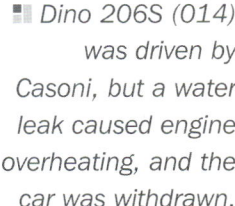 *Kolb and Follmer drove the Dino 206S (008), but clutch trouble forced the car to retire.*

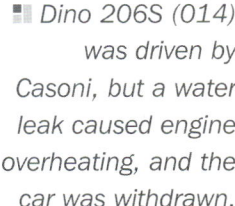 *The 365 P2 (0838) sits next to the Dino 206S (014) in the pit area prior to the race.*

A series of disappointments

A view of the 'White Elephant' in the pits at Le Mans.

The inclusion of this car was not as puzzling as one might think, as there was a definite link with Ferrari regarding the very existence and future development of the car. At the end of the 1950s, Ferrari started testing a GT prototype with a four-cylinder engine of 850cc, installed in a modified chassis and body of a Fiat 1200 Pininfarina. Throughout the development, Ferrari would not allow his Prancing Horse emblem to be used on the car and, when produced, would not allow Ferrari dealers to market or sell the car, with one exception – Luigi Chinetti, who had the rights to market and sell the car in North America. A number of road-going models were made and, in addition, four fibreglass-bodied examples known as the ASA RB613, three of these having a six-cylinder 1300cc engine directly derived from the Ferrari 250 engine. It was one of these examples that NART entered in the Le Mans 24-hour race for French drivers François Pasquier and Robert Mieusset. Chinetti had come up with the idea of introducing a new award for Le Mans, the Trophée Chinetti which, in effect, was in the form of a NART entry for two promising French drivers. Unfortunately, the NART-entered ASA did not last very long: it was involved in an accident after covering 50 laps in the race, and ended up buried in sand.

Two Dino 206S, two P-cars, and a 275 GTB made up the NART entry, but none of them made it through to see the chequered flag. First to be eliminated was the Dino 206S of Vaccarella and Casoni, the car rapidly expelling water from the engine compartment after just seven laps. Following closely behind was the second Dino 206S of Kolb and Follmer, a shattered clutch forcing them out after nine laps. The two P-cars fared a little better, the 365 P2 (0838) went out with gearbox problems on lap 88, and the Rodríguez/Ginther 330 P3 was also eliminated with gearbox failure after 151 laps. The car that lasted longest was the least likely to do so, the 275 GTB of Biscaldi and de Bourbon-Parme. The car covered 218 laps, before it too went out with gearbox problems.

While this was not a good showing for Ferrari in particular, to put the situation into perspective, only 15 of the 55 cars that started crossed the finish line. Despite the poor performance, the drivers received their due payments as follows, Bondurant $500, Vaccarella $790, and Kolb $920.

For the Bridgehampton Can-Am race in September, NART entered a Dino 206S (014) for Pedro Rodríguez to drive. The car was not suited to the class of large-engine opposition and struggled to make any impact. After covering 39 laps of the race, the car lost a wheel and was instantly retired. Bob Hutchins had obtained an entry through NART to use the 275 GTB (9057 GT), but in the production race it was involved in an accident, and failed to finish after rolling the car on lap 2. The damaged car was returned to Chinetti for repairs before it could be used again in 1967.

An interesting article appeared in the *New York Times*, 28 September 1966, written by Frank M Blunk. Talking about the US F1 Grand Prix to be held at Watkins Glen, he states:

> Ferrari is represented this year by only one car. According to Luigi Chinetti, the American representative for Ferrari, the new engine of twelve-cylinder design is somewhat different than the Ferrari run at Monza earlier this month. The car has not been entered by the factory but by the North American Racing Team which Chinetti directs. Lorenzo Bandini of Italy will be the driver.

Pedro Rodríguez was present for the Laguna Seca Can-Am race, using the Dino 206S that

Pedro Rodríguez in the Dino 206S (014) at the Bridgehampton Can-Am race.

A series of disappointments

he had at Bridgehampton. This time, though, the car had been leased by Chinetti to Bill Harrah for Rodríguez to drive. It fared no better than at Bridgehampton, finishing 14th in the first heat, and 25th in the second heat of the race, consequently not making it through to the final. In a consolation race, the car could do no better than ninth place.

The same Chinetti/Harrah arrangement was in place two weeks later, when Rodríguez and the Dino 206S turned up at Riverside. The car was still uncompetitive; so much so, that it failed to qualify for the race.

1967 started on a promising note for the North American Racing Team at the Daytona 24-hour race. It had three cars in attendance: two Ferraris and an ASA RB613. The ASA was most likely leased to Baker Racing, which was sponsored by Ring Free Oil.

NART's Dino 206S (014) was at Laguna Seca, where Rodríguez drove the car to a ninth place finish in the consolation race.

A small selection of cheques made out as payment to drivers from Luigi Chinetti Motors Inc.

A concise history of the North American Racing Team 1957 to 1983

6 | 1966-69

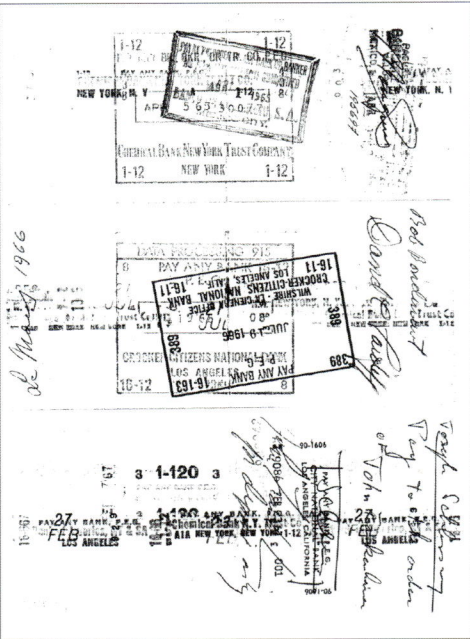

The reverse side of each cheque is countersigned by the driver.

On 20 January, Chinetti purchased chassis 0844 from Ferrari. It had been run in 1966 by the factory as a 330 P, but, before being sold, was upgraded to a P4 specification, and was officially designated a 412 P. Chinetti paid $20,000 for the car, and it was given to Pedro Rodríguez and Jean Guichet for the 24-hour race, while Gregory, Schlesser and Gregg were given the Dino 206S (008). Baker Racing had the knack of getting publicity through employing all-female drivers for some of its cars. Daytona was one of those occasions, with Suzy Dietrich and Donna Mae Mims piloting the ASA RB613. In addition, Liane Engeman, Janet Guthrie, Rosemary Smith, Smokey Drolet and Anita Taylor were in attendance. That would have been some team photograph!

The Ferrari 412 P (0844) was driven by Pedro Rodríguez and Jean Guichet to a third place finish in the 24-hour race at Daytona.

148 | N.A.R.T.

A series of disappointments

■ A temporary repair on the course was necessary for the 412 P when a suspension rod broke.

■ NART entered an ASA RB613 in the Daytona race, and it finished in 24th place.

■ NART's ASA RB613 overtakes a Volvo during the 24-hour race.

For Ferrari it turned out to be a dream race, with the factory P4s finishing first and second, and the NART 412P in third place. A relatively trouble-free 24 hours was in stark contrast to the large Ford entry, all of their GT40's suffering the effects of a bad batch of transmission shafts. Rodríguez only had one scare, when a bolt fell out of the transmission linkage on his car. A temporary repair on course, followed by a more permanent fix in the pits, saw him drop out of contention for first place, but he at least secured a third spot finish for the car.

Fred Baker used a NART entry for the Dino 206S. He had just bought the car, and had Chinetti rebuild the engine and overhaul the gearbox. However, the work had not been completed in time to qualify at Daytona, and the car had to start from the back of the grid. After coming through the field and managing to reach tenth place, Gregory came into the pits for a routine stop, only to have the engine misfire when it restarted, the problem being a stripped distributor drive. After covering 338 laps the car had to be retired. The ASA RB613 covered 459 laps to finish in 24th place overall, third in the under-2000cc prototype class.

For the first time in years, Luigi Chinetti's NART was officially missing from the Sebring entry list, because, Chinetti said "I don't want to be put in jail." Chinetti had made a last minute decision not to bring his North American Racing Team Ferraris, after a flurry of lawsuits made headlines a few days prior to the races. The races in 1966 had been marred by the death of four spectators, and the two families affected had filed lawsuits against Alec Ulmann as an individual; the Auto Racing Club, of which Ulmann was president, with failing to give spectators adequate protection; Mario Andretti (NART Ferrari); and Porsche driver Don Wester. As Andretti had been at the wheel of one of Chinetti's cars, Chinetti feared there would be a writ of foreign attachment issued, which would prevent removal of his cars after the race. Chinetti prudently decided to stay

6 | 1966-69

Pedro Rodríguez was one of the long-term regular drivers used by Luigi Chinetti, mainly through arrangements made between Chinetti and 'Papa' Rodríguez. His first drive for NART was in 1958, and his final was in 1970.

The 412 P (0844) turned up at Monza, where it was driven by Rodríguez and Guichet, but lasted only 46 laps before retiring.

at home, to avoid any legal unpleasantness. Chinetti was highly critical of what he termed "inadequate insurance coverage" at the Sebring course situated on an old airfield. "We run experimental cars and we do not know what will happen. There should be coverage that fully protects the entrants." Following Andretti's crash, Chinetti had to make the car available to the insurance company for one month, for a series of technical inspections.

Despite what it might have said on paper, four cars consigned to Chinetti were in attendance at Sebring. Rodríguez and Guichet were there in the Dino 206S (014) entered under Rodríguez's name, and the ASA RB613 (21004) for Suzy Dietrich and Donna Mae Mims. This was the same car that was entered at Daytona earlier in the year. There was also the entry under Fred Baker's name, of the Dino 206S (008). The car had qualified in 20th place on the grid, but at the green light the car failed to pull away, as it broke a half shaft on the start line. The fourth car was a 275 GTB4 NART Spyder entered under Denise McCluggage's name, sponsored by CITGO. Details of this are given in Chapter 12.

A series of disappointments

The Dino 206S entered under Rodríguez's name covered 101 laps before having to retire due to overheating problems, so it was left to the diminutive ASA to record a finish position, Dietrich and Mae Mims bringing the car home in 25th place having covered 159 laps.

The first of four European races followed for the North American Racing Team. The first of these was at Monza for the 1000km event. NART transported the 412 P to the event for Rodríguez and Guichet, and they were fourth on the grid for the start of the race. The 412 P ran just behind the leading group of cars until, on lap 44, Rodríguez decided to fight for position. The fight lasted for two laps, before Rodríguez left his braking too late at the first chicane, hit a guard rail, and abruptly stopped; his race was over.

NART's next excursion was to the Targa Florio in Sicily, where the Sicilian drivers Ferdinando Latteri and Ignazio Capuano piloted the Dino 206S (018). They managed three laps before going out of the race.

There were six places allocated to Luigi Chinetti for the Le Mans 24-hour race, but only three of those were taken. The 412 P (0844) had been repaired at Ferrari for Chinetti, and was given to Rodríguez and Baghetti to drive, while the older, long-tailed 365 P2 (0838) was given to Parsons and Ricardo Rodríguez (not Pedro's brother). The car had been dubbed 'the white elephant,' and had an elephant motif attached on the rear end of it. The third car was an Alpine-Renault M64 (1710) entered for two French drivers, Jean-Luc Thérier and François Chevalier, under the Trophée Chinetti scheme.

It was an early exit for the Parsons/Rodríguez 365 P2, when it didn't make the corner at Mulsanne, and slid deep into the sand. No amount of digging by Ricardo Rodríguez would extract the car. Bob Grossman said:

NART's 365 P2 (0838) was back at Le Mans sporting an elephant emblem on the rear wing. Driven by American Ricardo Rodríguez and Parsons, the car failed to finish.

The Ferrari factory and NART cars arrive at Le Mans.

" The handling of the car was so bad several drivers refused to drive it. The rear Perspex window distorted rear vision and dissipated the headlight beams from following vehicles. Because of this problem it was difficult to take the right line into corners – especially with other quicker cars behind. Eventually an incident occurred in practice, when I moved over at White House and was hit by Klass' Ferrari. I felt a bump but the car appeared undamaged so I continued.

1966-69

Klass' car ended up on the side of the road. Later the officials asked about the accident but I denied any knowledge of the incident. "

Pedro Rodríguez had made a great start to the race and led the way before being overtaken by Paul Hawkins' Ford GT40. The 412 P was consistently showing in the top ten cars as the laps went by, then had an unscheduled pit stop. It finally pitted again at two o'clock on Sunday morning with continuous engine problems, putting the car out of the race, having covered 144 laps. The Alpine-Renault M64 lasted longest before it also had engine failure, putting the car out of the race after covering 201 laps.

After the Le Mans race, Chinetti sent the 412 P back to the Ferrari factory, with a request to transform it into a car that he could enter in the Can-Am series in America, otherwise the car would be obsolete due to the new three-litre engine capacity limit, announced by the Commission Sportive International for Group 6 prototypes.

On 25 June the Reims 12-hour race took place. There was a Dino 206S entered by NART for Rodríguez and Guichet to drive. There is no obvious candidate for a chassis number of the car that was entered, though one can only surmise that the car was already in Europe, and not flown in from America for this one event. The only positive information on this race was that the Dino 206S retired.

The Can-Am series in America was attracting drivers from around the world, and Chinetti employed the services of Scarfiotti for the

Nereo Iori stands by the 412 P Can-Am Ferrari, with Wayne Sparling behind the wheel in the Bridgehampton paddock.

A series of disappointments

race at Bridgehampton in September. Chinetti entered the new-look modified 412 P (0844) against some formidable opposition. The transformation to the car included the deletion of the spare wheel and luggage compartment, as these were not necessary under Can-Am specification rules, and the nose section was lowered as the oil cooler now sat astride the gearbox. The coupé top had been dispensed with, and a low windscreen fitted, flaring into small Perspex side screens mounted in the doors. It soon became apparent to Scarfiotti that the car was too heavy to compete against six-litre Chevrolet blocks squeezed into lightweight bodies. The Bridgehampton track had been hit by hurricane Dora a few days previously, and was still drenched. Scarfiotti literally slid to a seventh place finish in the car, and for his tenacity won $1000 in prize money.

One week later at Mosport, Scarfiotti qualified in 11th place out of 17 entrants, and following a slow start suffered a flat tyre, and then a crash that put him out of the race after covering 44 laps.

The CSI ruling of 1967 was to see the end of the large-engine prototypes in Group six, a move probably mourned by as many organisations as it pleased others. The three-litre limit on engine capacity gave the advantage to those manufacturers of Formula One cars, as they were already producing that size of engine for those cars, whereas Ford and General Motors were left to respond to the new challenge. It also opened the door to other manufacturers to try their luck in the new form of Group 6 racing.

Consequently when NART went to Daytona in 1968, it was left to Chinetti to field the smaller cars, with the big 412 P at the factory undergoing work that would see it as a Can-Am specification car. The 1965 Le Mans-winning Ferrari 250 LM was entered for David Piper and Masten Gregory in the Sports category, and a Dino 206S for Pedro Rodríguez and Charlie Kolb in the Prototype category. There was also a third entry made, this for a 275 GTB/C but no drivers were nominated and the car failed to show.

■ *The 412 P Can-Am car (0844) was at Mosport.*

■ *Kolb and Rodríguez drove the Dino 206S (008) at Daytona, but the car failed to last the distance.*

A concise history of the North American Racing Team 1957 to 1983

250 LM (5893) was driven by Masten Gregory and David Piper at Daytona, but the car failed to finish.

Pedro Rodríguez made a strong start to the race, and was seventh overall after one hour, just before the head gasket blew, putting the Dino 206S out of the race. Three hours and 40 minutes into the race, there was an accident involving several cars, in which Gerhard Mitter's Porsche had a puncture, flipped, and spilt all its oil over the track. Just behind Mitter was Gregory in the 250 LM, who slammed on his brakes, right over the invisible spilt oil. The car flipped sideways, went end-over-end into the infield, and was badly damaged, though fortunately there were no injuries to those concerned. Gregory, who must be the most-crashed, still-surviving driver in the world, calmly jumped out of the hole where the Ferrari's windscreen had been. In practice, Gregory had trouble with a leaking fuel tank, and as he clambered out of the car his only thought was "God, I hope Sparling fixed that gas tank!"

There were no further NART entries until the Watkins Glen 6-hour race was held in July. Two cars were entered, the Dino 206S (014) was allocated to Pedro Rodríguez and Charlie Kolb, while Bob Grossman and Ronnie Bucknum had a 275 GTB4 (10311 GT). Neither car contested the leading positions, but did at least reach the finish line, the Dino 206S covering 247 laps to finish seventh, and the near-standard specification 275 GTB4 covering 241 laps to finish ninth overall.

There followed two Can-Am races in September, at Elkhart Lake and Bridgehampton. In 1967, the Ferrari factory had converted a

A series of disappointments

330 P4 (0860) to a Group 7 Can-Am specification for Bill Harrah to enter in the West Coast Can-Am races, after which it went back to Ferrari. Chinetti bought the car in July for $16,700, to use in the Can-Am races on the East Coast with Pedro Rodríguez driving the car.

At Elkhart Lake, Rodríguez excelled to qualify in tenth place on the grid then, in a rain-soaked race, did well to finish 13th in the Ferrari, covering 45 laps after coming from last place, following a ten minute pit stop in the second lap, to correct a rain-shorted ignition. Despite being well down the field, Rodríguez still collected $700 in prize money.

Two weeks later, the same car was at Bridgehampton. Another good qualifying session put Rodríguez 11th on the start grid, but this time he was not so lucky,

Ronnie Bucknum was a regular NART driver.

Pedro is pointing, "I think we will go this way," at Road America.

A concise history of the North American Racing Team 1957 to 1983

6 | 1966-69

Nereo Iori and Dick Fritz give Pedro a helping hand to get the 330 P4 Can-Am Ferrari from the paddock to the track.

Pedro Rodríguez drove the 330 P4 Can-Am Ferrari (0860).

Rodríguez drove the 330 P4 Can-Am at Bridgehampton, but failed to make an impression.

as on lap 12 he and Sam Posey made contact on the short back straight. Rodríguez slid off the track and broke the suspension on the car. Chinetti presented Rodríguez with a cheque for $1265 to cover both of the Can-Am races.

NART's final appearance of 1968 was at Le Mans for the 24-hour race, and it must be said that it appeared to be a half-hearted affair by NART. Three cars appeared, but by race day only two were on the start grid. Bob Grossman had a 275 GTB4, but lost his ride when the car, which sounded awful, was not permitted to start because of slow practice times. The venerable 250 LM (5893) had been repaired, after the crash at Daytona earlier in the year, though hardly looked in top condition, and was given to Gregory and Kolb to drive. The equally well-used Dino 206S (014) was there as a Trophée Chinetti entry for the French drivers, Chevalier and Lagier. The Dino 206S was the first car to fail, going out after 54 laps with a blown head gasket. Meanwhile, the 250 LM was faring better, making its way up to ninth place, despite continuous clutch problems.

A series of disappointments

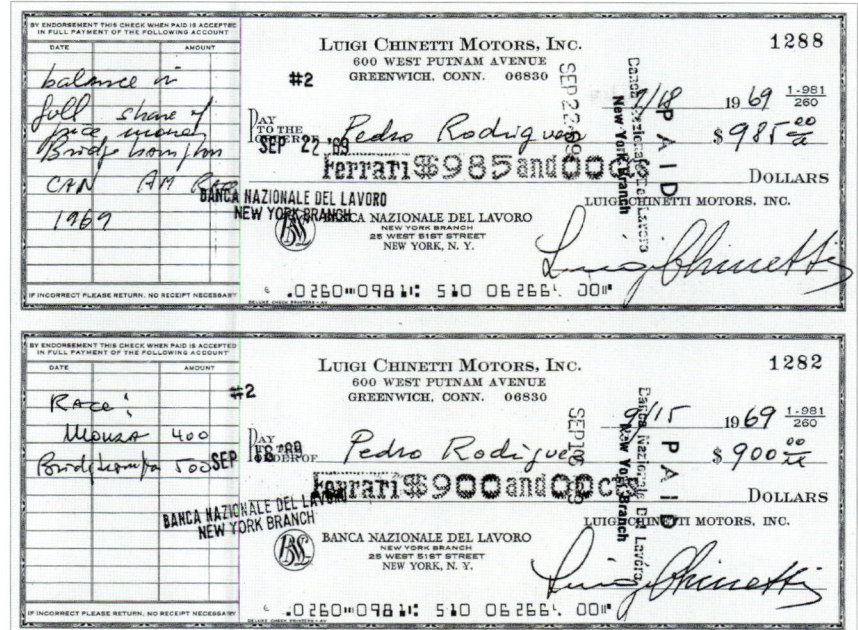

Two cheques paid to Pedro Rodríguez for his drives at Bridgehampton and Mosport.

■ Gregory and Kolb piloted the 250 LM (5893) but it retired from the race at Le Mans following an accident.

■ NART's Dino 206S (014) suffered a blown head gasket and was also retired from the race.

After covering 209 laps, Kolb negated all Gregory's efforts by going off the road at Tertre-Rouge and out of the race.

1969 saw some new faces driving for NART. One was Sam Posey, who was interviewed by the author at Posey's home in Connecticut. Talking of his first experiences of NART he stated:

❝ My first race for NART was at Daytona, and came about through an introduction to team manager Dick Fritz by Ron Meade who, at that time, was acting as a PR man at Autodynamics. Looking around the pit garage, the first thing that struck me was the stark contrast between NART and the highly efficient Penske organisation. NART looked to be very casual. Anyway, I was told by Dick that there could be an opening for a driver, but he would have to check with Chinetti. I was hanging around the pits, so Dick said to drive the 275 back to the garage from the pits – my first NART drive!

6 | 1966-69

Kolb and Biscaldi failed to finish at Daytona driving NART's Dino 206S (014)

NART's 275 GTB4, driven by American Ricardo Rodríguez and Sam Posey, finished in 23rd place at Daytona, after a prolonged stop to mend the gearbox.

Having got clearance from Luigi I was allowed to practice in the GTB, and after several laps I was convinced that it needed suspension changes. A good idea said Dick, but actually we don't have any other parts for the car. 99

The car had been repurchased from Jan de Vroom by Chinetti specifically for this race. The Daytona organisers were well aware of the lack of Ferrari entries, and had asked Dick

A series of disappointments

Fritz if he could help out. There was not much time for preparation, so very little was done to it. The fenders were removed, an outside exhaust system installed, a roll-bar inserted, an external fuel filler installed to feed the twin tanks, and Borrani wheels fitted.

Sam Posey was driving the car around the banking at around 3am, when the right rear tyre exploded, but he managed to spin the car onto the grass infield. Having run back to the pits, he had to set about collecting the spare wheel, jack and hammer, and change the wheel himself before driving off again. A while later the gearbox failed. Since there were no spares available, Dick Fritz decided to try and rebuild the gearbox in the pits. Fritz remembers seeing mechanic François Sicard covered in oil, as he set to work on the gearbox. Three hours later the car exited the pits, and eventually managed to cross the finish line in 23rd place (second in class). It was a meaningless achievement in terms of racing, but quite extraordinary for a car right off the showroom floor. The Kolb/Biscaldi Dino 206S circulated for 152 laps before the engine called 'enough,' and the car was retired.

For the Sebring 12-hour race Chinetti entered three cars. Sam Posey and Bob Dini were given a new production Dino 206 GT, straight off the boat, and the Dino 206S (014) was given another outing, again in the hands of Rodríguez and Kolb. The third car was described as a 330 P3, however, the Group 6 engine capacity limit for cars was 3-litre, so the car could not have had a 330 engine in it. It would appear that Major Cooper's 275 P (0816) was used instead. However, an engine swap would still have been needed, so that it conformed to a 3-litre capacity. Originally, Chinetti had been expecting to have a 312P for Sebring but,

Sam Posey's first drive with NART was in 1969, and he continued to drive for Luigi Chinetti in endurance races for the next four years.

Kolb and American Ricardo Rodríguez finished in ninth place at Sebring driving the Dino 206S (014).

A concise history of the North American Racing Team 1957 to 1983 | 159

6 | 1966-69

Zeccoli and Posey drove the 250 LM (5893) to an eighth place finish at Le Mans.

with industrial disputes in Italy, he had taken the precaution of preparing the spare P-car. The old 250 P was circulating as high as tenth, but did not finish due to transmission problems after covering 163 laps, while the two Dinos did better. The Dino 206 GT finished in 36th place, but still managed to win its class, while Ricardo Rodríguez and Kolb steered the Dino 206S to a creditable ninth-place finish, having completed 215 laps. For Rodríguez it meant a payment of $1975.

Three NART entries appeared for the Le Mans 24-hour race. Sam Posey and Theodoro Zeccoli, Alfa Romeo's chief test driver at the time, were given the four-year old 250 LM (5893), which won the race in 1965, while Bob Grossman and Ricardo Rodríguez had a new Ferrari 365 GTB, which had yet to be homologated, so would run as a prototype. French drivers Jimmy Mieusset and François Migault were driving the Dino 206S (014) within the provisions of the Trophée Chinetti.

Luigi Chinetti had driven the new 365 GTB from Maranello to Le Mans for the race, but during a practice session with Rodríguez taking the car out, it collided with the NART-entered Dino 206S being driven by Bob Grossman. Both cars were damaged beyond repair in the time available, and neither car started the race, depriving Migault and Mieusset, a chance at

A series of disappointments

glory in their home race. The traditional 4pm start was brought forward two hours, to allow race-goers the opportunity to vote in the presidential referendum the next day. Zeccoli had the honour of starting with the remaining NART entry, and both he and Posey maintained a consistent pace throughout the 24 hours, despite transmission problems, to finish in eighth place, a considerable feat considering the age and condition of the car. For his work Zeccoli was rewarded with two cheques totalling $950.

Sam Posey remembered:

> During the early hours of Sunday morning a car directly in front of me blows up. The resultant spray from the oil spill was deposited over the windscreen of my car, so I have to make an unscheduled stop in the pits. To my amazement nobody was there, so I jumped out, wiped the screen and drove back onto the track. At the end of the driving stint I got out of the car and Dick Fritz is busy checking the lap times. He noticed that I took some time longer on one of the laps, and enquired if there was any reason for it.

The reply was barely printable but, in essence, he said "Yes, I've a damn good reason why the lap took longer."

Jean Louis Lebreton was a mechanic who worked for Chinetti for several years. Before officially being employed full-time by Chinetti, he lived in France in a village close to Le Mans. He already had mechanics qualifications, and offered his services to Chinetti when his cars arrived from the factory for the Le Mans races in 1969. He worked on the cars prior to, and alongside, the regular mechanics that were flown in from America. He remembered how the team worked through the night trying to repair the 365 GTB4 but, as it was a new car, there were too few spares and no body parts. Attention was given instead to the Dino 206S, but to no avail.

On 4 September Chinetti bought a 312P (0870) from the factory, initially paying $8750 for the privilege of having this ex-factory car which ran at Le Mans. This was to be his entry into the Bridgehampton Can-Am race on 14 September, with Pedro Rodríguez driving the car. Looking to offset some of the costs, Dick Fritz had approached Goodyear to see if it would give financial support for the car. Whilst happy to supply the tyres, its support budget was exhausted for the remainder of the year. After qualifying 11th on the grid, Rodríguez made his way through the field to finish in fifth place out of 20 starters, gathering $1485 for his efforts.

1969 had been a poor year for the Ferrari Formula One team. Its 312 V12 was uncompetitive, and by the end of the European rounds of the World Championship, the team had lost interest in the car. With three races still to be run, Ferrari decided to loan a 312 Formula One car to NART. As far as Ferrari concerned, this was a convenient means of staying on the periphery of the Grand Prix scene, without losing any more face due to the poor performance of its cars. Chassis number 0017 was to see action in America, Canada and Mexico before being returned to the factory. Pedro Rodríguez was nominated to drive, as Ferrari knew he would squeeze everything there was out of the car.

In the Canadian Grand Prix at Mosport, Rodríguez retired on lap 37 with loss of oil

6 | 1966-69

pressure after starting 13th on the grid. Two weeks later at Watkins Glen, Ferrari fortunes improved as Rodríguez finished fifth, though seven laps in arrears after a pit stop to change all four wheels. At the final race in Mexico City, Rodríguez finished in seventh place, two laps behind the winning car, after being 15th on the grid. It must have been a difficult race for him knowing that his brother, Ricardo, had been killed on that very same track.

1968. Pedro Rodríguez drove the Ferrari 330 P4 (0860) at Road America, but could 13th position only.

7
1970-72
Overcoming adversity

7 | 1970-72

> The beginning of 1970 saw the introduction of the Ferrari 512S into Chinetti's armoury. $20,000 deposit was paid for chassis 1014, a $10,000 deposit, in addition to an initial deposit of $5000 paid in September 1970 on chassis 1006, and an additional sum for 1028.

The Daytona 24-hour race presented the first opportunity for Chinetti to try one of the 512Ss in competition. 1014 was used, slightly modified by having the roof extended to accommodate Gurney's tall frame. In addition to the 512S there were two 312Ps for Posey/Parkes (0872) and Adamowicz/Piper (0870), a 250 LM for Young/Chinetti Jr, a 365 GTB4 for Cluxton/Tatum and a 275 GTB/C for Bucknum/Pickett entered under the NART banner.

Marvin Davidson, who had guided Adamowicz to the F5000 Championship in 1969, counted Luigi Chinetti as one of his close associates, resulting in Adamowicz being offered a Ferrari to drive at Daytona. A special deal had also been arranged with Chinetti, whereby Carroll Smith was brought in to supervise the preparation of the Adamowicz/Piper car. Carroll Smith had been Adamowicz's team manager in the successful 1969 F5000 campaign. He ended up looking after both 312Ps, leaving Dick Fritz to concentrate on the 512S.

The 512S had been running well, but at midnight lost 16 minutes in the pits to have the front brake discs replaced, then later the car collided with another 512S, requiring

Parkes and Posey guided the 312P (0872) to a fourth place finish at Daytona.

NART's well-used 250 LM (5893) came seventh at Daytona, driven by Chinetti Jr and Young.

Overcoming adversity

The 312P (0870) was driven by David Piper and Tony Adamowicz, and finished in fifth position at Daytona.

Gurney and Parsons failed to finish the race in the 512S (1014).

7 | 1970-72

Cluxton and Tatum drove the 275 GTB/C (9063 GT), but failed to complete the race after cooling problems led the engine to overheat.

Mechanics hard at work, preparing the 365 GTB4 (12547) at Daytona for Gregory and Pickett.

the car to pit again for repairs. In the end the gearbox expired, and the car was retired after covering 464 laps. Despite not finishing, Gurney earned $3000 start money.

The 312P cars had given a good account of themselves, though not without problems. Parkes, during his long driving stint, had become tired, and crunched the front end of the car against the banking wall. The radiator had to be replaced, and Wayne Sparling built and installed a whole

Overcoming adversity

new aluminium fender in just 12 minutes. The other 312P suffered from a leaking radiator, but the replacement had already been used on the Parkes/Posey car, so additional pit stops were the order of the day. The Posey/Parkes 312P managed to finish in a commendable fourth place, ahead of the Adamowicz/Piper 312P in fifth place, with the venerable 250 LM ending the race seventh. Cooling system problems saw the demise of the 275 GTB/C on lap 142, and the same problem was to see the 365 GTB4 out of the race, after completing 308 laps.

The Sebring 12-hour race was held in mid-March, with NART bringing three cars – two 312Ps and a 512S. Parkes and Parsons had 0872, and Chinetti Jr and Adamowicz had 0870. The 512S was in the hands of Posey and Bucknum.

New safety regulations banned the traditional Le Mans-style start, so the 68 starters passed the line in a rolling start, following the pace lap. First casualty for NART was Chinetti Jr's 312P, going out on lap 56 with overheating problems caused by a broken water pump. The second setback occurred when Sam Posey was involved in a five-car crash after three hours of the race. Three slower cars, a Lancia, a Porsche 911 and a Fiat, were too intent on

Mike Parkes drove twice for NART in 1970. He shared a car with Sam Posey at Daytona, finishing in fourth place, then at Sebring, where he and Parsons finished sixth overall.

American legend Dan Gurney's first drive for NART was in 1958, though he was not a regular driver for Chinetti due to his commitments in other forms of motor sport. His final race for NART was in 1970.

Parsons and Adamowicz finished in tenth place after a series of delays in the 312P (0872) at Le Mans.

7 | 1970-72

The 312P (0872) going for inspection by the ACO at Le Mans.

Posey and Bucknum drove the 512S (1014) to a fourth place finish at Le Mans.

Overcoming adversity

The 512S (1014) in the pit area at Le Mans prior to the race.

their own race to notice Posey's 512S and Elford's Porsche 917 coming up quickly behind them. The Lancia pulled out in front of Posey, and there was nothing he could do about it, crashing into the rear of the car, while Elford went into the Porsche, and was hit in the side by the Fiat. The NART crew spent an hour patching the Ferrari's crumpled nose and repairing the steering, only to have the car suffer from fuel pump failure, 90 minutes later. The remaining car also had its troubles, though of a different nature. In the fifth hour, Parsons entered the long bend past the esses, working up to top gear. At that moment, a corner worker walked onto the track picking up debris, and there was no yellow flag or yellow lights showing. Parsons described what happened: "I was turning 140 or better when he started to run back then froze. I was set up on the right and got over as far as I could. If I had moved, I would have run right over him. The spoiler must have cut the hell out of his leg." It did, the corner worker was flown to a hospital with very serious leg injuries. Despite the accident and the resultant delay, the car continued in the race, and finished in sixth place, having covered 240 laps.

The Le Mans 24-hour race took place over 13-14 June, and NART had entered five cars for the race. It was a very rainy affair, and for some teams a very confusing race due to changes in the regulations for this year. The most obvious difference for the spectators was the change to the start of the race. The cars were lined up as usual, but the drivers did not run across the track to their cars – they were already seated in them.

Of the five cars entered, only three made a start to the race. The 312P (0870) had been qualified by Sam Posey, and was due to be co-driven by François Migault, but a sponsorship deal involving Migault fell through, so Chinetti decided to withdraw the car, and the 365 GTB4 for Mieusset had not been accepted by the ACO. Even then when it came to scrutineering, the 312P (0872) passed, but one of its drivers, Chuck Parsons, was deemed unfit to drive because of an old injury to his leg that left him with a bad limp. Despite Sam Posey intervening to argue Parson's case, the officials would not budge. When Chinetti heard of this, he approached the race organisers and threatened to withdraw his cars from the race, and have Enzo Ferrari withdraw the factory cars unless they changed their minds. It certainly focused the minds of the officials, and suddenly they were honoured to have 'Monsieur Parsons' in their race.

The three NART participants were outpaced during practice, though made a good start to the race as others around them had an early exit from the proceedings. The Kelleners/Loos 512S went out after 54 laps with handling problems caused by accident damage, but the other two cars crossed the finish line. The Posey/Bucknum 512S limped home to fourth place, firing on 11 cylinders, the first Ferrari home, while the Parsons/Adamowicz 312P was in tenth place, having covered 281 laps. The 312P had been affected by the heavy rain that fell, a fair amount coming into the supposedly closed cockpit, and sloshing around on the floor. During a pit stop, the pit crew was obliged to drill some holes in the floorpan for drainage. Needless to say, the water affected the electrical system, but the drivers carried on regardless. A spin on track caused damage to the rear section of the car, but after a prolonged pit stop for repairs the car made it to the finish.

After the Le Mans race, Chinetti Jr decided to transform 0872 in order to keep it competitive in American races during 1971. He decided to remove the Berlinetta roof section, and create a simpler, lighter front and rear end, in order to improve downforce on the car. This work was conducted by Wayne Sparling during the latter half of 1970, using aluminium panels wherever possible to reduce the weight of the car.

Chinetti's 512S entry into the Can-Am race at Lexington Mid-Ohio was a gamble, and the stakes were high with plenty of prize money available. Although the Ferrari engine was of small capacity when compared to most of the opposition, Chinetti wanted to promote Ferrari in the series, to help keep the retail side of his business to the fore. His greatest sales point was that engines normally seen on the track would filter down to the street cars, something the other manufacturers could not boast.

The Can-Am series was basically a number of races for Group 7 sports racing cars. It was organised in the traditional American style of 'race for the money,' as opposed to the European system of having start money for long distance races to entice teams and better drivers to attend and participate.

Pedro Rodríguez was offered the drive and, after finishing surprisingly high on the grid in fifth place, had to be content with an 11th place finish in the race, ten laps down on the winning McLaren M8D-Chevrolet driven by Denny Hulme.

One week later, the car was at Elkhart Lake for the next round of the Can-Am championship. A disappointing qualifying session left the car

Overcoming adversity

in 20th place on the start grid, but Rodríguez guided the car to an encouraging seventh place finish, winning $3300 for the team.

The first race of the 1971 Manufacturers' Championship series was held at Buenos Aires on 10 January. NART brought along a lone 512S (1006) to support the factory team, and was driven by Posey/di Palma/García-Veiga. After qualifying in ninth place on the start grid, the 512S finished the race in eighth position, having covered 148 laps.

It was in this race that Italian driver Giunti was fatally injured, and Sam Posey attended his funeral and accompanied the casket back to Italy. Whilst there, he was asked by Chinetti to go to the Ferrari factory and inspect the new 512M.

Two weeks later the Argentina trial Grand Prix took place for Formula One and Formula 5000 cars. The race was broken into two heats of 50 laps each, the overall winner being determined by aggregate times.

There were two cars that Luigi Chinetti had put his name to. One was a Surtees TS5A driven by Nestor García-Veiga, and the second car a McLaren M10B, driven in one heat by Gregg Young, and the other heat by Carlos Marincovich. Both were under the supervision of NART's Enio Gherardi, affectionately called 'prof,' because of his efforts to introduce a form of digital timing to the team. García-Veiga had to retire from Heat One on lap 11, because of an oil leak, and the Surtees TS5A did not reappear for the second heat. The McLaren M10B appeared in the first heat with Marincovich driving, but did not finish due to mechanical failure on lap nine. The fault was rectified in time for the second heat in which Gregg Young drove the car to a sixth place finish.

Ronnie Bucknum and Tony Adamowicz piloted 512S (1006) to a second place finish at Daytona.

The 312P took a fifth place finish at Daytona, driven by Chinetti Jr and García-Veiga.

With a busy schedule for the remainder of the year, Chinetti committed to use Goodyear tyres on his entries. In response, The Goodyear Tire & Rubber Company sent Chinetti a cheque for $25,000 in late March, in addition to an unknown sum that was paid on 25 January.

The Daytona 24-hour race was to see the revised version of NART's 312P (0872) in attendance, along with three other cars, a 512S for Bucknum/Adamowicz, and two 512M versions for Young/Gregory and Posey/Revson. The Young/Gregory car was entered as a joint venture between NART and Young American Racing. As 0872 had raced at Daytona in 1970, there was a direct comparison to be made between the performance of the car in its previous configuration, and its current one.

The result showed the current configuration to be one second quicker. In the race it briefly held third spot, before minor problems put the car down to a fifth place finish, with García-Veiga and Chinetti Jr driving. The Bucknum/Adamowicz 512S had a strong race, leading for a while, but with 45 minutes to go, was overtaken by Rodríguez in the Gulf-Porsche, when the Ferrari slowed by ten seconds a lap due to worn valve springs robbing the five-litre engine of power. The Young/Gregory and Posey/Revson 512Ms never made it to the finish line. After starting third on the grid, Posey lost several laps to rectify faulty brake lights, then, when lying in fourth place, the engine blew up, putting the car out of the race after covering 202 laps. The Gregory/Young car covered only 16 laps before the engine expired, the result of throwing a rod.

The Sebring 12-hour event was something of an anti-climax, as rumours circulated that it was to be the final 12-hour event. Each year the organisers promised to update the track, only later to say that there were no funds available. NART entered five cars in the race, Chinetti Jr and Eaton driving the revised-bodied 312P, with two additional headlights fitted in the nose section just ahead of the dashboard, Cluxton and Grossman in Cluxton's newly purchased 365 GTB4 (14107), Revson and Savage in the 512M, and two 512S models driven by Bucknum/Posey and Parsons/Weir.

It would appear that NART underestimated the number of staff it would require at the race, not that it was ever over-staffed, but this time it was chaotic. The new 365 GTB4 had been delivered in street form to the race, and all the mechanics were busy with it, even though the factory had already charged $1000 for race preparation. When Savage brought his car to the pits in the practice session with an unworkable gearshift, he was told to wait his turn. Just before the start of the race, Revson was seen tightening the screws on his rear view mirror, using a borrowed penknife. "Nobody remembered to bring a screwdriver," he said. The pit crew was exceptionally busy during the race. Revson came in for a routine fuel stop but the car would not restart, despite using a jump cable and a new battery. In the end they had to fit a new master electrical switch, which cost 45 minutes.

On lap 20, the throttle on Parson's 512S jammed going into the hairpin, and the car went into a carefully placed pile of sand. He managed to dig out the car and get it back to the pits, only to be told that the whole front end had been knocked out of shape, and the car's retirement was announced. The Bucknum/Posey 512S lasted until lap 114 when the left rear tyre blew. Bucknum drove it back to the pits, the rear tyre flailing badly, destroying the rear bodywork and breaking the dry-sump oil tank, so the engine seized. A single flat tyre had suddenly escalated into $30,000 worth of damage. Meanwhile, there was more action in the NART pit, as Eaton brought the 312P in for fuel and a driver changeover. Chinetti Jr was due to relieve Eaton, however he could not

The 512S (1006) reappeared at Sebring where Bucknum and Posey drove the car, but failed to finish the 12-hour race.

Overcoming adversity

find his crash helmet, so Eaton was ushered back into the car for another driving stint. After a frantic search, the helmet was found in the team trailer and a driver change accomplished at the next refuel stop.

The Revson/Savage 512S gearshift linkage never was fixed properly during practice, and became progressively worse, at every other pit stop it had to be hammered back into place, until on lap 169 it finally broke. This left the 312P and the new 365 GTB4 circulating to the finish of the race, the 312P finishing eighth, covering 215 laps despite some delays due to ignition and light problems, and the 365 GTB4, which started the race with only 273km on the clock, in 12th place, having covered 195 laps. Bob Grossman said "We were breaking the car in during the race; it just seemed to get faster and faster as the hours went by."

After Sebring, Chinetti Jr took the decision to dismantle 0872. He had plans to build a car that looked similar in style to the new 312PB that Ferrari was building. By utilising the engine, gearbox, steering and suspension from 0872, in a new chassis and fibreglass body fabricated by Wayne Sparling, a new car emerged, though could not be badged as a Ferrari. The original 0872 chassis and body panels were stored by Chinetti for a while, then went to NART mechanic François Sicard.

The Le Mans 24-hour race never ceases to come up with surprises. NART had entered four cars in the race, two 512Ms and a 512S in the prototype class, and a 365 GTB4 in the GT class. The last of these was rejected as a GT class entry by the race organisers, on the grounds that the engine was not a production car unit (the car had yet to be homologated), and therefore the car was placed in the prototype

The 512S (1006) being unloaded for the 24-hour Le Mans race.

The 512S (1006) appears to be the subject of an inspection by gentlemen in white coats.

Finishing in fifth place, the 365 GTB4 (12467), driven by Grossman and Chinetti Jr, leads a Lola T212 and two Porsches through the Esses.

class. However, someone forgot to let Chinetti know, and the team ran the car happily as a GT class entry. It was only when Grossman and Chinetti Jr had finished in fifth place overall in the 365 GTB4, thinking they had won the GT class, that the team learned the truth.

7 | 1970-72

The race is over and the NART crew celebrates its fifth-place finish.

Preparation for the race was not without its problems. Mechanic Jean Le Breton said:

> The 512M (1020) was being prepared the day before the start of Le Mans, but the team could not solve an oil leak problem. Working all night, the team were exhausted and were sleeping in the garage. On the ramp, it became evident that an oil pump seal was leaking, but because of its position could not easily be removed. A hole was drilled in the aluminium body from the cockpit compartment, so a wrench could be inserted to remove the oil pump. A new Volkswagen seal was fitted and the problem was solved.

The bright spot for the team was the performance of the Posey/Adamowicz 512M. Having been 12th quickest in practice, it survived numerous pit stops to try and cure a low oil pressure problem, and finished in third place, albeit some 29 laps behind the second place car. The Gregory/Eaton 512S had a short and torrid race, failing to pull away from the rolling start (used for the first time at Le Mans), and giving everyone a half-hour advantage, before finally taking to the track. The car stuttered around 15 times in three hours, before being retired with fuel system problems. Donohue and Hobbs in their 512M were entered under the NART banner as a flag-of-convenience, after Penske's late entry for the car had been rejected by the

Overcoming adversity

ACO. The car entered France as a registered street car, displaying its number plate so as to avoid posting an import bond. At the track it was attended to by the Penske pit crew, but even it could do nothing to help when the car ground to a halt after four hours, suffering from engine failure due to dirt clogging up an oil passage to the cam bearings.

On 24 and 25 July, two races were held at Watkins Glen. The first of these was the 6-hour race, in which Chinetti entered a 512M (1020) with Posey and Bucknum as drivers. They qualified fifth on the grid, and held a top-six spot until a routine pit stop midway through the race. Having refuelled, the starter motor failed, leaving them stranded in the pits after covering 126 laps. The 6-hour race signalled the end of an era, as it was the final race for Group 5 sports cars having 5-litre engine displacement. The next day was the Can-Am race, and again the 512M was in action. Sam Posey qualified the car in tenth place on the grid, and this time had better luck, finishing sixth and winning $3200, although he was three laps behind the leading car driven by Pete Revson.

The beginning of 1972 saw a number of changes in the way that NART would operate in future. It was becoming obvious to Chinetti that Ferrari was tightening its purse strings when it came to development of sports cars, and left the racing customers without any offerings. Gone were the large engine cars, as they were no longer eligible for World Cup races, and the 3-litre cars had come in, in the form of the new 312PB, a successor to the 1971 312P. These were intended for use purely as factory entries, and when Chinetti suggested to Ferrari that a second-string team of 312PBs be created for NART, Maranello Concessionaires and Charles Pozzi to run on a maintenance-payment deal, the idea was rejected. Ferrari put it bluntly, "You fellows could not afford to run them and I could not afford to support you." Chinetti saw the likely alternative as being able to run the 365 GTB4 in the GT Championship.

The good news for NART was that The Goodyear Tire & Rubber Company would continue to support the team in 1972 and to this end a sum of $50,000 was contributed to NART, in addition to a commitment to supply Goodyear racing tyres for practice, qualifying and participation in races for all its cars.

The other news was that Luigi Chinetti and Al Garthwaite formed a partnership to become the importer for Ferrari in the whole of the United States region east of the Mississippi river and through the lower half of Texas. This was arranged in part by friend, Marchese Carlo di Boyle, an Italian with close connections to the Agnelli family, which was increasingly interested in Ferrari's continual development as a marque of distinction in North America. Why would Chinetti do this? According to Dick Fritz, Chinetti had said "He would get out of the business when too many cars came into America and he could no longer sell to the people he wanted to." It was the classic scenario of the pressures of a large commercial enterprise (Ferrari), and the selective specialised approach by Luigi Chinetti, in selling a product of limited availability to special customers. The good news for Chinetti was that Al Garthwaite had no desire to dabble with the intricacies of motor racing, and he left the running of NART entirely to Chinetti.

First up on the calendar was the race at Daytona, a 6-hour affair this year, and there was no doubting that the Ferraris were the centre of attention, although not those of NART.

7 | 1970-72

A sparse scattering of spectators gathered to watch the progress of NART's Ferrari 365 GTB4 at Sebring.

Finishing in 13th place at Sebring was the 365 GTB4, driven by Posey and Adamowicz. The car suffered from fuel starvation problems throughout.

Chinetti Jr and Grossman drove the 365 GTB4 (14885) to an eighth place finish at Sebring.

Chinetti Jr succeeded in entering his adapted 312P, now called the Chinetti Special, after putting in a lot of hard work on the car over the winter, and it was joined by a 365 GTB4 for Posey and Bucknum. It was intended that Bucknum and Posey would drive separate cars, but Bucknum's 365 GTB4 (14889) was withdrawn due to late delivery.

Chinetti Jr's new car qualified in 16th place on the grid, but in the race only lasted for seven laps before the fuel tank split. The 365 GTB4 (14885) did a little better, lasting 119 laps before it expired. Sam Posey was not surprised, the car was new and as he put it "a street car with racing tyres."

Despite all of the rumours that 1971 would be the last Sebring 12-hour event, one year later the same rumour was still in force. However, the cars were there for another 12-hour race. NART entered two 365 GTB4 cars into the GT class, one for Posey

Overcoming adversity

and Adamowicz, the other for Chinetti Jr and Grossman. Again, the focus of attention was on the sports category, with the factory 312PBs dominating the scene, but further down the field the pair of 365 GTB4s continued to circulate to the finish of the race. Chinetti and Grossman finished eighth, covering 210 laps, while Posey and Adamowicz covered 199 laps, driving the 365 GTB4 (14889) that should have been present at Daytona in February. It could have finished higher up the field, but was subject to prolonged pit stops to sort out fuel starvation problems.

The NART cars in attendance for the 24-hour race at Le Mans had a more significant role than usual, as the Ferrari factory had declined to send any cars this year. The team arrived a week early, and took over the service department of a Volkswagen agency on the road to Chartres. NART entered three untried 365 GTB4s, together with a new Dino 246 GT, and an interesting addition in the form of a Chevrolet Corvette. The 365 GTB4s were assigned to Posey and Adamowicz (15685 GT), Jarier and Buchet (13855) and Chinetti Jr and Gregory (14141), while the Dino 246 GT was a late substitute for a withdrawn car, and was the Trophée Chinetti

Tony Adamowicz started driving for Luigi Chinetti in 1970, and was used by Chinetti on an irregular basis for nine years, his final drive for NART earning him a second place finish in the Daytona 24-hour race in 1979.

Jarier and Buchet finished in ninth spot at Le Mans, driving the 365 GTB4 (13855).

7 | 1970-72

A rare sight: a Corvette, entered by the North American Racing Team, going through ACO inspection.

The Heinz/Johnson Corvette did well to finish in 15th place.

car for French drivers Laffeach and Doncieux. Some doubts were expressed as to the qualifying time for the Dino 246 GT, but Chinetti argued that the officials had mistimed the car, and that the NART timers had the accurate times. A great deal of attention revolved around the fifth entry, not so much for what the car was, a Chevrolet Corvette, but more because Luigi Chinetti had entered it under the NART banner.

Back in America, the R.E.D. team (Race Engineering & Development) had successfully entered and won two GT

Overcoming adversity

The NART-entered Corvette was driven by David Heinz and Robert Johnson.

victories, and had impressed their sponsors, The Goodyear Tire & Rubber Company, to such an extent that it suggested that R.E.D. should enter the Le Mans race. This they did, but there was a major mix-up on the original Corvette entry paperwork, and the ACO were not going to allow them to run. Larry Truesdale of The Goodyear Tire & Rubber Company became involved and, as they were also sponsoring NART, Larry approached Luigi Chinetti to see if he would enter the car under the NART banner. It was coincidental that NART had a spare entry slot, and a deal was set up between Chinetti and the Corvette owner Dana English, on the understanding that the car would be painted in NART livery.

Dana decided to start from scratch in preparing his car, and purchased a $500 1968 small block convertible wreck from an insurance auction in Miami. The Corvette was dismantled and the damaged parts, including the frame, were discarded. The body was repaired to FIA-specification and a new frame was purchased from Ferman-Chevrolet in Tampa for $189. Affectionately called 'Old Scrappy,' the car looked resplendent when finished, but an accident in practice rearranged the front end of the car, and it ended up on the start grid weighed down with duct tape, for Heinz and Johnson to drive.

The race provided the spectators with some close racing in the GT class, with five

7 | 1970-72

Gregory and Chinetti Jr's 365 GTB4 is subject to inspection by the ACO, prior to the 24-hour race at Le Mans.

365 GTB4s no more than nine laps apart at the finish. The Chinetti Jr/Gregory car was not one of them, having retired from the race with gearbox problems after covering 226 laps. Despite some damage to his gearbox following a spin at the Indianapolis Turn, Posey guided his and Adamowicz's new 365 GTB4 to a sixth place finish, while Jarier and Buchet finished in ninth spot in their 365 GTB4. Brakes had been a weak point on the 365 GTB4s, but Dick Fritz countered the problem by using undrilled vented discs from the 1972 Corvette. Dick had called Bill Mitchell at General Motors, who had a box load of the discs pulled off the production line before they were drilled, and sent them to Le Mans. Much to the delight of the team, Heinz and Johnson brought their Corvette across the line in 15th place, after an early scare. Rain had forced Heinz into the pits to fit intermediate tyres for better grip in the wet, but he had a major drama along the Mulsanne straight. Heinz said "I was accelerating in fourth

Overcoming adversity

NART's 365 GTB4 for Jarier and Buchet awaits inspection at Le Mans.

In sixth place at Le Mans was the 365 GTB4, driven by Posey and Adamowicz.

7 | 1970-72

The Posey/Adamowicz 365 GTB4 (15865) ran well at Le Mans.

gear when I hit a wall of standing water at nearly 200mph. Surprised, I held the wheel tight, but the car spun 360 degrees, and when the spin stopped I was heading in the right direction, and the car had hardly slowed down." The French pairing of Laffeach and Doncieux finished 17th in the Dino 246 GT after covering 265 laps. When asked why the Dino 246 GT was entered, team manager Dick Fritz said "The Dinos weren't selling that well in the USA, and the GTS version was new to the market, so it was decided to race one in the hopes of it doing well and perking up sales of the model."

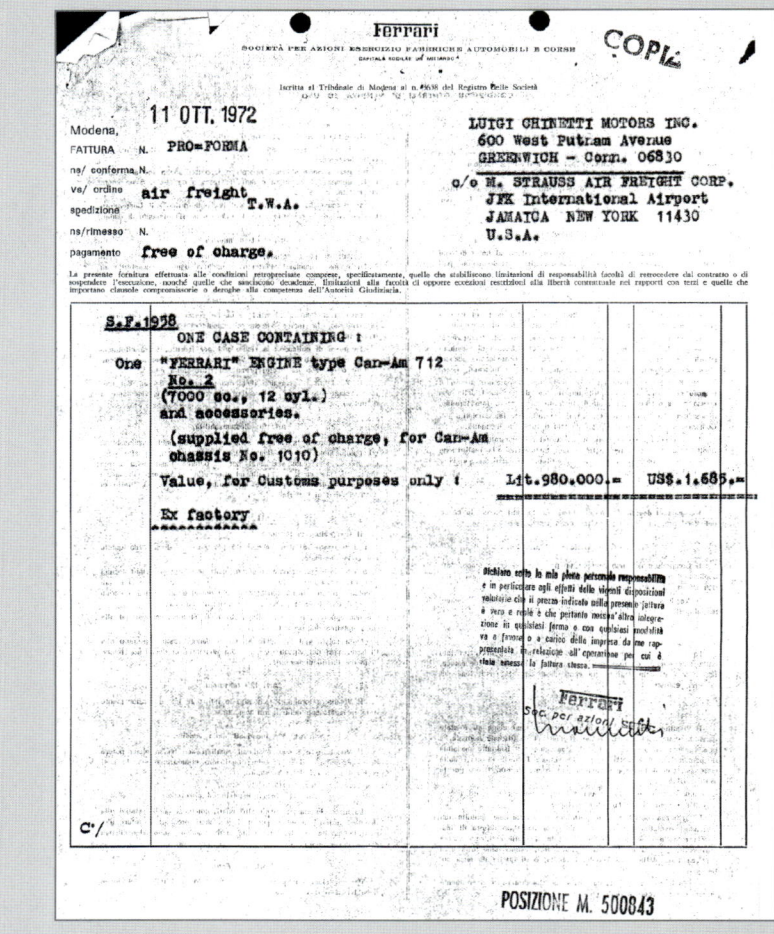
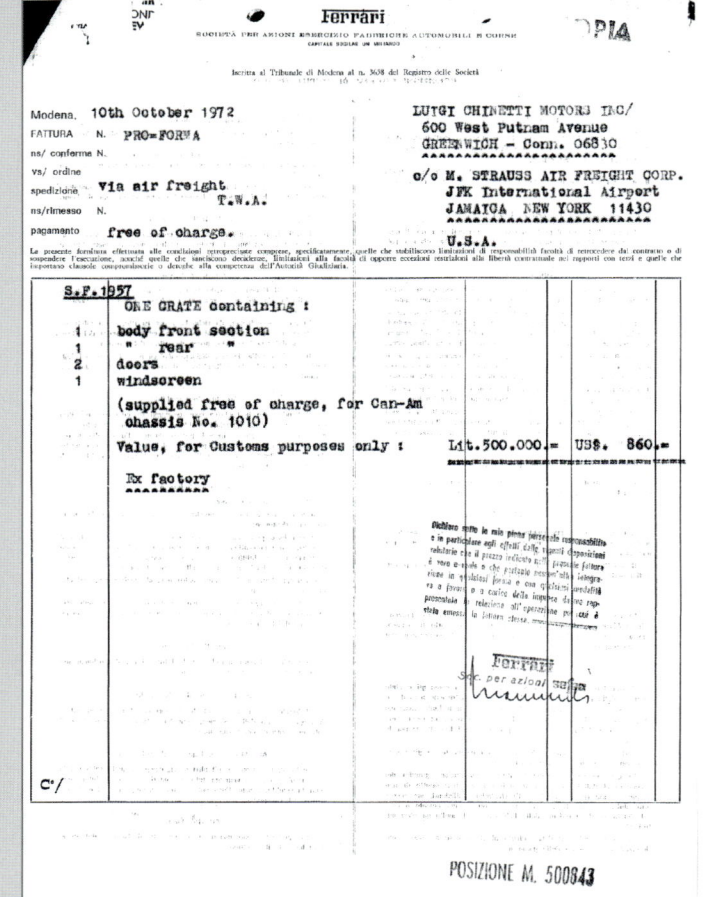

Overcoming adversity

The Watkins Glen 6-hour race was held on 22 July. Chinetti sent three cars to compete in the GT category, however, the Dino 246 GT that had done so well at Le Mans failed to qualify. The Hobbs/Posey 365 GTB4 led the GT section until the engine blew, putting it out of the race on lap 117, leaving the Jarier/Young 365 GTB4 (15685), which had finished sixth at Le Mans, to win the GT Group 4 section, finishing the race in sixth place overall.

On the day following the 6-hour race at Watkins Glen, the Can-Am race was held. NART had entered their newly acquired Ferrari 712 P, and Sam Posey had been given a practice run in the car. It was a machine that demanded the utmost respect, and Posey was not at ease with the car, especially when the throttle stuck open, so he declined to drive it in the race. Overnight, Nereo Iori rebuilt the system out of bits and pieces, using parts from other vehicles, in an attempt to keep the car running on race day. Chinetti had not paid out some $30,000 to have the car stand idle, so employed the services of Jean-Pierre

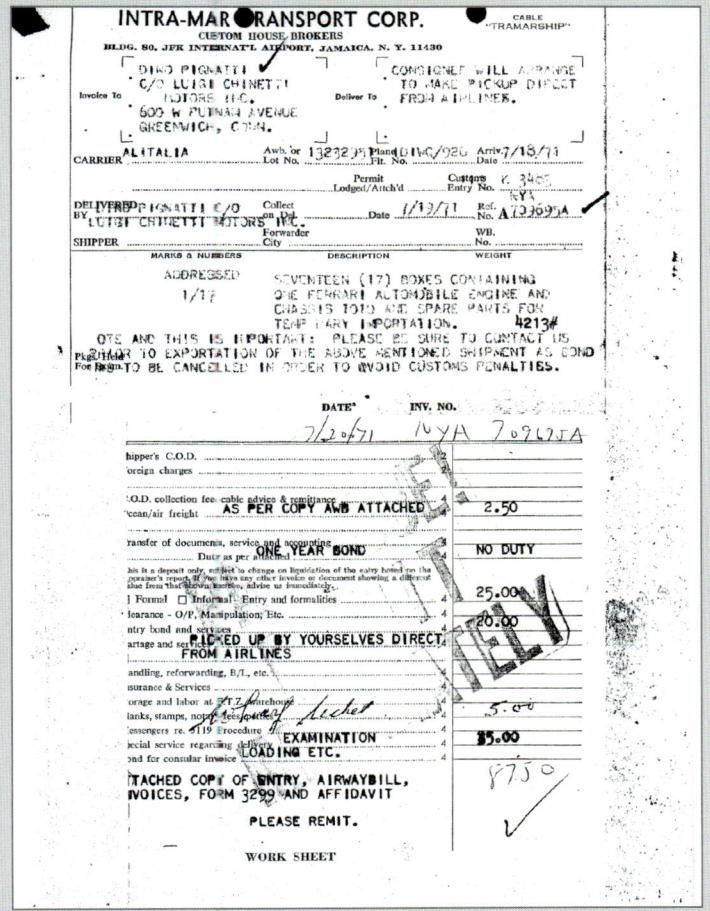 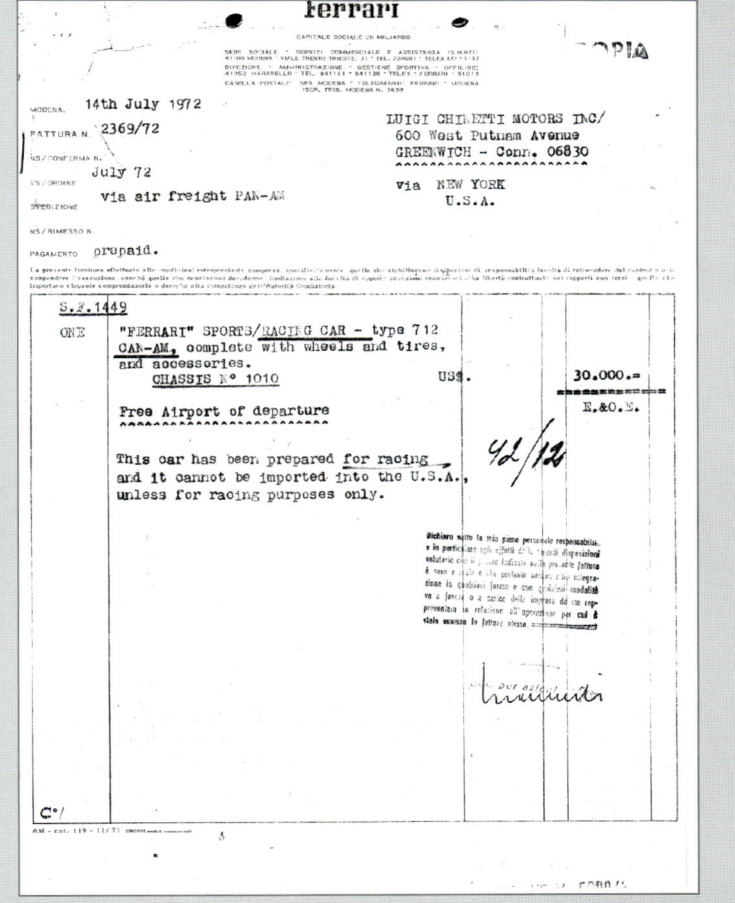

The paperwork trail for the sale of chassis 1010 from Ferrari to Luigi Chinetti.

A concise history of the North American Racing Team 1957 to 1983

7 | 1970-72

Jarier to drive the car instead. Ted Johnson, who worked for Chinetti, was there that day:

> Jarier took the car out and went round in a remarkably quick time, despite the throttle jamming again when he was touching 200mph. When Jarier was asked about how he coped with the problem he replied that when he came to the corner he turned the ignition off, went round the corner and switched it back on again.

The car had been entered at the same venue in 1971 by the factory, with Mario Andretti behind the wheel, where he brought the car home in fourth place. He remembers:

> It was a terrible car. It didn't really have the power it should have produced, and the handling was awful. The only thing going for it was the fact that most Can-Am cars were unreliable – at least you could be sure it would run for two hours. It was the worst Ferrari I ever drove.

As a last-minute stand-in driver, Jarier had no qualifying time, so was put to the back of the start grid, from where he gradually worked his way through the field to end the race in tenth place having covered 48 laps, and in doing so earned $2000 in prize money.

Four weeks later the 712 P made an appearance at Elkhart Lake, again with Jarier behind the wheel. NART had been busy making modifications to the bodywork to increase downforce on the car, with apparent success, as Jarier qualified in ninth spot on the grid. He carried his momentum forward from the Watkins Glen race, finishing in fourth place to win $5500 for his efforts.

NART's final entry for 1972 was at the Paris 1000 km race in October. In the past this race had traditionally been held at Montlhéry, but this year was held at the Rouen les Essarts circuit. Chinetti sent a 365 GTB4 (14889) for Jarier and Laffite to drive, with Iori, Spalding and Lebreton in attendance. After qualifying 24th on the grid, the car performed well and finished in ninth spot, the first of three 365 GTB4s in the race, and third in the GT class behind two Porsche entries.

8
1973-74
Further troubled times

8 | 1973-74

> For the North American Racing Team, 1973 would see them entering five race events, all of their entries being the 365 GTB4 in the GT category. It would also see them continue to be sponsored by The Goodyear Tire & Rubber Company, who this year would contribute $75,000 towards the team efforts.

The first race was held at Daytona in February, and as the Ferrari factory had declined to enter, Arturo Merzario was given a drive in one of the four NART entries. The pairings for the team were Migault and Minter, Chinetti Jr and Grossman, Ballot-Lena and Andruet, and Jarier and Merzario. The highest qualifying pair was Ballot-Lena and Andruet in 16th place, but was the first of the NART quartet to retire, on lap 284. Their direct competition came from the Chevrolet Corvettes, but the 365 GTB4s were holding them at bay at the halfway point of the race, the leading Corvette being 20 laps adrift of Minter and Grossman's cars. The Merzario/Jarier car succumbed to clutch failure on lap 394, leaving the other two GTB4s to grind their way steadily towards the finish. The Minter/Migault car climbed to second place, though 22 laps behind the winning Porsche, while the Chinetti Jr/Grossman/Shaw Jr car finished in fifth place.

Sebring continued to appear on the endurance race scene, though this year did not count towards any world championships. NART entered a solitary 365 GTB4 for Sam Posey and Harley Cluxton to drive, but the car never made it to the start grid, as it suffered terminal overheating problems during practice.

Chinetti Jr and Grossman finished fifth at the Daytona 24-hour race in their 365 GTB4 (14889).

A NART cluster, three 365 GTB4s make their way around the infield at Daytona.

Further troubled times

François Migault and Milt Minter steered their 365 GTB4 (14141) to a second-place finish at Daytona.

To celebrate the 50th Anniversary of the Le Mans 24-hour race, a special 2-hour feature race was arranged for specific cars that had previously taken part. With so many cars eligible, it was by invitation only. Luigi Chinetti, a three times winner at Le Mans, brought with him a car similar to that which he drove to victory in 1949, the Ferrari 166 MM. Whereas the original Le Mans winning car was 0008 M, this one was 0012 M painted to look similar to the original. Dressed in a business suit and tie, he donned a crash helmet, and took the Ferrari out for practice. After a lap he was back in the pits and explained to Phil Hill, who was to drive the car in the race that the Ferrari was wobbling very badly at the front. "Everything is a blur over 60mph – just like in the race when the steering arm nearly fell off." The mechanics looked under the car and, to everyone's amazement, the same steering arm as on the original car was about to fall off. The car was repaired, and Chinetti drove it for a few more laps, before handing the car over to Phil Hill.

A concise history of the North American Racing Team 1957 to 1983

An advert placed by Luigi Chinetti Motors Inc, capitalizing on the NART Grand Touring class victory at Daytona.

Further troubled times

Two NART cars, both 365 GTB4s, turned up for the 4-hour practice run at Le Mans. One, driven by Migault/Guitteny/Bodin, recorded a fifth position finish, but the other, driven by Jarier and, again, Migault, didn't participate. In the 24-hour race held in June, four 365 GTB4s were in attendance: the two used in the four-hour practice run plus two others, a new one (16407) for Posey/Minter and 16367 for di Palma/García-Veiga, the latter being an entry taken under NART's wing. Three of the NART cars had bodywork modifications made to them, by incorporating front fins attached to the front wings, and one of the cars also tried rear wing devices, to try to stabilise high-speed handling.

From a rolling start, Grossman brought his 365 GTB4 into the pits to have a wheel changed, as the tyre had split on the rolling lap. The inauspicious start was followed by Grossman coming off the road, and badly damaging the car, and it eventually retired after 19 hours of toil. The di Palma/García-Veiga car went out an hour earlier with clutch problems, and the Posey/Minter car was retired with a cracked piston in the 21st hour. This left Chinetti Jr and Migault to save some honour for NART, by finishing in 13th place after some minor electrical trouble. Chinetti Jr had stopped out on track due to electrical failure, and a new battery was required to get the car back to the pits. It was not within the rules to fit a new battery on the circuit, however, mechanic Jean Le Breton walked round to the car with one, and while the track marshals were distracted, handed the battery to Chinetti Jr. It got the car back to the pits, where it was found that an alternator belt had broken. Once changed, the car was on its way again.

In July, the Watkins Glen 6-hour race was held and Chinetti sent one 365 GTB4 (16407) to represent NART, driven by Posey and Migault. Starting in 25th spot on the grid, they fought their way up to 14th place, covering 160 laps by the finish, despite having a few unscheduled pit stops caused by overheating problems and a split header-tank.

All of motor racing received a rude awakening to the problems of the real world, with the Arab States' oil embargo in late 1973. Many of the scheduled events were postponed or cancelled. This energy crisis drifted into the early months of 1974, and only in the latter half of the year did things in the motor racing world start resembling normality.

The Daytona and Sebring races were cancelled, and the Ferrari factory team withdrew from sports car racing to concentrate its efforts and resources on Formula One racing. With no new sports cars coming from the factory, this left its customer teams, such as NART, Charles Pozzi and Maranello Concessionaires, with nothing in their teams that met current regulation specification, or was competitive in World Championship racing. This in turn led to

Migault and Guitteny attained the 12th quickest lap time at the Le Mans 4-hour practice race held in April, finishing fifth overall.

1973-74

the better drivers being lured into other teams and classes of racing, and the downwards spiral continued into what would become terminal decline within a decade for NART.

Despite the races at Daytona and Sebring being cancelled, The Goodyear Tire & Rubber Company continued to act as sponsor to NART, the 1974 contribution amounting to $100,000. As the offer was made in September 1973, it is unclear if the agreement stood, with so few races for NART to participate in.

With the American endurance races cancelled, NART's first opportunity to enter cars was at Le Mans, where three 365 GTB4s, a Dino 308 GT4 and the Chinetti Special turned up. Two of the NART cars did not last very long. The race had hardly started, when Paoli crashed into a barrier after locking-up the brakes, and the 365 GTB4 was out of the race with only four laps completed. French driver Jean-Pierre Paoli had paid Chinetti for a drive in the race, and it proved to be a short and expensive experience for him. The new Dino 308 GT4 had been upgraded to Group 5 race car specification, with Daytona pistons and conrods, and ported and polished heads. It was in 18th place when gearbox and clutch problems put the car out of the race, after completing 30 laps. The other three cars all finished the race, Ethuin and Guitteny finished in 11th place after experiencing trouble with locked brakes, while Cudini and Heinz finished sixth. Cudini had sustained accident

A sixth place finish was attained by Heinz and Cudini at Le Mans in the 365 GTB4 (14141).

Further troubled times

Zeccoli and Andruet drove the 312P V12 (0872) to a ninth place finish at Le Mans, delayed by breaking a series of accelerator cables.

NART's 365 GTB4 (16407) finished in 11th place at Le Mans.

Christian Ethuin and Lucien Guitteny drove the 365 GTB4 (16407) at Le Mans.

damage resulting in a cracked petrol tank. Soap was used to fill the crack, then it was taped over. It worked, though they had to be careful how the car was refuelled, so as not to create too much pressure in the tank. The Chinetti Special had been modified since its last appearance in 1972, having a smaller windscreen, a different roll-bar and a modified rear section with vertical fins. The car started in 24th spot, working its way up to fifth place before being delayed by several broken throttle cables and a broken gearshift. The car eventually finished ninth. For their efforts Cudini had a cheque from Chinetti for $2000, while Andruet and Ethuin both received $500.

The Watkins Glen 6-hour race, held on 12 July, had two NART entries, one for Cudini and Hiss, the other for Rutherford. On the day, only one 365 GTB4/C turned up. After qualifying 23rd on the grid the car retired with mechanical failure, having covering 83 laps.

Brian Redman piloted the 712 P (1010) in the Can-Am race held at Watkins Glen, but failed to finish.

The Ferrari Can-Am 712 P was resurrected by Chinetti to appear at the Watkins Glen Can-Am race the next day, and Sam Posey was invited to drive the car. During practice, something went wrong with the brakes, as when Posey pressed the pedal it went sharply to the floor, and in doing so broke a bone his foot. Brian Redman volunteered to drive the car in the race, but had to start from the back of the grid, as he had not recorded a practice time. A remarkable drive saw Redman bring the Ferrari up to a second-place finish in the 20 lap sprint held on Saturday, but was not so fortunate in the 33 lap race on Sunday. After starting well again, Redman was looking for another top-three finish, but the car suffered rear suspension failure that saw him park the car on the infield after 11 laps. Even though the car failed to finish, Redman's personal bank balance increased by $1000 for his weekend's contribution.

With NART's short racing season over, Chinetti Jr decided that it would be fun to go to Bonneville, in an attempt to break some old speed records. To do this would entail taking three cars (one a spare), and a pit crew. Having raised about $40,000 in sponsorship deals it was a viable proposition.

Two 365 GTB4s, one as a spare car (16343), and a 512M, were dispatched together with an eclectic mix of drivers. Former Formula One world champion Graham Hill, actor Paul Newman, and current NART driver Milt Minter

Further troubled times

joined Luigi Chinetti Jr, to discover what could be achieved under the direction of team manager Dick Fritz. It was projected that the 512M would use about 50 per cent more fuel than would be used in normal circuit racing. The passenger seat was exchanged for a 22 gallon fuel cell. With this modification the car was rechristened, and listed as a 512MB – the added B standing for Bonneville.

There were two courses at Bonneville: the straight-line course and also a ten-mile oval. It was the latter that was being used, with its straights of just over two miles in length, and the curves at each end that, through necessity, were very long and gradual. The whole course was marked with stakes at intervals, black barrels at the start of the curves, mileage banners, and a thick black line around the inside of the track. Initial tests of the cars on the circuit, confirmed the many dangers that lurked on a seemingly open expanse of salt. Only with experience and nerve, was it possible to go into the curves at over 170mph and, as Milt Minter put it, "I was always glad to see the straight markers appear." One test run, conducted by Chinetti Jr in the 512M, ended when a puncture in a rear tyre resulted in adjacent bodywork being removed, together with damage to an oil tank, fuel pump and radiator. It kept the mechanics, Sicard, Craige, Iori and Zanesi, busy for the remainder of the day and night.

The shorter distance records were attempted first in the 512M, then the progressively longer ones in the 365 GTB4 (14141), each record falling as the string of drivers took their turn at the wheel. The whole thing seemed surreal, having two cars circulating in the middle of nowhere, coming in for rapid refuelling and driver change-over, and at the same time the whole event being filmed for CBS.

The only unfortunate thing was that the 24-hour record remained unbroken, as the 365 GTB4's front right tyre burst, affecting the suspension. A half hour's work to rectify the problem took the car out of the equation for breaking the record, so the team gave up the unequal struggle. After the event Chinetti Jr said "It was easy to see how the old record had stood for so long."

In late November 1974, Chinetti Motors took delivery of a new Ferrari model, a 365 GTBB (18139) costing $25,000, a rear-engine street car, to replace the 365 GTB4. After trying the car, Chinetti Jr and Dick Fritz thought it possible to transform it into a successful track car. François Sicard and Bob Craige were given the responsibility of working on the mechanics and electrics, and Joe Randazzo worked on the bodywork over the winter months, so as to be ready for the Daytona and Sebring races of 1975.

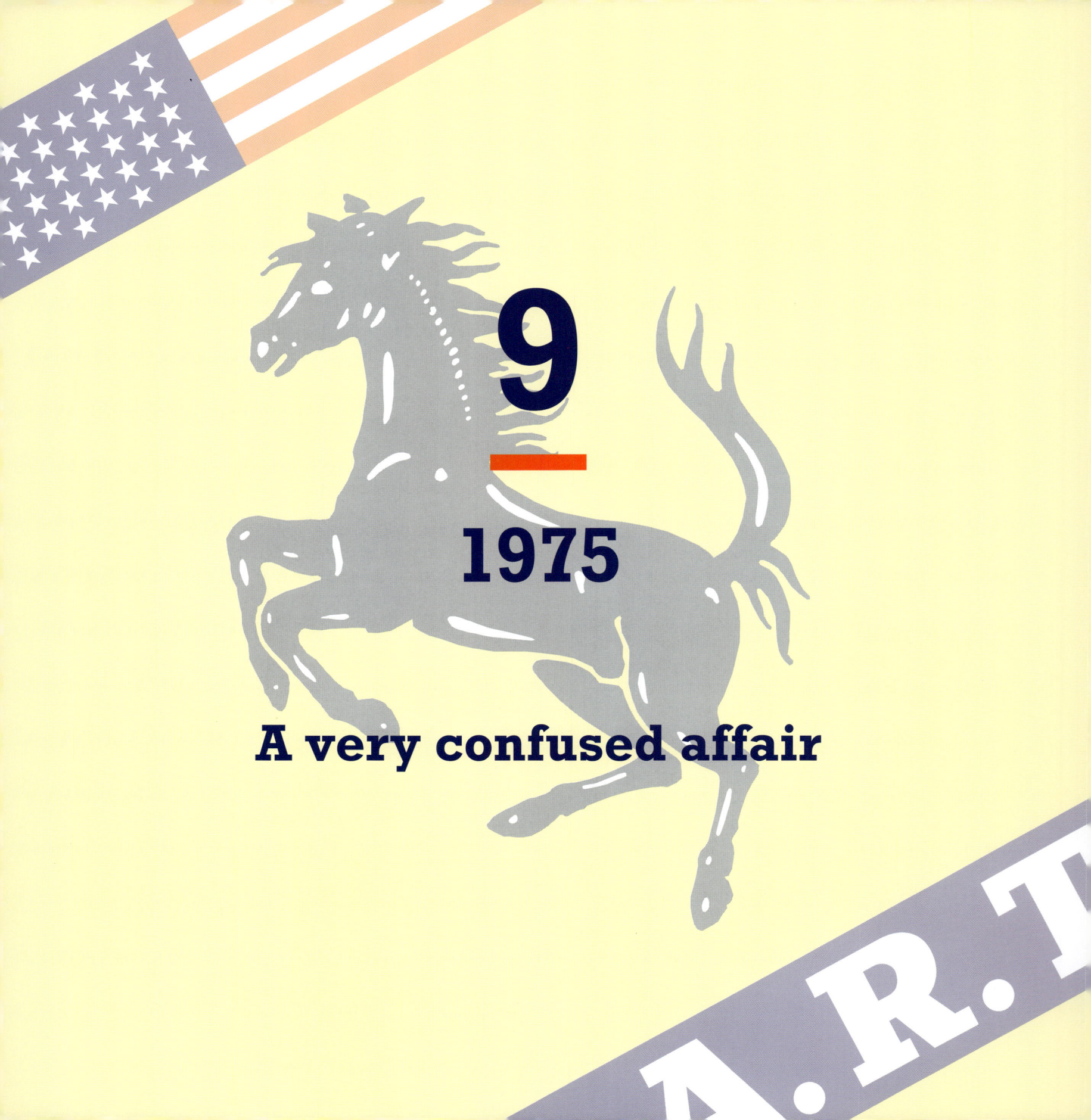

A very confused affair

> For the 1975 Daytona race, NART entered two cars, the 365 GTBB, and the 365 GTB4 that had been used at Bonneville. It would appear from the activity in the NART pit that there was still a fair amount of work to be done on the new 365 GTBB, "a good seven hours of work" according to team manager Dick Fritz.

Months of work came to nothing, as the suspension of the car collapsed during practice. A temporary repair was good enough to complete a lap, so as to receive 'race start money,' but no parts were available for proper repairs, and Claude Ballot-Lena declared the car undrivable after falling behind the field on the pace lap. Meanwhile, the well-used 365 GTB4 (14141) lasted for 392 laps, before a broken driveshaft caused the team to retire the car.

The 12-hour race at Sebring was to be a far happier affair for the North American Racing Team. Only one car was entered – the 365 GTBB – that had failed so miserably at Daytona. Things did not look so good to start with, as the car was not ready for practice and, as such, had to start at the back of the grid in 70th place. A long steady effort by both drivers ensured a sixth place finish behind a BMW CSL and four Porsche 911 RSRs, despite changing an alternator and the car catching fire in the pits during refuelling. Jean-Louis Lebreton related what had happened:

> The fire was indirectly attributed to the fitting of a long range rubber fuel tank. During the race it proved to be unreliable whilst being filled, air pockets formed, causing the tank to overflow inside the car. During one refuelling stop the fuel was an inch deep inside the car. Dick Fritz, unaware of the problem, urged Minter back onto the track. As soon as the car fired up, a spark ignited the fumes and the car went up in a ball of flames. I was caught in the flames and was badly burned.

With prompt action by the pit marshals the flames were doused, enabling the car to continue the race. It covered 215 laps, with Minter and Wietzes both picking up a cheque for $1000 for their success.

Road Atlanta in Georgia was NART's next destination. Although the 365 GTBB attended, it never made it to the start grid of either 100-mile heat of the Camel GT Challenge, due to a broken hub carrier in practice.

In May, the same car turned up for the Camel GT Challenge races held at Lime Rock, the engine now fitted with factory supplied competition cams and pistons, with Milt Minter behind the wheel. There were two 100-mile races, with the total laps covered determining the final positions. In the first race Minter covered 58 laps, but did not finish. He was classified as being 18th on distance covered. In the second race a broken connecting rod put paid to his efforts, having covered just 24 laps, and he was put in 26th place. Overall, Minter was classified as finishing in 20th place.

Chinetti put forward an entry of four cars to the Le Mans 24-hour race in June. They were a 365 GTBB (18095), two 365 GTB4s (16407 and 15965), and a Ferrari Dino 308 GT4 (08020). Whereas #16407 was a Pininfarina designed Daytona Coupe, chassis 15965 had been transformed from

9 | 1975

■ Jean-Pierre Malcher's 365 GTB4 (18095) was bodied by Michelotti, pictured on track during a practice session at Le Mans.

■ Bucknum and Facetti practised in the 365 GTB4 (16407) at Le Mans.

Chinetti discusses the situation regarding his cars with the press in the pits at Le Mans.

a Pininfarina Daytona Coupe to a Daytona Spyder, with a Targa-type roof by Giovanni Michelotti, to the order of Luigi Chinetti. The Spyder was quite unusual in appearance, resembling the Chevrolet Corvette in certain aspects, and had appeared at the Geneva Auto Salon earlier in the year. Ferrari was not keen on Chinetti entering either the 365 GTBB or the Ferrari Dino 308 GT4, as they were deemed to be 'under-developed for sustained periods of racing,' and Ferrari representative Gaetano Florini was present at Le Mans, to try and persuade Chinetti not to race them.

What followed was a complete disaster for all parties concerned. Practice for Le Mans held little difficulty for three of the four NART entries. Qualifying times were achieved in daylight practice for numbers

A very confused affair

NART's cars are withdrawn to the back of the pits after the ACO refused to let the Dino GT4 race.

Spectators appear bemused to see the NART cars in the paddock so close to the start of the race.

9 | 1975

Close up of the NART-entered 365 GTBB in the paddock at Le Mans.

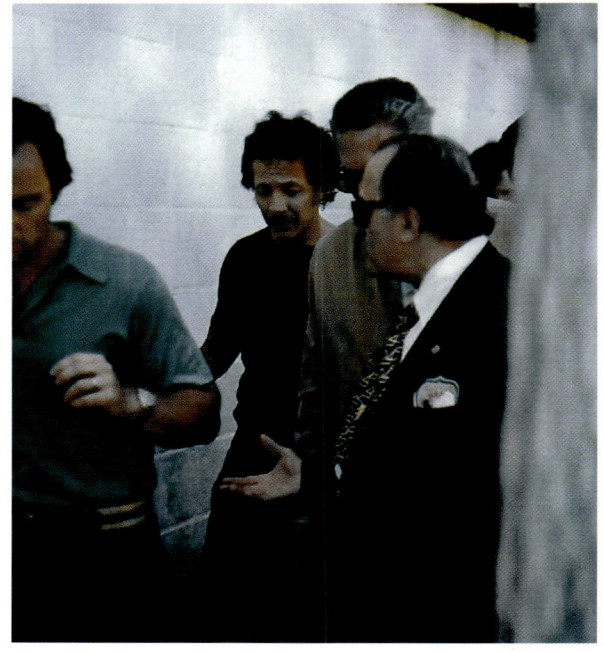

Chinetti (right), Baus (next to him), and Cluxton (left) are seen leaving the final meeting with the ACO. There appears to be some difference of opinion on how the meeting went, as Chinetti over-played his hand.

Luigi Chinetti in discussion with John Baus after the meeting with the ACO.

A very confused affair

43, 46 and 99, although there had been some questions regarding one of the GTB4's fuel consumption, which was quickly dealt with. There was also the little matter of not having enough tyres for both 365 GTBs, and a good deal of tyre-swapping took place during qualifying; this annoyed Ronnie Bucknum, who insisted on having the best sets on his car. Qualifying was delayed for number 17, as Chinetti argued with the officials that the Ferrari Dino 308 GT4 was a 2-door Grand Touring car, and should have been placed in the Grand Touring class, not in Group 5 with the fastest sports cars. Losing that argument, Chinetti sent the Ferrari Dino 308 GT4 out for practice driven by Harley Cluxton, who had paid for his ride with NART, but he achieved a slower qualifying time than necessary. He also failed to match the necessary time for driving during the hours of darkness, at the same time as suffering the effects of an unstable rear wing on the car.

Back at the Volkswagen garage where NART was based, the mechanics decided that the rear spoiler needed extra support. They required thin tubing, but had none to hand until they discovered a bike leaning against the garage wall – the frame tubing was just the right diameter – so they 'borrowed' the bike and cut up the frame, using the tubing to support the wing. The bike belonged to the garage owner's wife – she never did find out who stole it!

With the rear spoiler fixed, the car had recorded a reasonable time of 4.32.9 in the hands of Gagliardi. The ACO chairman, Pierre Allanet, informed NART's manager, John Baus, on Thursday evening that "... all his cars and drivers had fulfilled the qualification criteria, during both daylight and darkness." Chinetti and Baus interpreted that statement to mean that the full team had achieved starting status, only to find out ahead of the Friday morning drivers' meeting that number 17 had been taken from the qualifying list of starters. The Dino had apparently been pushed out by a Porsche, driven by three local Frenchmen. Enquiries with ACO officials were met with the explanation that Cluxton's qualifying times at night were generally slower than other drivers, and did not meet the necessary parameters (having already being told they did). As many other cars had also been quicker in daylight hours, the ACO felt that the car had failed to meet the requirements as laid down in the rules, in light of another late entry Porsche going quicker than the Dino 308 GT4.

Chinetti was furious and challenged the ruling, in perhaps not the most logical way, ranting that he was a three times winner at Le Mans – how could they treat him this way? The officials were having none of it, and still refused the Dino 308 GT4 a starting place. It got worse; Chinetti said that the organisers then asked him to sign a document saying "that the Dino was being thrown out of the race for poor performance." "That would have been like signing my death warrant," said Chinetti, "if I sign it is like saying the Dino is a jalopy. How can I do that? I sell 6000 of those cars in the United States."

After the Friday morning drivers' meeting, Chinetti put the pair of French drivers, Guitteny and Haran, into the Dino 308 GT4 and they circulated all morning. It appeared that Chinetti was prepared to abandon one of the 365 GTB4s if necessary, just to have the Dino running.

In a last-ditch attempt to resolve their differences, the ACO and Chinetti, along with John Baus and Harley Cluxton, had a final meeting late on Saturday morning. At that meeting

A concise history of the North American Racing Team 1957 to 1983

9 | 1975

■■ *NART's 365 GTB4 driven by Muniz and Young in Mexico City, pictured prior to the start of the race.*

■ *The 365 GTB4 placed first in the race in Mexico.*

The Muniz and Young rent-a-car entry on the grid at the start of the race.

Chinetti made a tactical error by putting all his cards on the table, issuing his ultimatum "Let the Dino 308 start the race or I withdraw the whole team." The officials called his bluff, sticking to their ruling. The ACO was already in a tight spot regarding some other excluded cars and, seeing the opportunity to admit three of those cars, it seized the chance with both hands. Chinetti tried a different tactic, saying that the French public may accept the cars not running, but how would the officials explain why they refused to let two pairs of French drivers (Malcher/Langlois and Guitteny/Haran) appear in their home race? There was still no positive response from the ACO officials, and the meeting ended on a sour note.

On Saturday early afternoon, the Dino 308 GT4, along with the other Ferraris belonging to NART, appeared in front of the pits ready for the race later that day. Again the ACO officials refused point blank to allow it to start. As a consequence, Chinetti told his pit crew to wheel the cars away. By this time, crowds of photographers and spectators were aware something was going on, and milled around the NART pits. The situation became impossible to control, so Chinetti reluctantly acceded to the officials' ruling, and carried out his threat to withdraw the cars. At the same time the ACO were clearing the NART spares and tools away from the pits, making the decision final. It was long suspected that the ACO officials were pressurised to get one of the Ferraris out, to

A very confused affair

make way for a Japanese entry, though it was never proven.

With so much confusion around the pits and paddock, Chinetti gave an impromptu press conference behind the pits as the race was being started. Excerpts of the press conference were supplied by an eye-witness to the event.

> The Dino is a good example of the Le Mans GTX, but I was obliged to enter in Group 5. That was unthinkable. Unfortunately, it only achieved 11th best time in this group. The ACO refused to waiver the requirements of the Group, so it fell to me to search for a precedent. They [ACO] refused to qualify Gagliardi without me signing a paper saying that Ferrari would present the Type at the Geneva Salon. At the show [in March '75] the ACO encouraged me to be present at Le Mans. At Le Mans they said they wanted a model that gentleman-racers would use the following year [1976]. I hoped to finish in style ... now it is over. Le Mans is finished for me. This is not the end I wished for. I was hoping to finish in style, giving an honest performance. To return here in any way I would have to come in a Porsche, and with that I do not agree. I love the beautiful machines [Ferraris]. Where is Le Mans headed? I do not know. I think it will be a championship without interest in the Porsche. This is unfortunate after the great contests of the past.

ACO President Pierre Allanet responded:

> [It was] a simple application of the regulations. We do not understand the attitude of the American, and are not in agreement with the Chinetti proposal [to change the car to the GTX class]. After the second supplemental qualifications, one of the cars was not going to be permitted to start. It would have been unfair to make an exception, even for Mr Chinetti, a devotee of Le Mans. His car was not allowed. It was also unacceptable to change the drivers and replace them with strangers [a tentative proposal to have Guitteny and Haran drive the car]. On this point we were in complete disagreement.

After hearing this Chinetti said "That is not our custom. We regret having to forfeit. The complete responsibility is on them."

There were no winners that day. Everyone ended up the poorer, rashness on Chinetti's side, stubbornness on the ACO side, with the paying spectators left to wonder what was happening, as this sad episode unfolded.

There was one more race to report, but it is unclear if the race took place in 1975 or not. The venue was Mexico. François Sicard could not remember exactly when, but stated:

> Chinetti arranged with a Mexican driver, Muniz, to a rent-a-drive in a 365 GTB4, and Gregg Young was to co-drive the car for this 1000km race. I and Wayne Sparling went to Mexico with the car, and for this package Muniz paid $10,000. The car won the race and very little work was done on it.

There was a Marco Antonio Muniz who was a friend of the Rodríguez brothers when they were getting started, and this entry could be associated with the same person.

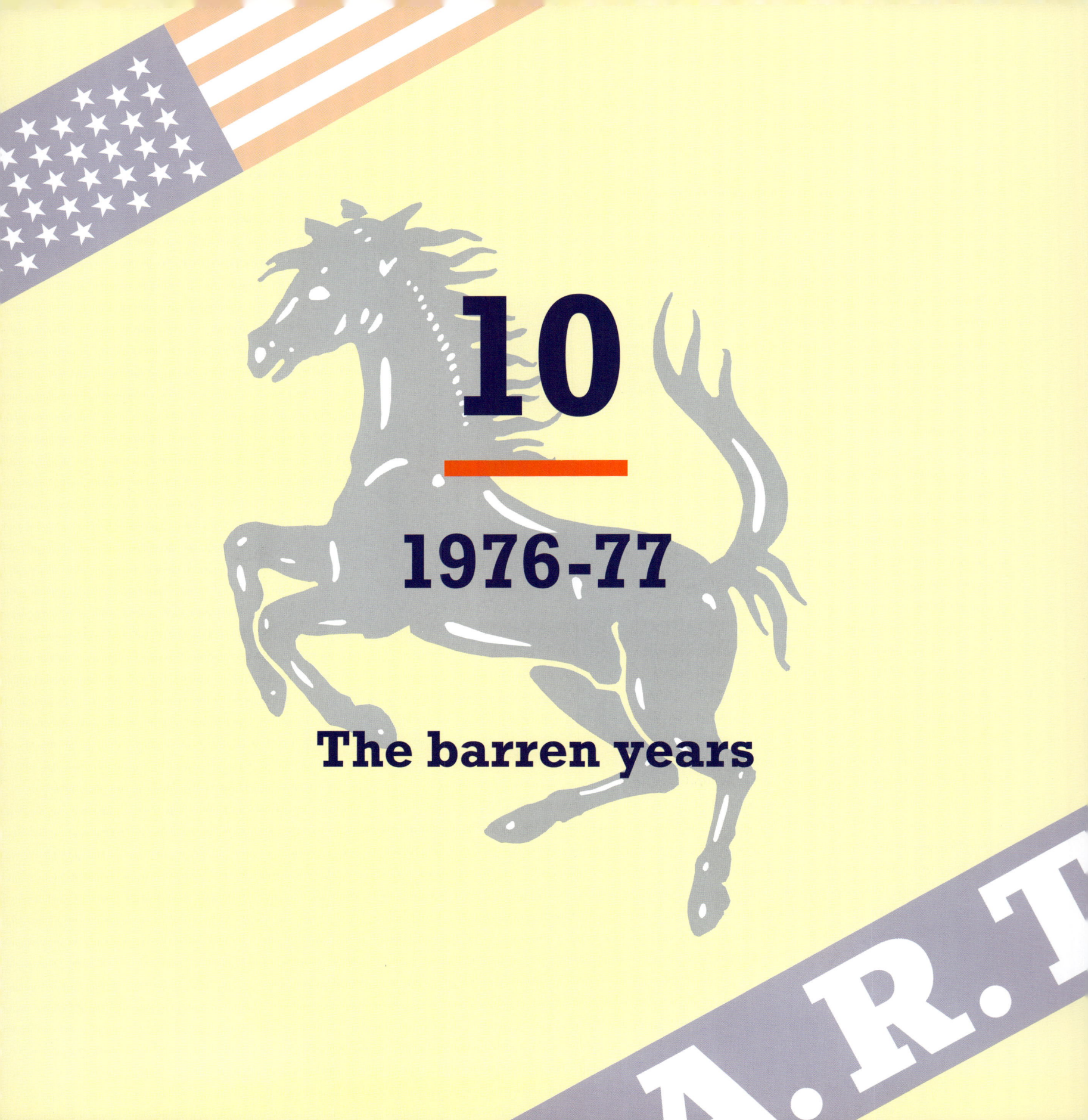

The barren years

> "Turmoil within the Luigi Chinetti Motors organisation led to the entire operation being put up for sale, and as a consequence 1976 proved to be a year of non-participation for the North American Racing Team."

Despite the arguments between Chinetti and the ACO in 1975, plans had been formulated for an entry in Le Mans, but the changing face of the endurance racing game, with altered regulations, saw no 365 GTB4s, no Dino 308 GT4s, or aged modified sports prototypes as viable contenders for honours. Lack of opportunities within NART led to team manager Dick Fritz leaving the Chinetti organisation early in the year, to set up his own business, Amerispec Corporation, in Danville, Connecticut.

Earlier in the year, discussions had taken place between Luigi Chinetti Jr and John Woodner from Berkeley CA (who had previously raced at Le Mans), to see if a package could be created to enter a 365 GTBB under NART's wing, with Woodner and Minter driving the car. Sponsorship was required for a suggested development of the engine by Joe Huffaker, but, as the car was not entered, it would seem likely that the sponsorship fell short of what was required, despite Woodner's efforts to raise the funds.

In 1977 there was just one Ferrari entered for the Le Mans 24-hour race, the NART-entered 365 GTBB, under the guidance of John Baus, the same car (18139) that performed for NART in 1975. To assist in the expense

François Migault and Lucien Guitteny drove the 365 GTBB (18139) to 16th place at Le Mans.

of undertaking this race Chinetti-Garthwaite Imports contributed $15,000 to NART. The car was now officially in the ownership of Howard O'Flynn, of Banker's Discount in New York, but for entry purposes the car was still under the NART banner. Driven by Migault and Guitteny the Ferrari, sporting a modified back wing, qualified 48th fastest. Thanks to some consistent steady driving, the Ferrari climbed up the field and finished the race in 16th place, despite losing two hours to replace a flywheel gasket.

According to an article that appeared in the *Greenwich Times* as late as 31 May 1979, it confirmed that portions of Luigi Chinetti Motors Inc were sold to Tom Parker in 1977. At a shareholders meeting held on 15 September 1977, the sale of the majority of Luigi Chinetti Motors Inc was agreed. Assets relinquished included the Greenwich facility, the New York showroom, and a portion of the car inventory.

The parts inventory was sold separately, while certain prominent cars that usually languished in the showrooms were retained, as they belonged to either Marion or Luigi Chinetti Jr. At the time of the sale, Luigi Chinetti Sr and Marion Chinetti each owned 21 per cent of the shares, Luigi Chinetti Jr had 33 per cent, and Al Garthwaite, 25 per cent. Luigi Chinetti stated: "What we did was to get rid of the selling and servicing portion of the business, so we could concentrate on the parts that excite us, the designing and racing."

After about six months, Parker stopped making payments on his purchase of the business and the Chinettis reclaimed portions of the business by court order. During that period of time, the business records had been disbursed, all the cancelled cheques with drivers autographs sold, and other cheques and business files also parcelled out.

11
1978-80
Limited participation

11 | 1978-80

1978 was a year of upheaval for the Chinetti-Garthwaite Imports organisation and, because of this, racing was not foremost in the minds of those concerned. Ferrari was 50 per cent owned by Fiat, and worldwide changes were being sought as to how Ferrari should operate its distribution of cars.

Ferrari North America wanted to make sweeping changes, and issued notice of termination to Modern Classic Motors in Reno, who distributed to the western side of America as well as to Chinetti-Garthwaite Imports, the importer for the eastern side of America.

Chinetti-Garthwaite Imports took out an injunction in the US District Court, Eastern District of Pennsylvania, to stop Ferrari from terminating the franchise, on the basis that a) there was no justification for that action to be taken; and b) irreparable damage would be caused to Chinetti-Garthwaite Imports if that action went ahead. (A full judgement document is available, Chinetti-Garthwaite Imports, Inc v Ferrari Societa per Azioni Esercizio Fabbriche Automobili e Corse, CIV.A No 78-2998).

In brief, the judgement stated:

> After balancing the relevant factors, I hold that CGI is entitled to the preliminary injunction that it seeks. CGI has proved that without the injunction it will be irreparably harmed while Ferrari will not be harmed and has shown that it likely to succeed on the merits. CGI has therefore fulfilled the requirements for receiving preliminary injunction relief.
>
> *District Judge Cahn*

A write-up in the *New York Times* of 24 November 1979 confirmed the verdict given by the District Court in the case of Chinetti-Garthwaite Imports v Ferrari case. "Ferrari North America wanted to take back the Chinetti-Garthwaite distribution rights in December 1978 when it took back the rights in Reno from Modern Classic Motors, but Chinetti-Garthwaite obtained an injunction blocking the move." It appears that a financial agreement was eventually reached between the two parties.

However, during 1978, a limited amount of time and money was spent on the North American Racing Team.

The 1978 Daytona 24-hour race saw more action for the 365 GTBB (18139). In an endeavour to make the car more competitive, significant changes had been made by NART, but were only the first steps in improving the car. The 365 engine was replaced with a 512 engine, though it was virtually a stock motor; a competition specification engine wasn't made available until shortly prior to the car racing at Le Mans, by which time the car had been entered by Howard O'Flynn. The 365 GTBB qualified in 17th spot and the combination of Guitteny, Migault and Young covered 521 laps; during this time, the car experienced electrical problems, which caused the car to drop from eighth place to finish in 22nd place.

The same lone NART 365 GTBB turned up at Road Atlanta for the 100-mile race. Migault qualified the car in 21st place, and that is precisely where the car finished the race.

NART entered a Ferrari 512 BB (24131) for the Le Mans 24-hour race with Guerin, Delaunay and Young driving the

Limited participation

Guerin, Delaunay and Young piloted the 512 BB at Le Mans, but the car retired with gearbox failure after covering 232 laps.

car. The 512 BB qualified in 36th place on the grid, and after travelling through the night, and being as high as 11th place, the gearbox failed, and the car was withdrawn. It had covered 232 laps, and had looked likely to take a class win.

In 1979, NART raised enough enthusiasm and sponsorship money to enter a new 512 BBLM (26683) in the Daytona 24-hour race, one of three supplied by Ferrari to private teams after they had been prepared by the Assistenza Clienti department at Modena. Only at the last moment did a second car come under its control, a 365 GTB4, originally entered by Otto Zipper. It came as a blow to everyone to hear that Zipper had died from a heart attack in his hotel room the evening before the race, and his entry was about to be withdrawn from the race, when Chinetti stepped in and offered to look after the car with drivers John Morton and Tony Adamowicz, both familiar with the way that NART worked.

Industrial action in Italy had hindered preparation of the 512 BBLM – the wheelmakers were on strike. Only a personal unofficial visit by Luigi Chinetti to somebody at the factory secured the required materials to complete the car, so it was with some satisfaction that Chinetti saw the car in the NART pit at Daytona.

11 | 1978-80

NART's venerable 365 GTB4 (16407) remained remarkably reliable, and took second place at Daytona driven by Adamowicz and Morton.

Bedard, Delaunay and Tulius piloted NART's 512 BBLM at Daytona, but failed to last the 24-hours due to tyre failure resulting in an accident.

Limited participation

The 512 BBLM (26683) turned up at Le Mans with Grandet, Delaunay and Henn driving the car. It lasted for only 54 laps before coming off the road and sustaining enough damage for NART to withdraw the car from the race.

When the 365 GTB4 appeared on the start grid in 24th place, a black sash had been painted across the bonnet in respect for Otto. The 512 BBLM was further up the grid in 16th place, with Bob Tullius, Jean-Pierre Delaunay and Patrick Bedard driving. Practice had shown to Chinetti and everyone else that watched, that the 512 BBLM was going to be a handful to control, with its vary flared back end and long tail. It skipped from one side of the banking to the other and, sure enough, three hours into the race, the NART-entered 512 BBLM clipped the banking wall, and in doing so demolished the front end and shortened the back end of the car by a couple of feet. For the second time, a Michelin tyre had failed on the banking at 180mph. Both failures had been on the right rear of the BBLM. Michelin didn't allow for the sustained loading. That was the signal for the other two 512 BBLMs being run by Charles

11 | 1978-80

- Front end damage to 512 BBLM (26683).

- Rear end damage to 512 BBLM (26683). NART mechanic Al Roberts standing to the right of the car.

Pozzi to call it a day, before anything worse happened to his cars. Meanwhile the 365 GTB4 was making its way forward through the field, and nobody could quite believe that this venerable car was lying in second spot, with less than an hour to go. A faultless display of driving was rewarded with a second spot finish, a true but remarkable tribute to Otto Zipper, and a pleasing one for Luigi Chinetti knowing that he had helped in achieving this result.

The 512 BBLM was hastily rebuilt in time to fulfil the NART entry at Le Mans. While rebuilding the car, pneumatic jacks were added to the specification for the first time. The car

Limited participation

A concise history of the North American Racing Team 1957 to 1983

11 | 1978-80

The 512 BBLM (26683) heads a line of cars early in the race.

A view of the business end of the 512 BBLM in the pits at Le Mans.

was driven by Delaunay, Henn and Grandet, it qualified 36th on the grid and covered 54 laps, before Preston Henn came off the road at the Tertre-Rouge bend while in 20th place, damaging the car.

The same Ferrari 512 BBLM (26683) was back in action at the Daytona 24-hour race in 1980. Driven by 'gentlemen' drivers, Dieudonne and Henn, the car qualified in 23rd place on the grid. In the race it covered 341 laps before going out with fuel problems, later diagnosed as stemming from a broken fuel tank.

NART's visit to Le Mans was short and expensive. The 512 BBLM (30559) that was entered never made it past the end of practice, when the engine seized with a lubrication problem. Such was the damage that it was beyond immediate repair, much to the disappointment of the team, as the car had posted a competitive time of 4'11.2sec in early practice.

Regarding the retail side of the business, the Chinetti-Garthwaite partnership was finally disbanded in 1980, when Ferrari established a factory-controlled entity for US distribution.

12
1981-83
The passing of an era

The passing of an era

> The imminent demise of NART was confirmed in 1981. There was just one entry this year, to the Le Mans 24-hour race, where the new Ferrari 512 BBLM (35527) was wheeled into the pit lane for the start of the race to be driven by Morton, Cudini and Gurdjian.

After qualifying quickest of the small Ferrari contingent in 29th place, the car was running in fourth place overall, and stayed there for several hours. NART's 512 BBLM was so much quicker than the other 512 BBs, questions were asked as to whether or not he had a special engine from the factory. Chinetti denied it, simply pointing out that all of the engines were dyno tested, and he had selected number 023, which he considered to be the best one. The Ferrari had covered 247 laps when Gurdjian, on one of his driving stints, left the road and hit a guard rail, forcing retirement of the car.

A deal between Chinetti and business entrepreneur, Preston Henn, ensured a presence at the Daytona 24-hour race in 1982. The 512 BB (30559) was entered by

NART's lone entry to Le Mans in 1981, 512 BBLM (35527), was driven by Cudini, Gurdjian and Morton, but failed to finish.

A concise history of the North American Racing Team 1957 to 1983

NART's 512 BBLM in action during the 24-hour race at Le Mans.

Chinetti on behalf of Preston Henn's T-Bird Swap Shop, sponsor of the car. The driver team of Bob Wollek, Edgar Doeren and Randy Lanier qualified the car in 15th spot on the grid. It ran strongly for 523 laps, but was retired with gearbox ailments.

Encouraged by the strong showing of the 512 BB at Daytona, the Chinetti/Swap Shop combination entered the Sebring 12-hour race with confidence, fielding an all-woman team of Janet Guthrie, Desire Wilson and Bonnie Henn. The Ferrari 512 BB started the race in 17th place but suffered from suspension trouble while Desire Wilson was driving. The car was stopped out on the course while she made temporary repairs, before getting it back to the pits. For her efforts the team was penalized three minutes – the crime, taking a short cut back to the pits. Despite the efforts of the pit crew, the car was eventually retired, after covering 163 laps.

NART put one entry forward to the Le Mans 24-hour race, the 512 BBLM (35527), the same car that had crashed at Le Mans the previous year. Not so many sponsor decals appeared on the car this year, though one legend around the number circle on the nose did create interest. It read "In God we trust." "Why do you have that? Your car was totally wrecked last year," was the question. Chinetti's answer was "Yes, but the driver, he was not hurt!"

There in person again this year, Chinetti stood out from the crowd, as he maintained certain old ways; a necktie and smart blue blazer in the pits, where other owners flashed polo shirts, and a narrow brim hat pulled down to his ears, instead of the fashionable baseball hat. Pure class, little wonder he received the respect as a driver and team owner who had seen it all during 50 years at Le Mans, and was given the honour of starting the race this year, the differences of 1975 put to one side. The new Group C rules in force in 1982, caused much speculation as to how many cars would see the finish flag this year, partly due to the rule to maintain a minimum fuel mileage – a rule easy

The passing of an era

The 512 BBLM (35527) in the pit area at Le Mans prior to the 24-hour race, showing very few sponsorship decals.

NART's 512 BBLM (35527), driven by Cudini, Morton and Paul, finished in ninth place at Le Mans in 1981.

The 512 BBLM captured at speed at Le Mans on its way to a ninth place finish.

Luigi Chinetti stands alongside the NART entry at Le Mans for the final time.

enough to enforce, by simply limiting fuel tanks to 100 litres, and pit stops for fuel to 25 for the race. The NART drivers were Cudini, Morton and Paul, who qualified the car down in 37th place, though still quickest of the Ferraris. 15 hours in from the start, the NART Ferrari was running in fourth place and leading its class. All around them cars had dropped out of the race, 30 of the 55 starters had succumbed to mechanical failure or had run out of fuel. Unfortunately the Ferrari hoodoo struck the NART car again, as the gearbox lost first, second and fifth gears, and by the 20th hour just fourth and fifth gear were left. As a result, the car's lap times slowed dramatically, and the Ferrari ended up ninth overall and fourth in class. It was the second year in a row that the NART entry was headed for a top five finish, before misfortune struck. Little did the spectators realise that this was to be the final appearance of the North American Racing Team at a race event.

By the beginning of 1983, NART, as a force in motor racing, had basically diminished to nothing. Only one entry was recorded as a potential starter, that of the 24-hour race held at Le Mans in June. However, the proposed car,

The passing of an era

A special dinner was laid on for Luigi Chinetti Sr on 16 October 1982 – 'Salute to Luigi Chinetti.' Menu signed by Carroll Shelby.

a 512 BBLM (35527), was withdrawn, as it was discovered that the tail section did not conform to the new regulations issued by the organisers of the race.

Although the same car had raced at Le Mans in 1981 and 1982, it had become obsolete, as rule changes were introduced. Indecision led to a delay in Chinetti authorising the necessary expenditure on the car, to bring it to the correct specification. It would have meant that the Assistenza Clienti in Modena would only have two weeks to carry out the modifications, and they reluctantly informed Chinetti that it would not be possible to complete the work within the given timescale. Consequently, Chinetti abandoned the idea, and the Le Mans organisers were notified of the withdrawal of the North American Racing Team entry.

So as to keep the records straight, it should be noted that a Le Mans entry was lodged by NART in both 1984 and 1985 for a 512 BBLM, with Alain Cudini and Dany Snobeck nominated as drivers for 1984. The Ferrari did not attend in 1984 and the entry was not accepted by the ACO in 1985. The final entry was lodged in 1987, but again no details of the car have come to light, although it would have been in the IMSA GTO class.

A concise history of the North American Racing Team 1957 to 1983

13
Spyder

The NART 275 GTB4

The NART 275 GTB4

> "It would have been churlish to disregard Luigi Chinetti's influence on the sales of Ferrari in the United States. Certainly NART's indirect contribution to the success of Ferrari sales was outstanding."

However, as an individual Chinetti held sway with his elite customer base, and he would usually be able to produce 'something special' for his customers when asked to.

His influence at the Ferrari factory, and with the various coachwork manufacturers in Italy, had already allowed him to order a few cars to the customers' own specification.

In 1967 Ferrari was producing a 275 GTS, but Chinetti's clients were asking for something more 'sporty' than this production model.

Chinetti's idea was to have a 275 GTB4/Spyder produced by Scaglietti, loosely based on a design he had seen created by Carrozzeria Autocourse, a one-off so-called Nembo Spyder. He eventually convinced the Ferrari factory to build a series of ten units, though his original ambitious plan was to have 25 built.

These ten genuine Spyders built in 1967/68 were 275 GTB4 Berlinettas converted by Scaglietti in Modena, and, when complete, were identical to the 275 GTB4 Berlinetta, apart from the soft-top and a horizontal trunk lid; to keep the costs down no additional bracing was added to the frame.

Three-quarter front view of the 275 GTB NART Spyder standing outside of Carrozzeria Autocorse, June 1966.

13 | Spyder

Three-quarter rear view of the 275 GTB NART Spyder.

The NART 275 GTB4

The ten cars were never recognised as official Ferrari models, so, because Chinetti was instrumental in the ordering and subsequent production of the cars at Scaglietti, they became known as NART Spyders. They turned out to be a little more difficult to sell than anticipated, hence some of Chinetti's customers' invoices showed charges for the bodywork conversion, while others did not.

The first NART Spyder (09437 GT) was shipped to America in February 1967, just in time for the Sebring 12-hour race where it was driven by Denise McCluggage and Pinkie Rollo. They finished in a respectable 17th place, a good result considering that mechanically, it was a standard production specification car.

Potential legal complications (explained in Chapter Six) meant that Luigi Chinetti would not be in attendance but, according to Denise McCluggage, he sent the Spyder to Sebring, the car entered in her name, accompanied by a couple of his mechanics to look after the car. The car was sponsored by the Cities Service Oil Company (CITGO) to the tune of $6000. When asked what they got for $6000, part of Chinetti's reply was "$3000 for race car depreciation and overall cost after the 12-hour race." This would imply that title rights to the car remained with Chinetti and, in all but name, was entered by NART. Consequently the car has been listed in this book as a tenuous NART entry.

However, the records show that Denise McCluggage was the official entrant. She had NART stickers, cut out the A, turned it upside-down, took out the crossbar from the A and used it as a letter V to form NVRT (North Vermont Racing Team). It would appear that very little needed to be done to elude the potential legal ramifications of the previous year's race.

Of the ten NART Spyders built, the 09437 GT was the only one to be entered in a race before going to a retail customer. Eight others were also sold in America, but the tenth car (11057 GT) went to the Spanish Ferrari importer and was sold in Europe.

Epilogue

One cannot claim that the North American Racing Team was the greatest privately run racing team in the world, for that statement is subjective. However, what is indisputable is that the team, linked with Chinetti Motors and the Ferrari factory, was unique in both the way it operated, and the results that were attained in both National and International races over three decades.

Chinetti was fiercely proud of the fact that no driver was killed while driving a car for the North American Racing Team, and not many teams could boast the same thing during the period that NART was competing.

Bob Grossman said that Chinetti was the antithesis of Briggs Cunningham. While Cunningham appeared more orderly in the way his team functioned, Chinetti was more informal, as some of the pit crew performances bore witness to. Irrespective of appearances, the team were genuinely competitive, but at the same time they enjoyed themselves.

There is the story that Dick Fritz told of a race at Le Mans, that typifies the informal fun nature of the organisation:

> We were racing an aluminium-panel Daytona and there was a weight limit that had to be met, but the car was underweight. We put some weight in the car, and the car went through inspection, but it was still too light. I told Chinetti, who said he thought that I had put extra weight in the car. I replied that I had. I had added a big tool box and a nine-year-old boy in the trunk of the car, and it was still too light; and I was worried about the boy and the exhaust fumes. Chinetti approached an official who had the car reweighed and mysteriously it passed. Somewhere out there this nine-year-old boy is telling people this story and nobody believes him.

Dick Fritz said

> Chinetti was not always easy to work for. He was demanding, and did not pay particularly well and was also set in his ways and was reluctant to change his work practises. He was also a shrewd businessman, seemingly being able to do deals and wield influence with Enzo Ferrari like other people could not – their friendship counted for a lot.

Importantly, the staff that worked for Chinetti Motors and NART were loyal and dedicated, for, I am told, some of the pay cheques remained uncashed at the end of a week. It wasn't that the recipients did not need the money, but more to the point that circumstances were sometimes difficult, and the money was not there to honour the cheques. That did not stop or deter those enthusiasts who would come to the workshop in an evening and work on the competition cars alongside the skilled mechanics, indeed they felt it a privilege to be able to do so.

The NART 275 GTB4

Dick Fritz said

> Chinetti employed possibly no more than 20 people at any one time, hence race mechanics did customer cars in the day, and prepared race cars at weekends and evening. When François (Sicard) joined the team he found this hard to understand at first. Only four or five people went to races to look after the cars, sometimes on an expenses only basis.

In some ways it summed up part of Chinetti's legacy. It would have been all too easy for people to miss an opportunity, because of being inhibited or concerned about failing in what they were striving to achieve, but Chinetti encouraged individuals to pursue their dreams and ambitions. No matter if it was as a helping hand in the workshop, or endeavouring to become a racing driver, he would be there to give encouragement.

He was keen to give young drivers a chance, and was honest in his opinion of them. Rich or poor they were offered equal opportunities to prove themselves. Sam Posey said

> He made more opportunities for me, without asking anything in return except my enthusiasm. He never asked me to find a sponsor, and never paid me any more than I was due.

As with most things in life there are achievements and disappointments, and Chinetti experienced both in equal measure. Those, like Luigi Chinetti, who accomplished significant achievements in life, will be praised by some and scorned by others, but their accomplishments will never be diminished.

Luigi Chinetti Sr died at the age of 93 on 17 August 1994, a man respected and honoured by the many people he knew and helped. Phil Hill said

> He has always been renowned for his tenacity in getting young drivers started. He will be remembered by many, many people who owe their successes to him.

Ultimately, Chinetti's place in history will be determined not just by his accomplishments, but by his passion for life. It was this that fuelled his successes on and off the track, and it was this also, at that Christmas Eve meeting, that shaped the future of both Ferrari, the man, and Ferrari, the company. For that accomplishment alone, Chinetti will never be forgotten.

Can you imagine ...

14

1957-1983

Statistical review

Statistical review

CN	MAKE & MODEL	CHASSIS No	NOMINATED DRIVER(S)	RACE RESULTS
		1957		

22–23 June — Le Mans 24-hour
CN	MAKE & MODEL	CHASSIS No	NOMINATED DRIVER(S)	RACE RESULTS
10	Ferrari 290 MM	0616	Arents G/de Vroom J	DNF

December — Bahamas Speed Weeks, Nassau
CN	MAKE & MODEL	CHASSIS No	NOMINATED DRIVER(S)	RACE RESULTS
44	Ferrari 315 S	0684	Greenspun G	Gov Tr 20 OA 12cl C
44	Ferrari 315 S	0684	Greenspun G	Nassau Tr 15 OA 6cl C
105	Ferrari 290 MM	0628	Moss S	Memorial Tr 1 OA 1cl C
105	Ferrari 290 MM	0628	Moss S	Nassau Tr 1 OA 1cl C

CN	MAKE & MODEL	CHASSIS No	NOMINATED DRIVER(S)	RACE RESULTS
		1958		

11–12 January — Masters Field NAB, Florida
CN	MAKE & MODEL	CHASSIS No	NOMINATED DRIVER(S)	RACE RESULTS
96	Ferrari 250 GT TdF	0773 GT	Arents G (NART SOUTH)	R1 17 OA
96	Ferrari 250 GT TdF	0773 GT	Arents G (NART SOUTH)	R5 13 OA

24 February — Cuban Grand Prix, Havana
CN	MAKE & MODEL	CHASSIS No	NOMINATED DRIVER(S)	RACE RESULTS
4	Ferrari 335 S	0674	Moss S	1 OA
10	Ferrari 315 S	0656	Von Trips W	4 OA
14	Ferrari 290 MM	0628	Crawford E	8 OA

23 March — Sebring 12-hour
CN	MAKE & MODEL	CHASSIS No	NOMINATED DRIVER(S)	RACE RESULTS
22	Ferrari 250 GT TdF	0773 GT	Kessler B/O'Shea P/Cunningham D	5 OA
21	Ferrari 250 GT TdF	0893 GT	Arents G/Reed G/O'Dell D	7 OA

8 June — Thompson Raceway
CN	MAKE & MODEL	CHASSIS No	NOMINATED DRIVER(S)	RACE RESULTS
25	Ferrari 335 S	0674	Andrey G	2 OA

21–22 June — Le Mans 24-hour
CN	MAKE & MODEL	CHASSIS No	NOMINATED DRIVER(S)	RACE RESULTS
25	Ferrari 500 TR	0600 MDTR	Rodríguez P/Behra J	DNF
18	Ferrari 250 TR	0666	Gurney D/Kessler B	DNF
19	Ferrari 250 TR	0730 TR	Marchtin E/Tavano F	DNF

29 June — Monza 500
CN	MAKE & MODEL	CHASSIS No	NOMINATED DRIVER(S)	RACE RESULTS
16	Ferrari 375 Indy Monoposto	0388	Schell H	Heat 1 12 OA

Abbreviations

CN = Car Number
DNF = Did Not Finish
DNA = Did Not Attend
DNQ = Did Not Qualify
U2L = Under 2-litre
O2L = Over 2-litre
NK = Not Known
OA = Overall
WDN = Withdrawn

CN	MAKE & MODEL	CHASSIS No	NOMINATED DRIVER(S)	RACE RESULTS
16	Ferrari 375 Indy Monoposto	0388	Schell H	Heat 2 13 OA
16	Ferrari 375 Indy Monoposto	0388	Schell H	Heat 3 DNS
16	Ferrari 375 Indy Monoposto	0388	Schell H	Final placing 13 OA

7 September — Lime Rock

CN	MAKE & MODEL	CHASSIS No	NOMINATED DRIVER(S)	RACE RESULTS
4	Ferrari 860 Monza	0602 M	Kessler B	2 OA

7 September — Road America

CN	MAKE & MODEL	CHASSIS No	NOMINATED DRIVER(S)	RACE RESULTS
25	Ferrari 335 S	0674	Andrey G/Reventlow L	1 OA

13–14 September — Bridgehampton

CN	MAKE & MODEL	CHASSIS No	NOMINATED DRIVER(S)	RACE RESULTS
99	Ferrari 860 Monza	0602 M	Grossman R	R4 DNF
99	Ferrari 860 Monza	0602 M	Grossman R	R6 3 OA

20 September — Watkins Glen

CN	MAKE & MODEL	CHASSIS No	NOMINATED DRIVER(S)	RACE RESULTS
25	Ferrari 335 S	0674	Andrey G	3 OA

27–28 September — Watkins Glen Formula Libre

CN	MAKE & MODEL	CHASSIS No	NOMINATED DRIVER(S)	RACE RESULTS
3	Ferrari 290 MM	0628	Gurney D	2 OA
4	Ferrari 860 Monza	0602 M	Kessler B	3 OA

5 December — Governor's Trophy, Nassau Prelim

CN	MAKE & MODEL	CHASSIS No	NOMINATED DRIVER(S)	RACE RESULTS
10	Ferrari 250 TR	0728 TR	Rodríguez P	2 OA
25	Ferrari 335 S	0674	Andrey G	5 OA

5 December — Governor's Trophy, Nassau

CN	MAKE & MODEL	CHASSIS No	NOMINATED DRIVER(S)	RACE RESULTS
10	Ferrari 250 TR	0728 TR	Rodríguez P	4 OA
25	Ferrari 335 S	0674	Andrey G	DNF
28	Ferrari 290 MM	0628	Arents G	DNS

6 December — Nassau Ferrari

CN	MAKE & MODEL	CHASSIS No	NOMINATED DRIVER(S)	RACE RESULTS
10	Ferrari 250 TR	0728 TR	Rodríguez P	2 OA

7 December — Nassau Trophy

CN	MAKE & MODEL	CHASSIS No	NOMINATED DRIVER(S)	RACE RESULTS
10	Ferrari 250 TR	0728 TR	Rodríguez P	2 OA
25	Ferrari 335 S	0674	Andrey G	DNF

Abbreviations

CN = Car Number
DNF = Did Not Finish
DNA = Did Not Attend
DNQ = Did Not Qualify
U2L = Under 2-litre
O2L = Over 2-litre
NK = Not Known
OA = Overall
WDN = Withdrawn

Statistical review

'59

CN	MAKE & MODEL	CHASSIS No	NOMINATED DRIVER(S)	RACE RESULTS
		1959		|//
21 March				**Sebring 12-hour**
19	Ferrari 500 TR	0600 MDTR	Casner L/Hunt J/Collins D	13 OA
10	Ferrari 250 TR	0666	Carveth R/Geitner G	DNF
19	Ferrari 250 TR	0722 TR	Casner L/Hunt J	DNS
82	Ferrari 250 TR	0724 TR	Fulp J	DNS
20–21 June				**Le Mans 24-hour**
18	Ferrari 250 GT LWB	1461 GT	Pilette A/Arents G	4 OA
16	Ferrari 250 GT California	1451 GT	Grossman R/Tavano F	5 OA
17	Ferrari 250 TR	0666	Carveth R/Geitner G	DNF
25 July				**Lime Rock**
9	Maserati 300 S	3083	Rodríguez P	Heat 1 5 OA
9	Maserati 300 S	3083	Rodríguez P	Heat 2 5 OA
9	Maserati 300 S	3083	Rodríguez P	Heat 3 3 OA
9	Maserati 300 S	3083	Rodríguez P	3 OA
4 December				**Nassau Governor's Trophy Prelim**
9	Ferrari Dino 196S	0776	Rodríguez R	4 OA U2L
10	Ferrari 250 TR	0766 TR	Rodríguez P	7 OA O2L
4 December				**Nassau Governor's Trophy**
9	Ferrari Dino 196S	0776	Rodríguez R	2 OA U2L
10	Ferrari 250 TR	0766 TR	Rodríguez P	3 OA O2L
5 December				**Nassau Ferrari Race**
10	Ferrari 250 TR	0766 TR	Rodríguez R	2 OA
6 December				**Nassau Trophy**
10	Ferrari 250 TR	0766 TR	Rodríguez P	13 OA
9	Ferrari Dino 196S	0776	Rodríguez R	DNS

'60 — 1960

CN	MAKE & MODEL	CHASSIS No	NOMINATED DRIVER(S)	RACE RESULTS
28 February				**Cuba GP**
10	Ferrari 250 TR	0766 TR	Rodríguez P	2
	Ferrari Dino 196S	0776	Rodríguez R	DNA
26 March				**Sebring 12-hour**
10	Ferrari 250 GT SWB	1785 GT	Hugus E/Pabst A	4 OA
12	Ferrari 250 GT SWB	1539 GT	Sturgis W/D'Orey F	6 OA
11	Ferrari 250 GT SWB	1773 GT	Arents G/Kimberly W	7 OA
65	OSCA S 750	768	Cunningham D/Fulp J	23 OA
7	Ferrari 250 TR59/60	0774 TR	Daigh C/Ginther R	DNF
28	Ferrari Dino 196S	0776	Rodríguez P/Rodríguez R	DNF
8 May				**Targa Florio**
172	Ferrari Dino 196S	0776	Rodríguez P/Rodríguez R	7 OA
15 May				**Cumberland**
61	OSCA F J	0003	McCluggage D	2 OA
55	Ferrari 250 GT SWB	1785 GT	Hugus E	8 OA
22 May				**Nürburgring 1000km**
27	Ferrari Dino 196S	0776	Rodríguez P/Rodríguez R	DNF
29 May				**Bridgehampton**
731	OSCA F J	0003	Kaback S	DNF
19 June				**Roosevelt Raceway**
110	OSCA F J	0003	Rodríguez R	2 OA Prelim
110	OSCA F J	0003	Rodríguez R	DNF
26 June				**Le Mans 24-hour**
17	Ferrari 250 TR	0766 TR	Rodríguez R/Pilette A	2 OA
18	Ferrari 250 GT SWB	1931 GT	Arents G/Connell A	5 OA
19	Ferrari 250 GT SWB	1759 GT	Hugus E/Pabst A	7 OA
20	Ferrari 250 GT SWB California	2015 GT	Sturgis W/Schlesser J	DNF
54	OSCA S 750	768	Bentley J/Gordon J	18 OA

Statistical review

CN	MAKE & MODEL	CHASSIS No	NOMINATED DRIVER(S)	RACE RESULTS
28 August				**Bridgehampton**
195	Ferrari 500 TRC	0702 MDTR	Fulp J	NK
95	OSCA S 750	768	Fulp J	NK
96	Ferrari 250 GT SWB	1931 GT	Arents G	NK
11 September				**Road America**
77	Ferrari 250 TR60	0770 TR	Pabst A/Wuesthoff W	2 OA
12	Ferrari 500 TRC	0702 MDTR	Cunningham D/Fulp J/Constantine G	15 OA
3 December				**Nassau Governor's Trophy**
57	Ferrari 250 TR59/60	0746	Rodríguez R	1 OA
28	Ferrari 250 TR60	0770 TR	Rodríguez P	DNF
4 December				**Nassau Pan-American FJ**
8	OSCA F J	0003	Rodríguez R	DNF
4 December				**Nassau Trophy**
57	Ferrari 250 TR59/60	0746	Rodríguez P/Rodríguez R	2 OA
70	OSCA S 750	768	Fleming T	DNF

Abbreviations

CN = Car Number
DNF = Did Not Finish
DNA = Did Not Attend
DNQ = Did Not Qualify
U2L = Under 2-litre
O2L = Over 2-litre
NK = Not Known
OA = Overall
WDN = Withdrawn

CN	MAKE & MODEL	CHASSIS No	NOMINATED DRIVER(S)	RACE RESULTS
		1961		
24 March				**Sebring**
41	OSCA F J	0012	Rodríguez R	12 OA
25 March				**Sebring 12-hour**
17	Ferrari 250 TR59/60	0746	Rodríguez P/Rodríguez R	3 OA
22	Ferrari Dino 246S	0784	Hall J/Constantine G	7 OA
18	Ferrari 250 GT SWB California	2015 GT	Pabst A/Andrey G/Newman A/Publicker R	12 OA
37	Ferrari Dino 246S *Using 2-litre engine*	0776	Helburn W/Fulp J/Hudson S	18 OA
26	Ferrari Dino 246S	0778	Hugus E/Connell A	DNF
11	Ferrari 250 GT SWB	2455 GT	Tavano F/Arents G/Serena F	DNF

CN	MAKE & MODEL	CHASSIS No	NOMINATED DRIVER(S)	RACE RESULTS
69	OSCA S 1000	1001	Cunningham D/Price R/Fleming T	DNF

14 May — Cumberland

CN	MAKE & MODEL	CHASSIS No	NOMINATED DRIVER(S)	RACE RESULTS
73	OSCA F J	0003	Kaback S	11 OA

28 May — Nürburgring 1000km

CN	MAKE & MODEL	CHASSIS No	NOMINATED DRIVER(S)	RACE RESULTS
5	Ferrari 250 TRI 61	0780 TR	Rodríguez P/Rodríguez P	2 OA

10–11 June — Le Mans 24-hour

CN	MAKE & MODEL	CHASSIS No	NOMINATED DRIVER(S)	RACE RESULTS
20	Ferrari 250 GT SWB	2731 GT	Grossman R/Pilette A	6 OA
17	Ferrari 250 TR 61	0792 TR	Rodríguez R/Rodríguez P	DNF
18	Ferrari 250 GT SWB	2735 GT	Moss S/Hill G	DNF
19	Ferrari 250 GT SWB	2725 GT	Arents G/Reed G	DNF
43	OSCA S 1000	1001	Cunningham D/Hugus E	DNF

15 August — Le Mans 24-hour

CN	MAKE & MODEL	CHASSIS No	NOMINATED DRIVER(S)	RACE RESULTS
44	Ferrari 250 GT SWB	2725 GT	Arents G/Hammill S	4 OA

30 September — Mosport

CN	MAKE & MODEL	CHASSIS No	NOMINATED DRIVER(S)	RACE RESULTS
1	Ferrari 250 TRI 61	0794 TR	Rodríguez P	2 OA
20	Ferrari 250 TR59/60	0746	Constantine G	4 OA
3	Ferrari Dino 246S	0778	Fulp J	6 OA
8	OSCA S 1000	1001	Hayes F	9 OA
2	Ferrari Dino 246S	0784	Rodríguez R	DNF
63	Ferrari 250 TR	0770 TR	Reed G	Disq
75	OSCA S 498		Heppenstall R	
211	Ferrari 250 GT SWB	2731 GT	Grossman R	1 OA

15 October — Riverside

CN	MAKE & MODEL	CHASSIS No	NOMINATED DRIVER(S)	RACE RESULTS
68	Ferrari 250 TRI 61	0794 TR	Rodríguez R	DNQ
68	Ferrari 250 TRI 61	0794 TR	Rodríguez R	DNF

22 October — Montlhéry

CN	MAKE & MODEL	CHASSIS No	NOMINATED DRIVER(S)	RACE RESULTS
5	Ferrari 250 GT SWB	3005 GT	Rodríguez P/Rodríguez R	1 OA

8 December — Nassau Governor's Trophy

CN	MAKE & MODEL	CHASSIS No	NOMINATED DRIVER(S)	RACE RESULTS
2	Ferrari 250 TRI 61	0794 TR	Rodríguez P	1 OA
99	Ferrari Dino 246S	0778	Fulp J	4 OA
18	Ferrari 250 GT SWB California	2015 GT	Newman A	DNF

Abbreviations

CN = Car Number
DNF = Did Not Finish
DNA = Did Not Attend
DNQ = Did Not Qualify
U2L = Under 2-litre
O2L = Over 2-litre
NK = Not Known
OA = Overall
WDN = Withdrawn

Statistical review

CN	MAKE & MODEL	CHASSIS No	NOMINATED DRIVER(S)	RACE RESULTS
10 December				**Nassau Trophy**
2	Ferrari 250 TRI 61	0794 TR	Rodríguez P	3 OA
49	Ferrari 250 TR59/60	0746	Constantine G	6 OA
99	Ferrari Dino 246S	0778	Fulp J	9 OA
18	Ferrari 250 GT SWB California	2015 GT	Arents G	26 OA
7	Ferrari Dino 246S	0784	Rodríguez R	DNF

CN	MAKE & MODEL	CHASSIS No	NOMINATED DRIVER(S)	RACE RESULTS
		1962		
11 February				**Daytona 3-hour**
1	Ferrari Dino 246 SP	0796	Hill P/Rodríguez R	2 OA
18	Ferrari 250 GT SWB Exp	2643 GT	Moss S	4 OA
9	Ferrari Dino 196S	0784	Fulp J/Hudson S	8 OA
22	Ferrari 250 GT SWB	2725 GT	Roberts F	12 OA
50	Ferrari 250 TRI 61	0794 TR	Rodríguez R/Ryan P	15 OA
77	Ferrari 250 GT SWB	3005 GT	Thiem D/Grossman R	18 OA
24 March				**Sebring 12-hour**
24	Ferrari 250 GTO	3387 GT	Hill P/Gendebien O	2 OA
25	Ferrari 250 GT SWB	2725 GT	Hammill S/Serena F	4 OA
36	Ferrari Dino 248 SP	0806	Fulp J/Ryan P	13 OA
27	Ferrari 250 GT SWB	3327 GT	Hayes C/Haas C/Dietrich C	34 OA
34	Ferrari Dino 246 SP	0790	Rodríguez P/Rodríguez R	DNF
35	Ferrari Dino 246S	0784	Rodríguez P/Grossman R/Connell A	DNF
77	OSCA S 1000		McCluggage D/Eager A	DNF
58	OSCA 1600 GT	007	Publicker R/Litchie S	DNF
26	Ferrari 250 TRI 61	0794 TR	Ireland I/Moss S/Fulp J/Tavano F	Disq
3 June				**Bridgehampton**
23	OSCA FJ	0003	McCluggage D	6 OA
23-4 June				**Le Mans 24-hour**
17	Ferrari 250 GTO	3387 GT	Grossman R/Roberts F	6 OA
18	Ferrari 250 TRI 61	0794 TR	Fulp J/Ryan P	DNF

A concise history of the North American Racing Team 1957 to 1983

Abbreviations

CN = Car Number
DNF = Did Not Finish
DNA = Did Not Attend
DNQ = Did Not Qualify
DSQ = Disqualified
U2L = Under 2-litre
O2L = Over 2-litre
NK = Not Known
OA = Overall
WDN = Withdrawn

CN	MAKE & MODEL	CHASSIS No	NOMINATED DRIVER(S)	RACE RESULTS
57	Ferrari 250 TRI		Grossman R/Roberts F	DNA
37	OSCA 1600 GT	007	Arents G/Behra J/Hammill S	DNF

16 September — Bridgehampton Double 400

CN	MAKE & MODEL	CHASSIS No	NOMINATED DRIVER(S)	RACE RESULTS
8	Ferrari 330 TRI LM	0808	Rodríguez P	1 OA
57	Ferrari 250 GTO	3323 GT	Hugus E/Hayes C	3 OA
23	OSCA S 1000		McCluggage D/Eager A	DNF
3	Ferrari		Hayes C	DNA
6	Ferrari Dino 196 SP		Fulp J	DNA
69	OSCA 1600 GT	007	Arents G/Publicker R	DNA

23 September — Mosport

CN	MAKE & MODEL	CHASSIS No	NOMINATED DRIVER(S)	RACE RESULTS
44	Ferrari 330 TRI LM	0808	Rodríguez P/Rodríguez R	2 OA
41	Ferrari Dino		Rodríguez R	DNA
47	Ferrari Dino		Fulp J	DNA

21 October — Montlhéry

CN	MAKE & MODEL	CHASSIS No	NOMINATED DRIVER(S)	RACE RESULTS
1	Ferrari 250 GTO	3987 GT	Rodríguez P/Rodríguez R	1 OA

11 November — Puerto Rica

CN	MAKE & MODEL	CHASSIS No	NOMINATED DRIVER(S)	RACE RESULTS
	Ferrari Dino 268 SP	0798	Hill P	WDN
	Ferrari 330 TRI LM	0808	Rodríguez P	WDN

2 December — Nassau Tourist Trophy Prelim

CN	MAKE & MODEL	CHASSIS No	NOMINATED DRIVER(S)	RACE RESULTS
21	Ferrari 250 GTO	3223 GT	Bandini L	3 OA O2L
70	OSCA 1600 GT	007	Fleming T	5 OA U2L

2 December — Nassau Tourist Trophy

CN	MAKE & MODEL	CHASSIS No	NOMINATED DRIVER(S)	RACE RESULTS
21	Ferrari 250 GTO	3223 GT	Bandini L	2 OA
70	OSCA 1600 GT	007	Heppenstall R	DNF

7 December — Nassau Governor's Trophy Prelim

CN	MAKE & MODEL	CHASSIS No	NOMINATED DRIVER(S)	RACE RESULTS
64	Ferrari Dino 196 SP	0804	Fulp J	1 OA U2L
7	Ferrari 330 TRI LM	0808	Gregory M	2 OA O2L
21	Ferrari 250 GTO	3223 GT	Hayes C	5 OA O2L
70	OSCA 1600 GT	007	Fleming T	14 OA

7 December — Nassau Governor's Trophy

CN	MAKE & MODEL	CHASSIS No	NOMINATED DRIVER(S)	RACE RESULTS
21	Ferrari 250 GTO	3223 GT	Hayes C	3 OA
64	Ferrari Dino 196 SP	0804	Fulp J	4 OA

Statistical review

CN	MAKE & MODEL	CHASSIS No	NOMINATED DRIVER(S)	RACE RESULTS
70	OSCA 1600 GT	007	Fleming T	19 OA
7	Ferrari 330 TRI LM	0808	Gregory M	DNF

9 December — Nassau Trophy

CN	MAKE & MODEL	CHASSIS No	NOMINATED DRIVER(S)	RACE RESULTS
7	Ferrari 330 TRI LM	0808	Gregory M	4 OA
21	Ferrari 250 GTO	3223 GT	Hayes C	5 OA
3	Ferrari Dino 268 SP	0798	Bandini L	8 OA
64	Ferrari Dino 196 SP	0804	Fulp J	34 OA
70	OSCA 1600 GT	007	Fleming T	DNF

CN	MAKE & MODEL	CHASSIS No	NOMINATED DRIVER(S)	RACE RESULTS

1963

16 February — Daytona Challenge

CN	MAKE & MODEL	CHASSIS No	NOMINATED DRIVER(S)	RACE RESULTS
22	Ferrari 250 GTO	3223 GT	Roberts F	4 OA

17 February — Daytona 3–hour

CN	MAKE & MODEL	CHASSIS No	NOMINATED DRIVER(S)	RACE RESULTS
18	Ferrari 250 GTO	4219 GT	Rodríguez P	1 OA
22	Ferrari 250 GTO	3223 GT	Roberts F/Cannon J	15 OA
28	Ferrari 250 GTO		Ward R	DNA

24 March — Sebring 12-hour

CN	MAKE & MODEL	CHASSIS No	NOMINATED DRIVER(S)	RACE RESULTS
18	Ferrari 330 TRI LM	0808	Hill G/Rodríguez P	3 OA
28	Ferrari 250 GTO	4219 GT	Bonnier J/Cannon J	13 OA
32	Ferrari 250 GTO	3223 GT	Grossman R/Mayer T/Thiem D/Hayes C	18 OA
27	Ferrari Dino 268 SP	0798	Fulp J/Heuer H	34 OA
55	Sunbeam Harrington Alpine	B9106097	Theodoli F/Kneeland W	36 OA
57	OSCA 1600 GT	007	Fleming T/Baumann H/Heppenstall R	40 OA

15–16 June — Le Mans 24-hour

CN	MAKE & MODEL	CHASSIS No	NOMINATED DRIVER(S)	RACE RESULTS
26	Ferrari 250 GTO	4713 GT	Gregory M/Piper D	6 OA
11	Ferrari 330 LMB	4453 GT	Gurney D/Hall J/Rodríguez P	DNF
10	Ferrari 330 TRI LM	0808	Rodríguez P/Penske R	DNF
25	Ferrari 250 GTO		Rodríguez P	DNA

24 August — Goodwood Tourist Trophy

CN	MAKE & MODEL	CHASSIS No	NOMINATED DRIVER(S)	RACE RESULTS
15	Ferrari 250 GTO	4713 GT	Penske R	8 OA

A concise history of the North American Racing Team 1957 to 1983

CN	MAKE & MODEL	CHASSIS No	NOMINATED DRIVER(S)	RACE RESULTS
14–22 September				**Tour de France**
170	Ferrari 250 GTO	4713 GT	Schlesser J/Le Guezec C	DSQ
14–15 September				**Bridgehampton Double 500**
1	Ferrari 250 P	0810	Rodríguez P	2 OA
47	Ferrari 330 LMB	4453 GT	Gurney D	3 OA
28 September				**Mosport**
5	Ferrari 250 P	0810	Rodríguez P	1 OA
6	Ferrari Dino 268 SP	0798	Bandini L	DNF
27 October				**Virginia International Raceway**
26	Ferrari 250 P	0810	Fulp J	No result
			A driver was killed during the race, race declared void.	
6 December				**Nassau Governor's Trophy**
10	Ferrari 250 P	0810	Rodríguez P	2 OA
14	Ferrari Dino 268 SP	0798	Fulp J	5 OA
8 December				**Nassau Trophy**
10	Ferrari 250 P	0810	Rodríguez P	2 OA
14	Ferrari Dino 268 SP	0798	Fulp J	11 OA

CN	MAKE & MODEL	CHASSIS No	NOMINATED DRIVER(S)	RACE RESULTS
		1964		
15 February				**Daytona Challenge Cup**
33	Ferrari 250 LM	5149	Rodríguez P	DNF
16 February				**Daytona 2000km**
30	Ferrari 250 GTO	5571 GT	Rodríguez P/Hill P	1 OA
31	Ferrari 250 GTO	4713 GT	Grossman R/Hansgen W	3 OA
1 March				**Augusta**
26	Ferrari 250 LM	5149	Fulp J	8 OA
21 March				**Sebring 12-hour**
30	Ferrari 250 GTO	5571 GT	Rodríguez P/Piper D/Gammino M	7 OA
29	Ferrari 250 GTO	4713 GT	Thompson R/Grossman R	15 OA

Statistical review

CN	MAKE & MODEL	CHASSIS No	NOMINATED DRIVER(S)	RACE RESULTS
28	Ferrari 250 LM	5149	Kolb C/O'Brien T	DNF
25	Ferrari 330 P	0810	Rodríguez P/Fulp J	DNF
26	Ferrari 330 P	0814	Foyt AJ/Comite L	DNS

20–21 June — Le Mans 24-hour

CN	MAKE & MODEL	CHASSIS No	NOMINATED DRIVER(S)	RACE RESULTS
27	Ferrari 250 GTO	5573 GT	Grossman R/Tavano F	9 OA
26	Ferrari 250 GTO	5571 GT	Hugus E/Rosinski J	DNF
15	Ferrari 330 P	0810	Rodríguez P/Hudson S	DNF
58	Ferrari 250 LM	5909	Piper D/Rindt J	DNF
24	Ferrari 250 LM			DNA

5 July — Reims 12-hour

CN	MAKE & MODEL	CHASSIS No	NOMINATED DRIVER(S)	RACE RESULTS
8	Ferrari 250 LM	5909	Surtees J/Bandini L	2 OA
26	Ferrari 250 GTO	5571 GT	Rodríguez P/Vaccarella N	11 OA
27	Ferrari 250 GTO	5573 GT	Grossman R/Hudson S	DNF

29 August — Goodwood Tourist Trophy

CN	MAKE & MODEL	CHASSIS No	NOMINATED DRIVER(S)	RACE RESULTS
26	Ferrari 250 GTO	5573 GT	Surtees J	DNF

13 September — Mt Tremblant

CN	MAKE & MODEL	CHASSIS No	NOMINATED DRIVER(S)	RACE RESULTS
1	Ferrari 275 P	0812	Rodríguez P	1 OA

20 September — Bridgehampton Double 500

CN	MAKE & MODEL	CHASSIS No	NOMINATED DRIVER(S)	RACE RESULTS
81	Ferrari 275 P	0812	Rodríguez P	2 OA
82	Ferrari 330 P	0820	Fulp J	5 OA
80	Ferrari 330 P	0824	Scarfiotti L	DNF

26 September — Mosport

CN	MAKE & MODEL	CHASSIS No	NOMINATED DRIVER(S)	RACE RESULTS
4	Ferrari 330 P	0820	Rodríguez P	1 OA
3	Ferrari 330 P	0824	Scarfiotti L	2 OA
2	Ferrari 275 P	0812	Hansgen W	4 OA

4 October — Watkins Glen USA GP

CN	MAKE & MODEL	CHASSIS No	NOMINATED DRIVER(S)	RACE RESULTS
7	Ferrari 158	0005	Surtees J	2
8	Ferrari 1512	0007	Bandini L	DNF
7T	Ferrari 158	0006		DNS
8T	Ferrari Dino 156	0003		DNS

11 October — Montlhéry 1000km

CN	MAKE & MODEL	CHASSIS No	NOMINATED DRIVER(S)	RACE RESULTS
1	Ferrari 250 GTO	5573 GT	Rodríguez P/Schlesser J	2 OA

Abbreviations

CN = Car Number
DNF = Did Not Finish
DNA = Did Not Attend
DNQ = Did Not Qualify
DSQ = Disqualified
U2L = Under 2-litre
O2L = Over 2-litre
NK = Not Known
OA = Overall
WDN = Withdrawn

CN	MAKE & MODEL	CHASSIS No	NOMINATED DRIVER(S)	RACE RESULTS
25 October				**Mexico GP**
7	Ferrari 158	0006	Surtees J	2 OA
8	Ferrari 1512	0007	Bandini L	3 OA
18	Ferrari Dino 156	0003	Rodríguez P	6 OA
7T	Ferrari 158	0005		DNS
29 November				**Nassau GT**
11	Ferrari 250 GTO	5571 GT	Rodríguez P	7 OA
29 November				**Nassau Tourist Trophy**
11	Ferrari 250 GTO	5571 GT	Rodríguez P	6 OA
4 December				**Nassau Governor's Trophy**
10	Ferrari 330 P	0820	Rodríguez P	4 OA
6 December				**Nassau Trophy**
10	Ferrari 330 P	0820	Rodríguez P	3 OA
11	Ferrari 250 GTO	5571 GT	Hill P	11 OA
20	Ferrari		Surtees J	DNA

CN	MAKE & MODEL	CHASSIS No	NOMINATED DRIVER(S)	RACE RESULTS
		1965		
28 February				**Daytona 2000km**
77	Ferrari 330 P2	0838	Rodríguez P/Surtees J	DNF
88	Ferrari 330 P	0820	Hansgen W/Piper D	DNF
99	Ferrari 275 P	0814	Hansgen W/Fulp J/Hugus E/Rodríguez P/Grossman R	DNF
22 March				**Sebring 12-hour**
26	Ferrari 330 P	0810	Grossman R/Hudson S	DNF
32	Ferrari 275 P	0814	Hugus E/O'Brien T/Hayes C	12 OA
27	Ferrari 330 P	0822	Fulp J/Kolb C	DNF
21–22 June				**Le Mans 24-hour**
21	Ferrari 250 LM	5893	Rindt J/Gregory M/Hugus E	1 OA
18	Ferrari 365 P2	0838	Rodríguez P/Vaccarella N	7 OA
57	Ferrari 275 GTB/C			DNA

Statistical review

CN	MAKE & MODEL	CHASSIS No	NOMINATED DRIVER(S)	RACE RESULTS
3–4 July				**Reims 12-hour**
3	Ferrari 365 P2	0838	Rodríguez P/Guichet J	1 OA
	Ferrari 250 LM		Vaccarella N	DNS
23 August				**Zeltweg**
10	Ferrari 250 LM	5893	Rindt J	1 OA
19 September				**Bridgehampton Double 500**
20	Ferrari 365 P2	0838	Rodríguez P	2 OA
19	Ferrari 275 GTB/C	6885 GT	Arents G/Hutchins R	11 OA
18	Ferrari 275 P2	0814	Andretti M	DNF
25 September				**Mosport**
10	Ferrari 365 P2	0838	Rodríguez P	3 OA
3 October				**Watkins Glen USA GP**
14	Ferrari 1512	0007	Rodríguez P	5 OA
24	Ferrari 158	0006	Bondurant R	9 OA
24 October				**Mexico GP**
14	Ferrari 1512	0008	Rodríguez P	7 OA
2 December				**Nassau Tourist Trophy Prelim**
7	Ferrari 275 GTB/C	6885 GT	Kolb C	1 OA
2 December				**Nassau Tourist Trophy**
7	Ferrari 275 GTB/C	6885 GT	Kolb C	1 OA
3 December				**Nassau Governor's Trophy**
7	Ferrari 275 GTB/C	6885 GT	Durham A	11 OA
5 December				**Nassau Trophy**
	Ferrari 275 GTB/C	6885 GT	Durham A	DNF

Abbreviations

CN = Car Number
DNF = Did Not Finish
DNA = Did Not Attend
DNQ = Did Not Qualify
DSQ = Disqualified
U2L = Under 2-litre
O2L = Over 2-litre
NK = Not Known
OA = Overall
WDN = Withdrawn

CN	MAKE & MODEL	CHASSIS No	NOMINATED DRIVER(S)	RACE RESULTS
		1966		
5–6 February				**Daytona 24-hour**
21	Ferrari 365 P2/3	0838	Rodríguez P/Andretti M	4 OA
22	Ferrari 250 LM	5893	Rindt J/Bondurant R	9 OA

1957-1983

Abbreviations

CN = Car Number
DNF = Did Not Finish
DNA = Did Not Attend
DNQ = Did Not Qualify
DSQ = Disqualified
U2L = Under 2-litre
O2L = Over 2-litre
NK = Not Known
OA = Overall
WDN = Withdrawn

CN	MAKE & MODEL	CHASSIS No	NOMINATED DRIVER(S)	RACE RESULTS
32	Ferrari 250 LM	5901	Hawkins P/Follmer G/Wester D	DNF

26 March — **Sebring 12-hour**

26	Ferrari 365 P2/3	0838	Rodríguez P/Andretti M	DNF

17 April — **Vineland**

	Ferrari Dino 268 SP	0798	Hutchins R	5 OA

25 April — **Monza 1000km**

36	Ferrari Dino 206S	014	Bondurant R/Vaccarella N	DNS

1 May — **Virginia International Raceway**

11	Ferrari Dino 268 SP	0798	Hutchins R	Kn

15 May — **Cumberland**

	Ferrari Dino 268 SP	0798	Hutchins R	8 OA

21–22 May — **Watkins Glen**

	Ferrari 275 P	0814	Chinetti Jr L	1 OA (Sat)
	Ferrari 275 P	0814	Chinetti Jr L	2 OA (Sun)

4 June — **Vineland**

	Ferrari 275 GTB	9057 GT	Hutchins R	NK

5 June — **Nürburgring 1000km**

12	Ferrari Dino 206S	008	Rodríguez P/Ginther R	3 OA

12 June — **St Jovite**

3	Ferrari 275 P	0814	Chinetti Jr L/Kolb C	DNF

18–19 June — **Le Mans 24-hour**

26	Ferrari 275 GTB/C	9015 GT	Biscaldi G/de Bourbon-Parme M	DNF
18	Ferrari 365 P2	0838	Gregory M/Bondurant R	DNF
38	Ferrari Dino 206S	008	Kolb C/Follmer G	DNF
25	Ferrari Dino 206S	014	Vaccarella N/Casoni M	DNF
27	Ferrari 330 P3	0846	Rodríguez P/Ginther R	DNF
54	ASA RB613	21000	Pasqueier F/Mieusset J	DNF

18 September — **Bridgehampton**

3	Ferrari Dino 206S	014	Rodríguez P	C-A DNF
71	Ferrari 275 GTB	9057 GT	Hutchins R	Prod DNF

CN	MAKE & MODEL	CHASSIS No	NOMINATED DRIVER(S)	RACE RESULTS
16 October				**Laguna Seca**
21	Ferrari Dino 206S	014	Rodríguez P	Heat 1 14 OA
21	Ferrari Dino 206S	014	Rodríguez P	Heat 2 25 OA
21	Ferrari Dino 206S	014	Rodríguez P	Con 9 OA
30 October				**Riverside**
24	Ferrari Dino 206S	014	Rodríguez P	DNQ

CN	MAKE & MODEL	CHASSIS No	NOMINATED DRIVER(S)	RACE RESULTS
1967				
4–5 February				**Daytona 24-hour**
26	Ferrari 412 P	0844	Rodríguez P/Guichet J	3 OA
96	ASA RB613	21004	Dietrich S/Mae Mims D	24 OA
28	Ferrari Dino 206S	008	Gregory M/Schlesser J/Gregg P	DNF
27	Ferrari 330 P3		Gregg P/Schlesser J	DNA
1 April				**Sebring 12-hour**
25	Ferrari 275 GTB4 NART Spyder	9437 GT	McCluggage D/Rollo P	17 OA
63	ASA RB613	21004	Dietrich S/Mae Mims D	25 OA
32	Ferrari Dino 206S	014	Rodríguez P/Guichet J	DNF
35	Ferrari Dino 206S	008	Kolb C/Crawford E	DNF
26	Ferrari 330 P3	0844	Rodríguez P	DNS
24 April				**Monza 1000km**
9	Ferrari 412 P	0844	Rodríguez P/Guichet J	DNF
14 May				**Targa Florio**
186	Ferrari Dino 206S	018	Latteri F/Capuano I	DNF
10–11 June				**Le Mans 24-hour**
25	Ferrari 412 P	0844	Rodríguez P/Baghetti G	DNF
26	Ferrari 365 P2	0838	Rodríguez R/Parsons C	DNF
55	Alpine-Renault M64	1710	Thérier J-L/Chevalier F	DNF
32	Ferrari Dino 206S		Kolb C	DNA
27	Ferrari 275 GTB			DNA
50	ASA RB613			DNA

14 | 1957–1983

CN	MAKE & MODEL	CHASSIS No	NOMINATED DRIVER(S)	RACE RESULTS
	Ferrari 365 P2/3		Grossman R/de MortMarcht J	DNS

25 June — Reims 12-hour

CN	MAKE & MODEL	CHASSIS No	NOMINATED DRIVER(S)	RACE RESULTS
28	Ferrari Dino 206S	018	Rodríguez P/Guichet J	DNF

17 September — Bridgehampton

CN	MAKE & MODEL	CHASSIS No	NOMINATED DRIVER(S)	RACE RESULTS
32	Ferrari 412 P	0844	Scarfiotti L	7 OA

24 September — Mosport

CN	MAKE & MODEL	CHASSIS No	NOMINATED DRIVER(S)	RACE RESULTS
32	Ferrari 412 P	0844	Scarfiotti L	DNF

1968

3–4 February — Daytona 24-hour

CN	MAKE & MODEL	CHASSIS No	NOMINATED DRIVER(S)	RACE RESULTS
80	Ferrari Dino 206S	002	Rodríguez P/Kolb C	DNF
81	Ferrari 250 LM	5893	Gregory M/Piper D	DNF
82	Ferrari 275 GTB	9057 GT		DNA

23 March — Sebring 12-hour

CN	MAKE & MODEL	CHASSIS No	NOMINATED DRIVER(S)	RACE RESULTS
	Ferrari Dino 206S			DNA

14 July — Watkins Glen 6-hour

CN	MAKE & MODEL	CHASSIS No	NOMINATED DRIVER(S)	RACE RESULTS
21	Ferrari Dino 206S	014	Rodríguez P/Kolb C	7 OA
22	Ferrari 275 GTB4	10311 GT	Grossman R/Bucknam R	9 OA

1 September — Elkhart Lake

CN	MAKE & MODEL	CHASSIS No	NOMINATED DRIVER(S)	RACE RESULTS
22	Ferrari 330 P4	0860	Rodríguez P	13 OA

15 September — Bridgehampton

CN	MAKE & MODEL	CHASSIS No	NOMINATED DRIVER(S)	RACE RESULTS
22	Ferrari 330 P4	0860	Rodríguez P	DNF

28–9 September — Le Mans 24-hour

CN	MAKE & MODEL	CHASSIS No	NOMINATED DRIVER(S)	RACE RESULTS
14	Ferrari 250 LM	5893	Gregory M/Kolb C	DNF
36	Ferrari Dino 206S	014	Chevalier F/Lagier B	DNF
15	Ferrari 275 GTB4		Grossman R	DNQ
16	Ferrari 330 P4			DNA
19	Ferrari 330 P4			DNA

Abbreviations

CN = Car Number
DNF = Did Not Finish
DNA = Did Not Attend
DNQ = Did Not Qualify
DSQ = Disqualified
U2L = Under 2-litre
O2L = Over 2-litre
NK = Not Known
OA = Overall
WDN = Withdrawn

Statistical review

1969

CN	MAKE & MODEL	CHASSIS No	NOMINATED DRIVER(S)	RACE RESULTS

1 February — Daytona 24-hour

CN	MAKE & MODEL	CHASSIS No	NOMINATED DRIVER(S)	RACE RESULTS
41	Ferrari 275 GTB4	10311 GT	Posey S/Rodríguez R	23 OA
40	Ferrari Dino 206S	014	Kolb C/Biscaldi G	DNF

21 March — Sebring 12-hour

CN	MAKE & MODEL	CHASSIS No	NOMINATED DRIVER(S)	RACE RESULTS
37	Ferrari Dino 206S	014	Kolb C/Rodríguez R	9
38	Ferrari Dino 206 GT		Dini R/Posey S	36 OA
26	Ferrari 330 P	0816	Parsons C/Rodríguez R	DNF

15–16 June — Le Mans 24-hour

CN	MAKE & MODEL	CHASSIS No	NOMINATED DRIVER(S)	RACE RESULTS
17	Ferrari 250 LM	5893	Zeccoli T/Posey S	8 OA
16	Ferrari 365 GTB4	12547	Rodríguez R	DNS
61	Ferrari Dino 206S	014	Migault F/Mieusset J(Grossman R)	DNS
100	Ferrari 275 GTB/2			DNA

14 September — Bridgehampton

CN	MAKE & MODEL	CHASSIS No	NOMINATED DRIVER(S)	RACE RESULTS
12	Ferrari 312P	0870	Rodríguez P	5 OA

20 September — Mosport Canada GP

CN	MAKE & MODEL	CHASSIS No	NOMINATED DRIVER(S)	RACE RESULTS
12	Ferrari 312 F1	0017	Rodríguez P	DNF

5 October — Watkins Glen USA GP

CN	MAKE & MODEL	CHASSIS No	NOMINATED DRIVER(S)	RACE RESULTS
12	Ferrari 312 F1	0017	Rodríguez P	5 OA

19 October — Mexico City Mexico GP

CN	MAKE & MODEL	CHASSIS No	NOMINATED DRIVER(S)	RACE RESULTS
12	Ferrari 312 F1	0017	Rodríguez P	7 OA

1970

CN	MAKE & MODEL	CHASSIS No	NOMINATED DRIVER(S)	RACE RESULTS

31 January — Daytona 24-hour

CN	MAKE & MODEL	CHASSIS No	NOMINATED DRIVER(S)	RACE RESULTS
24	Ferrari 312P	0872	Parkes M/Posey S	4 OA
23	Ferrari 312P	0870	Piper D/Adamowicz T	5 OA
21	Ferrari 250 LM	5893	Young G/Chinetti Jr L	7 OA
22	Ferrari 365 GTB4	12547	Gregory M/Pickett W	DNF

CN	MAKE & MODEL	CHASSIS No	NOMINATED DRIVER(S)	RACE RESULTS
25	Ferrari 512S	1014	Gurney D/Parsons C	DNF
20	Ferrari 275 GTB/C	9063 GT	Cluxton H/Tatum G	DNF
31	Ferrari Dino 246 GT			DNA

21 March — Sebring 12-hour

CN	MAKE & MODEL	CHASSIS No	NOMINATED DRIVER(S)	RACE RESULTS
22	Ferrari 312P	0872	Parkes M/Parsons C	6 OA
23	Ferrari 312P	0870	Adamowicz T/Chinetti Jr L	DNF
24	Ferrari 512S	1006	Bucknum R/Posey S	DNF

13–14 June — Le Mans 24-hour

CN	MAKE & MODEL	CHASSIS No	NOMINATED DRIVER(S)	RACE RESULTS
11	Ferrari 512S	1014	Posey S/Bucknum R	4 OA
57	Ferrari 312P	0872	Parsons C/Adamowicz T	10 OA
10	Ferrari 512S	1018	Kelleners H/Loos G	DNF
32	Ferrari 365 GTB4		Mieusset R	Nac
39	Ferrari 312P	0870	Posey S/Migault F	DNS

23 August — Mid Ohio

CN	MAKE & MODEL	CHASSIS No	NOMINATED DRIVER(S)	RACE RESULTS
20	Ferrari 512S	1006	Rodríguez P	11 OA

30 August — Elkhart Lake

CN	MAKE & MODEL	CHASSIS No	NOMINATED DRIVER(S)	RACE RESULTS
20	Ferrari 512S	1006	Rodríguez P	7 OA

CN	MAKE & MODEL	CHASSIS No	NOMINATED DRIVER(S)	RACE RESULTS
		1971		

10 January — Buenos Aires 1000km

CN	MAKE & MODEL	CHASSIS No	NOMINATED DRIVER(S)	RACE RESULTS
22	Ferrari 512S	1006	Posey S/di Palma L/García-Veiga N	8 OA

24 January — Buenos Aires GP

CN	MAKE & MODEL	CHASSIS No	NOMINATED DRIVER(S)	RACE RESULTS
30	Surtees TS5A	006 TS	García-Veiga N	Heat 1 DNF
28	McLaren M10B		Marchincovich C/Young G	Heat 1 DNF / Heat 2 6

30–31 January — Daytona 24-hour

CN	MAKE & MODEL	CHASSIS No	NOMINATED DRIVER(S)	RACE RESULTS
23	Ferrari 512S	1006	Bucknum R/Adamowicz T	2 OA
21	Ferrari 312P	0872	Chinetti Jr L/García-Veiga N	5 OA
20	Ferrari 512S	1014	Young G/Gregory M	DNF
22	Ferrari 512S	1020	Posey S/Revson P	DNF

Statistical review

CN	MAKE & MODEL	CHASSIS No	NOMINATED DRIVER(S)	RACE RESULTS
24	Ferrari 365 GTB4		De Cadenet A/Weir D	DNA
25	Ferrari Dino 246 GT		Cluxton H/Tatum G	DNA

2 March — **Sebring 12-hour**

CN	MAKE & MODEL	CHASSIS No	NOMINATED DRIVER(S)	RACE RESULTS
21	Ferrari 312P	0872	Chinetti Jr L/Eaton G	8 OA
24	Ferrari 365 GTB4	14107	Cluxton H/Grossman R	12 OA
22	Ferrari 512M	1020	Revson P/Savage R	DNF
23	Ferrari 512S	1006	Bucknum R/Posey S	DNF
26	Ferrari 512S	1028	Parsons C/Weir D	DNF

12–13 June — **Le Mans 24-hour**

CN	MAKE & MODEL	CHASSIS No	NOMINATED DRIVER(S)	RACE RESULTS
12	Ferrari 512M	1020	Posey S/Adamowicz T	3 OA
58	Ferrari 365 GTB4	12467	Grossman R/Chinetti Jr L	5 OA
11	Ferrari 512M	1040	Donohue M/Hobbs D	DNF
14	Ferrari 512S	1006	Gregory M/Eaton G	DNF

24 July — **Watkins Glen 6-hour**

CN	MAKE & MODEL	CHASSIS No	NOMINATED DRIVER(S)	RACE RESULTS
14	Ferrari 512M	1020	Posey S/Bucknum R	DNF

25 July — **Watkins Glen Can-Am**

CN	MAKE & MODEL	CHASSIS No	NOMINATED DRIVER(S)	RACE RESULTS
14	Ferrari 512M	1020	Posey S	6 OA

Abbreviations

CN = Car Number
DNF = Did Not Finish
DNA = Did Not Attend
DNQ = Did Not Qualify
DSQ = Disqualified
U2L = Under 2-litre
O2L = Over 2-litre
NK = Not Known
OA = Overall
WDN = Withdrawn

1972

CN	MAKE & MODEL	CHASSIS No	NOMINATED DRIVER(S)	RACE RESULTS

6–7 February — **Daytona 6-hour**

CN	MAKE & MODEL	CHASSIS No	NOMINATED DRIVER(S)	RACE RESULTS
21	Chinetti Special	-	Chinetti Jr L/Eaton G	DNF
22	Ferrari 365 GTB4/C	12467	Posey S/Bucknum R	DNF
23	Ferrari 365 GTB4/C	14889	Bucknum R	DNQ

25 March — **Sebring 12-hour**

CN	MAKE & MODEL	CHASSIS No	NOMINATED DRIVER(S)	RACE RESULTS
22	Ferrari 365 GTB4/C	14885	Chinetti Jr L/Grossman R	8 OA
21	Ferrari 365 GTB4/C	14889	Posey S/Adamowicz T	13 OA

10–11 June — **Le Mans 24-hour**

CN	MAKE & MODEL	CHASSIS No	NOMINATED DRIVER(S)	RACE RESULTS
74	Ferrari 365 GTB4/C	15685	Posey S/Adamowicz T	6 OA
38	Ferrari 365 GTB4	13855	Jarier J-P/Buchet C	9 OA
4	Chevrolet Corvette		Heinz D/Johnson R	15 OA

Abbreviations

CN = Car Number
DNF = Did Not Finish
DNA = Did Not Attend
DNQ = Did Not Qualify
DSQ = Disqualified
U2L = Under 2-litre
O2L = Over 2-litre
NK = Not Known
OA = Overall
WDN = Withdrawn

CN	MAKE & MODEL	CHASSIS No	NOMINATED DRIVER(S)	RACE RESULTS
46	Ferrari Dino 246 GT	2678	Laffeach J-P/Doncieux G	17 OA
57	Ferrari 365 GTB4	14141	Gregory M/Chinetti Jr L	DNF

22 July — Watkins Glen 6-hour

CN	MAKE & MODEL	CHASSIS No	NOMINATED DRIVER(S)	RACE RESULTS
22	Ferrari 365 GTB4/C	15685	Jarier J-P/Young G	6 OA
21	Ferrari 365 GTB4/C	14889	Posey S/Hobbs D	DNF
24	Ferrari Dino 246 GT	2678	Cluxton H/Moran R	DNQ

23 July — Watkins Glen Can-Am

CN	MAKE & MODEL	CHASSIS No	NOMINATED DRIVER(S)	RACE RESULTS
40	Ferrari 712 P	1010	Jarier J-P	10 OA

27 August — Elkhart Lake

CN	MAKE & MODEL	CHASSIS No	NOMINATED DRIVER(S)	RACE RESULTS
40	Ferrari 712 P	1010	Jarier J-P	4 OA

15 September — Paris 1000km

CN	MAKE & MODEL	CHASSIS No	NOMINATED DRIVER(S)	RACE RESULTS
24	Ferrari 365 GTB4/C	14889	Jarier J-P/Laffite J	9 OA

1973

3–4 February — Daytona 24-hour

CN	MAKE & MODEL	CHASSIS No	NOMINATED DRIVER(S)	RACE RESULTS
22	Ferrari 365 GTB4	14141	Migault F/Minter W	2 OA
21	Ferrari 365 GTB4/C	14889	Chinetti Jr L/Grossman R/Shaw W Jr	5 OA
20	Ferrari 365 GTB4/C	15685	Merzario A/Jarier J-P	DNF
23	Ferrari 365 GTB4/C	16343	Ballot-Lena C/Andruet J-C	DNF

24 March — Sebring 12-hour

CN	MAKE & MODEL	CHASSIS No	NOMINATED DRIVER(S)	RACE RESULTS
21	Ferrari 365 GTB4	14115	Posey S/Cluxton H	DNS

1 April — Le Mans 4–hour

CN	MAKE & MODEL	CHASSIS No	NOMINATED DRIVER(S)	RACE RESULTS
33	Ferrari 365 GTB4/C	14889	Migault F/Guitteny L/Bodin J-P	5 OA
30	Ferrari 365 GTB4	14141	Migault F/Jarier J-P	DNS

9–10 June — Le Mans 24-hour

CN	MAKE & MODEL	CHASSIS No	NOMINATED DRIVER(S)	RACE RESULTS
38	Ferrari 365 GTB4	14141	Chinetti Jr L/Migault F	13 OA
6	Ferrari 365 GTB4/C	16407	Posey S/Minter W	DNF
36	Ferrari 365 GTB4/C	14889	Grossman R/Guitteny L	DNF
37	Ferrari 365 GTB4/C	16367	di Palma L/García-Veiga N	DNF

Statistical review

CN	MAKE & MODEL	CHASSIS No	NOMINATED DRIVER(S)	RACE RESULTS
21 July				**Watkins Glen 6-hour**
8	Ferrari 365 GTB4/C	16407	Posey S/Migault F	14 OA

CN	MAKE & MODEL	CHASSIS No	NOMINATED DRIVER(S)	RACE RESULTS
		1974		
15–16 June				**Le Mans 24-hour**
54	Ferrari 365 GTB4	14141	Heinz D/Cudini A	6 OA
1	Chinetti Special	-	Zeccoli T/Andruet J-C	9 OA
56	Ferrari 365 GTB4/C	16407	Ethuin C/Guitteny G	11 OA
55	Ferrari 365 GTB4/C	16343	Paoli J-P/Couderc A	DNF
18	Ferrari Dino 308 GT4	08020	Lafosse J-L/Gagliardi G	DNF
12 July				**Watkins Glen 6-hour**
55	Ferrari 365 GTB4/C	16407	Hiss M/Cudini A	DNF
54	Ferrari 365 GTB4		Rutherford J/Cudini A	DNA
13 July				**Watkins Glen Can-Am**
10	Ferrari 712 P	1010	Redman B	2 OA
				33-lap race
10	Ferrari 712 P	1010	Redman B	DNF
23–24 September				**Bonneville Salt Flats**
10-mile	Ferrari 512M	1020	Chinetti Jr L	174.763mph
500km	Ferrari 365 GTB4	14141	Hill G	171.255mph
500-mile	Ferrari 365 GTB4	14141	Minter M/Chinetti Jr L/Hill G	166.173mph
1000km	Ferrari 365 GTB4	14141	Newman P/Chinetti Jr L/Hill G	166.445mph
10km	Ferrari 512M	1020	Chinetti Jr L/Newman P	174.759mph
24-hour	Ferrari 365 GTB4	14141	Chinetti Jr L/Hill G/Newman P/Minter M	DNF

CN	MAKE & MODEL	CHASSIS No	NOMINATED DRIVER(S)	RACE RESULTS
		1975		
1 February				**Daytona 24-hour**
0	Ferrari 365 GTB4	14141	Minter M/Ballot-Lena C/Gagliardi L	DNF

14 | 1957-1983

Abbreviations

CN = Car Number
DNF = Did Not Finish
DNA = Did Not Attend
DNQ = Did Not Qualify
DSQ = Disqualified
U2L = Under 2-litre
O2L = Over 2-litre
NK = Not Known
OA = Overall
WDN = Withdrawn

CN	MAKE & MODEL	CHASSIS No	NOMINATED DRIVER(S)	RACE RESULTS
1	Ferrari 365 GTBB	18139	Cudini A/Ballot-Lena C/Minter M	DNF
22 March				**Sebring 12-hour**
111	Ferrari 365 GTBB	18139	Minter M/Wietzes E	6 OA
20 April				**Road Atlanta**
5	Ferrari 365 GTBB	18139	Minter M	DNS
3 May				**Lime Rock**
111	Ferrari 365 GTBB	18139	Minter M	R1.DNF, Classified 18
111	Ferrari 365 GTBB	18139	Minter M	R2.DNF, Classified 24
June				**Le Mans 24-hour**
45	Ferrari 365 GTB4/C	16407	Bucknum R/Facetti C	WDN
46	Ferrari 365 GTB4 Michelotti	15965	Malcher J-P/Langlois P/Facetti C	WDN
99	Ferrari 365 GTBB	18095	Guitteny L/Haran J/Bucknum R/Gagliardi G	WDN
17	Ferrari Dino 308 GT4	08020	Gagliardi G/Cluxton H	DNQ
				Mexico
48	Ferrari 365 GTB4		Young G/Muniz D	1 OA

CN	MAKE & MODEL	CHASSIS No	NOMINATED DRIVER(S)	RACE RESULTS
1976				
12 June				**Le Mans 24-hour**
5	Ferrari 512 BB			DNS
6	Ferrari 308 GTB			DNS
70	Ferrari 365 GTB4			DNS

CN	MAKE & MODEL	CHASSIS No	NOMINATED DRIVER(S)	RACE RESULTS
1977				
June				**Le Mans 24-hour**
75	Ferrari 365 GTBB	18139	Migault F/Guitteny L	16 OA

Statistical review

1978

CN	MAKE & MODEL	CHASSIS No	NOMINATED DRIVER(S)	RACE RESULTS

4–5 February — Daytona 24-hour

CN	MAKE & MODEL	CHASSIS No	NOMINATED DRIVER(S)	RACE RESULTS
5	Ferrari 365 GTBB	18139	Migault F/Guitteny L/Young G	22 OA

16 April — Road Atlanta

5	Ferrari 365 GTBB	18139	Migault F	21 OA

10 June — Le Mans 24-hour

87	Ferrari 512 BB	24131	Guerin J/Delaunay J-P/Young G	DNF

1979

3–4 February — Daytona 24-hour

CN	MAKE & MODEL	CHASSIS No	NOMINATED DRIVER(S)	RACE RESULTS
65	Ferrari 365 GTB4/C	16407	Adamowicz T/Morton J	2 OA
68	Ferrari 512 BB	26683	Bedard P/Delaunay J-P/Tullius R	DNF

9 June — Le Mans 24-hour

64	Ferrari 512 BB	26683	Delaunay J-P/Henn P/Grandet C	DNF

1980

2 February — Daytona 24-hour

CN	MAKE & MODEL	CHASSIS No	NOMINATED DRIVER(S)	RACE RESULTS
69	Ferrari 512 BB	26683	Dieudonne P/Henn P	DNF

14–15 June — Le Mans 24-hour

74	Ferrari 512 BB	30559	Henn P/Delaunay J-P	DNS

1981

June — Le Mans 24-hour

CN	MAKE & MODEL	CHASSIS No	NOMINATED DRIVER(S)	RACE RESULTS
49	512 BBLM	35527	Cudini A/Gurdjian P/Morton J	DNF

'82

CN	MAKE & MODEL	CHASSIS No	NOMINATED DRIVER(S)	RACE RESULTS
		1982		
30–31 January				**Daytona 24-hour**
6	512 BB	30559	Wollek R/Doeren E/Lanier R	DNF
20 March				**Sebring 12-hour**
6	512 BB	30559	Guthrie J/Wilson D/Henn B	26 OA
13–14 June				**Le Mans 24-hour**
72	512 BBLM	35527	Cudini A/Morton J/Paul J	9 OA

'83

CN	MAKE & MODEL	CHASSIS No	NOMINATED DRIVER(S)	RACE RESULTS
		1983		
June				**Le Mans 24-hour**
50	512 BBLM	35527		DNA

Abbreviations

CN = Car Number
DNF = Did Not Finish
DNA = Did Not Attend
DNQ = Did Not Qualify
DSQ = Disqualified
U2L = Under 2-litre
O2L = Over 2-litre
NK = Not Known
OA = Overall
WDN = Withdrawn

Also from Veloce Publishing ...

*All prices subject to change. P&P extra.

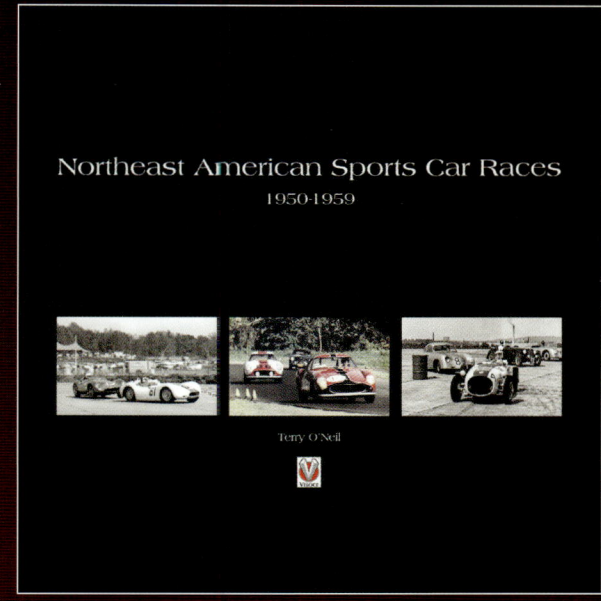

Northeast American Sports Car Races
1950-1959

Focuses on the different aspects that contributed to the emergence of Northeast.

American sports car racing during the 1950s. Its evolution was neither easy nor uneventful for drivers, clubs or track owners, and the politics, intrigue and tragedy that came to characterise the period are covered here in fascinating detail.

ISBN: 978-1-845842-54-3 • Hardback • 25x25cm • 432 pages
499 pictures • £49.99* UK/$99.95* USA

Runways & Racers
Sports Car Races held on Military Airfields in America 1952-1954

Examines the various factors that contributed to sports car races being held at American military bases in the early 1950s.

A fascinating insight to this two-year period, complemented by over 150 pictures, many previously unpublished.

ISBN: 978-1-845842-55-0 • Hardback • 25x25cm • 208 pages
202 pictures • £19.99* UK/$39.95* USA

For more info on Veloce titles, visit our websites, email info@veloce.co.uk or call +44(0)1305 260068
www.veloce.co.uk • www.velocebooks.com • digital.veloce.co.uk

Also from Veloce Publishing ...

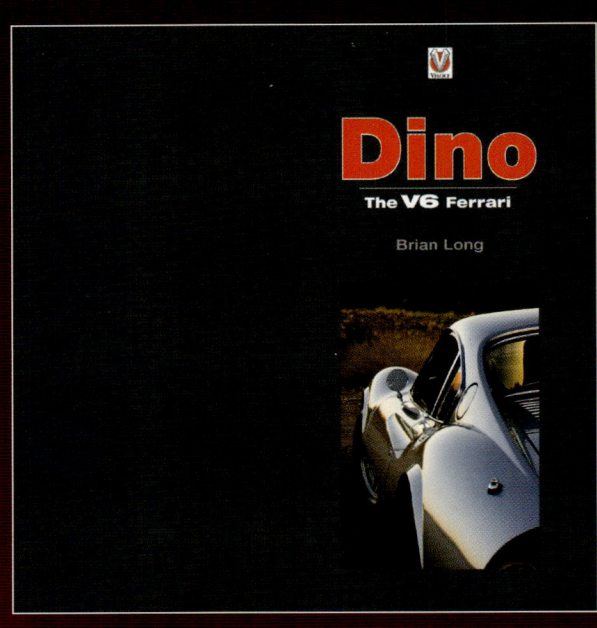

Dino
The V6 Ferrari

Although not the fastest or the most powerful Ferrari, the beautiful lines of the Dino have inspired generations of enthusiasts.

This book covers the full story of this classic, from Pininfarina concept car through to final production model, illustrated throughout with contemporary material.

ISBN: 978-1-904788-39-3 • Hardback • 25x25cm
250 pictures • 176 pages • £40* UK/$69.95* USA

Ferrari 333 SP
WSC Giants

Designed by Ferrari's Mauro Rioli, with British race car designer Tony Southgate.

The Ferrari 333 SP contested a variety of sports car championships, both in America and Europe, from the IMSA World Sports Car Championship, to the 24 Hours of Le Mans.

ISBN: 978-1-845847-58-6 • Paperback • 19.5x21cm • 128 pages
146 colour pictures • £16.99* UK/$27.95* USA

For more info on Veloce titles, visit our websites, email info@veloce.co.uk or call +44(0)1305 260068
www.veloce.co.uk • www.velocebooks.com • digital.veloce.co.uk

*All prices subject to change. P&P extra.

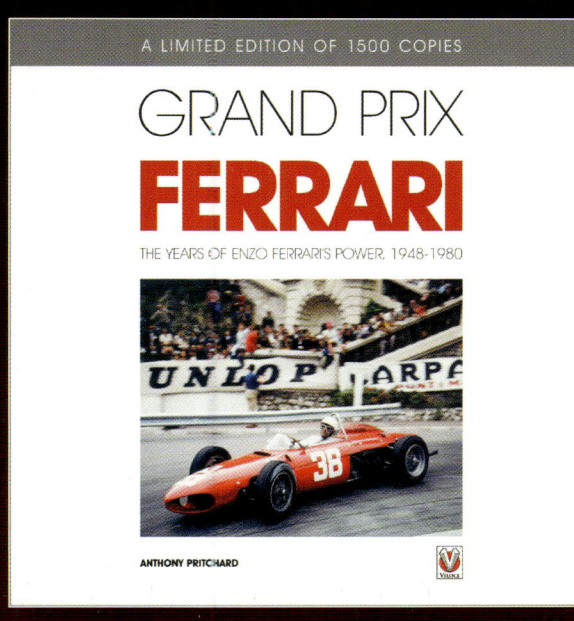

Grand Prix Ferrari

The Years of Enzo Ferrari's Power, 1948-1980

A limited edition of 1500 copies.

An enthralling, comprehensive, and highly readable account of the racing history of motor sport's most important marque, supported by over 200 colour and black and white photographs.

ISBN: 978-1-845846-23-7 • Hardback • 25x25cm • 416 pages
214 colour pictures • £85* UK/$135* USA

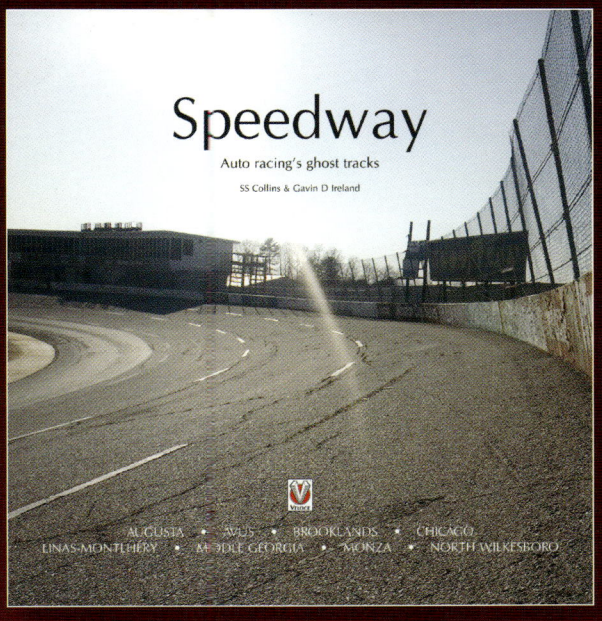

Speedway

Auto racing's ghost tracks

An evocative then and now look at eight abandoned race circuits in the USA and Europe, featuring both historic pictures plus stunning new photographs.

Features track diagrams & memorabilia, too. Note that some of these circuits featured in the much acclaimed Autodrome – The lost race circuits of Europe, but in this edition are illustrated by many new photographs.

ISBN: 978-1-845842-41-3 • Hardback • 25x25cm • 176 pages
186 colour pictures • £17.50* UK/$35.00* USA

Connect on social media   facebook www.facebook.com/VelocePublishing   @VeloceBooks

Also from Veloce Publishing ...

*All prices subject to change. P&P extra.

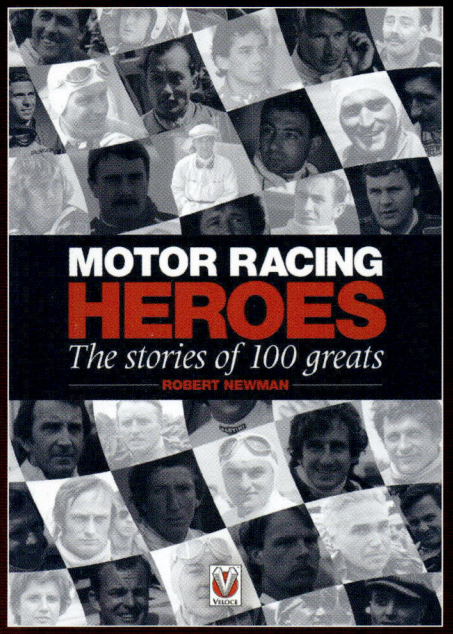

Motor Racing Heroes
The Stories of 100 Greats

100 heroes from almost 100 years of motor sport are covered in this book.

Revealing the determination, heroism, raw courage, skill at the wheel – and just plain humanity – that has elevated men and women into the special, rarified atmosphere of heroism.

ISBN: 978-1-845847-48-7 • Hardback • 21x14.8cm • 384 pages £19.99* UK/$32.99* USA

Ferrari 312P & 312PB
WSC Giants

Details the origin and history of the 3-litre Ferrari sports cars, which the famed Italian firm designed and built to contest the various versions of the World Sports Car Championship between 1969 and 1973.

Features over 100 photographs, many rare and previously unpublished.

ISBN: 978-1-845842-59-8 • Paperback • 19.5x21cm • 128 pages • 145 pictures • £16.99* UK/$29.95* USA

For more info on Veloce titles, visit our websites, email info@veloce.co.uk or call +44(0)1305 260068
www.veloce.co.uk • www.velocebooks.com • digital.veloce.co.uk

Index

Cars

NOTE: *Grey italicised* entries indicate cars that were entered in races, but not mentioned in the body of text, and therefore have no page number reference (see Chapter 14 *Statistical review*).

Alfa Romeo 14, 15
Alpine-Renault M64
  1710 151
  ASA RB613
  21000 142, 147
  21004 150
Chevrolet Corvette 178-180
Ferrari 166 MM 16, 17, 19, 23, 187
Ferrari 290 MM
  0616 29
  0628 29-31
Ferrari 375 Indy
  0388 20, 21, 35, 36
Ferrari 315 S
  0656 31
  0684
Ferrari 335 S
  0674 31, 33, 36-38
  0764 46
Ferrari 860 Monza 28, 41
  0602 36
Ferrari 250 GT TdF
  0773 31
  0893 32
  1461 44, 46
Ferrari 250 GT SWB 57, 71
  1539 51, 52
  1759 56
  1773 49
  1785 51, 53
  1931 59
  2455 63, 64
  2643 76, 79
  2725 67, 69, 76
  2731 66-68
  2735 69
  3005 73, 76
  3327 79
Ferrari 250 GT LWB California
  1451 44, 45
Ferrari 250 GT SWB California 71
  2015 56, 64
Ferrari 250 GTO 78, 86, 91, 95, 118, 120
  3223 88-90, 93
  3323
  3387 78, 80, 85
  3984
  3987 86
  4219 90, 93
  4713 93, 94, 96, 97, 102, 103, 106
  5571 102, 103, 108, 110, 119
  5573 107, 109, 110

Ferrari 500 TR 33-34, 44
  0600 44
  0666
Ferrari 500 TRC 42
  0702 57, 58
Ferrari 250 TR 33, 44, 46, 48, 51, 59, 78, 86
  0666 33, 44, 46
  0722 44
  0724 44
  0728 41
  0730 33
  0746 59, 60, 64
  0756
  0766 48, 55, 58, 61
  0770 59
  0774 50-52, 59
  0792 66, 68
  0794 69, 71, 76, 81, 82
Ferrari 250 TRI 61
  0780 65
  0794
Ferrari 250(275) LM 104, 110, 114
  5149 103, 104
  5909 109
  5893 125, 126, 136, 137, 154, 157, 160, 164
  5901 136, 137
Ferrari 250 P 99, 100, 103
  0810 98, 101, 103, 106, 108, 124
Ferrari 275 P 114, 122, 124, 133
  0812 111
  0814 141
Ferrari 330 P 111, 114, 118, 122, 124
  0814 112, 115, 132, 138
  0816 159
  0820 112, 119, 120
  0822 124
  0824 111, 113
Ferrari 275 P2
Ferrari 330 P2 122
  0838
Ferrari 365 P2 138
  0838 128, 130, 131, 136-138, 142, 144, 146, 151
Ferrari 330 P3 138
  0846
Ferrari 330 P4
  0860 155, 162
Ferrari 312P 166, 173
  0870 161, 164, 167, 170
  0872 164, 167, 170, 171, 191
Ferrari 312P V8 (Chinetti Special) 176, 191
Ferrari 412 P 152
  0844 148, 150, 151, 153
Ferrari 330 TRI 86
  0808 89, 92, 94
Ferrari 330 LMB

4453 94-96, 99
Ferrari 512S 170, 172
  1006 171-173
  1014 164, 165
  1018
  1020
  1028
Ferrari 512M 171, 172
  1020 174, 175
  1040
Ferrari 512MB 193
Ferrari 365 GTBB
  15965
  18095 195
  18139 193, 203, 206
Ferrari 512 BB
  24131 206
  30559
Ferrari 512 BBLM
  26683 207, 209-213
  35527 215-217, 219
Ferrari 712 P 183, 191
  1010 184, 192
Ferrari 275 GTB 145, 156
  9057 141, 142, 146
  10311 154
Ferrari 275 GTB/C 133
  6885 132, 134
  9015
  9063 166
Ferrari 275 GTB/NART Spyder 150, 221-223
  09437 223
Ferrari 365 GTB4 186, 190
  12467 173
  12547 166
  13855 177
  14107 172
  14115
  14141 177, 187, 190, 193, 195
  14885 176
  14889 177, 184, 186
  15685 177, 182
  15965 195
  16343 192
  16367 189
  16407 189, 191, 195, 208
Ferrari Dino 196S 62
  0776 47, 49, 51, 53
Ferrari Dino 246S 61-2, 74
  0778 64, 70, 71
  0784 62, 71, 74, 76, 79, 82
Ferrari Dino 196 SP
  0804 87
Ferrari Dino 246 SP
  0790 78, 82
  0796 76
Ferrari Dino 248 SP 83
  0806 78, 81

Ferrari Dino 268 SP
  0798 87, 89, 92, 93, 100, 101, 141
Ferrari Dino 206S 138, 145, 149, 151
  002
  008 139, 143, 144, 148, 150, 153
  014 144, 146, 147, 150, 154, 156, 157, 159, 160
Ferrari Dino 206 GT 159-160
Ferrari Dino 246 GT 183
  2678
Ferrari Dino 308 GT4 190
  08020 195
Ferrari F1 158
  0005 117
  0006
Ferrari F1 1512 118, 133, 134
  0007 116
  0008
Ferrari F1 312
  0017 161
Ferrari Dino F1 156
  0003 118
Maserati 300 S
  3083 47
McLaren M10B 171
OSCA S 750 53, 56
  768 58
OSCA S 1000 61, 64, 69-71, 78, 86
  1001
OSCA S 2000 70
OSCA Formula Junior 53, 59, 64, 83
  0003 55
  0012
OSCA 1600 GT 83, 85, 86, 90
  007 78, 89, 92
Sunbeam Harrington Alpine
  B9106097 92
Surtees TS5A
  006 TS 171

Drivers

Adamowicz, Tony 164, 167, 170-172, 177, 180, 207
Andretti, Mario 132, 133, 136, 138
Andrey, Gaston 33, 36-38, 64
Andruet, Jean-Claude 186, 191
Arents, George 26, 29, 32, 44, 46, 57, 58, 64, 69, 71, 74, 84-86, 132
Baghetti, Giancarlo 124, 151
Ballot-Lena, Claude 186, 195
Bandini, Lorenzo 87, 89, 90, 100, 104, 116, 118, 119, 133, 138
Baumann, Harold 92
Bedard, Pat 9
Behra, Jose 34, 85, 86
Bentley, John 58
Biscaldi, Giampiero 146, 159
Bondurant, Robert 127, 134, 136-138
Bonnier, Jo 93, 104, 118

Index

Buchet, Claude 177, 180
Bucknum, Ronnie 154, 167, 171, 172, 175, 176, 199
Cannon, John 91, 93
Capuano, Ignazio 151
Carveth, Rod 44, 46
Casner, Lloyd 44
Casoni, Mario 145
Chevalier, Francois 151, 156
Chinetti Jr, Louis 141, 142, 167, 172, 173, 176, 177, 186, 189, 192, 193, 203
Cluxton, Harley 172, 186, 199
Connell, Alan 46, 57, 62, 64, 78
Constantine, George 36, 59, 62, 70, 71, 74
Cudini, Alain 190, 191, 218
Cunningham, David 53, 59, 64, 69
Daigh Chuck 50
D'Orey, Fritz 51
De Bourbon-Parme, Michel 146
Di Palma, Luis 171, 189
Delauney, Jean-Pierre 206, 209, 212
Dietrich, Suzy 78, 148, 150
Dini, Robert 159
Doeren, Edgar 216
Doncieux, Gilles 178, 182
Donohue, Mark 174
Durham, Al 134
Eager, Alan 78
Eaton, George 172, 173
Ethuin, Christian 190, 191
Fleming, Tom 60, 89, 90, 92
Follmer, George 136, 166
Foyt, A J 101
Fulp, John 53, 57-59, 70, 71, 74, 76, 78, 83-86, 89, 92, 93, 101, 103, 111-114, 124
Gacia-Veiga, Nestor 171, 172, 189
Gagliardi, Giancarlo 199
Gammino, Mike 103
Geitner, Gil 42, 44, 46
Gendebien, Oliver 78, 81
Ginther, Ritchie 50, 139, 141, 146
Gordon, Jack 58
Grandet, Cyril 212
Gregg, Peter 148
Gregory, Masten 86, 88-90, 94, 126, 129, 130, 148, 149, 153, 154, 156, 171, 172
Greenspun, Gene 30
Grossman, Robert 37, 39, 44-46, 68, 70, 76, 78, 82, 85, 86, 93, 102, 104, 106, 107, 110, 111, 123-127, 151, 154, 156, 160, 172, 173, 177, 189
Guerin, Jacques 206
Guichet, Jean 130, 131, 148, 150-152
Guitteny, Lucien 189, 190, 199, 200, 204, 206
Gurdjian, Philippe 215
Gurney, Dan 33, 34, 71, 94-99, 100, 164, 166
Guthrie, Janet 216
Haas, Carl 78

Hall, Jim 62, 94-96
Hamill, Sterling 78, 83-86
Hansgen, Walt 55, 99, 100, 102, 111, 114, 122, 133
Haran, Jacky 199, 200
Hawkins, Paul 136
Hayes, Charles 78, 86, 88, 89, 93, 133
Hayes, Fred 70, 71
Heinz, David 190
Henn, Bonnie 216
Henn, Preston 212, 215
Heppenstall, Ray 70, 92
Heuer, Harry 92, 93
Hill, Graham 69, 92, 93, 97, 100, 104, 116, 118, 124, 192
Hill, Phil 59, 76, 78, 81, 87, 93, 102, 120
Hiss, Mike 191
Hobbs, David 174, 182
Hudson, Skip 76, 103, 110
Hugus, Ed 51, 53, 57, 62, 64, 69, 85, 103, 108, 123, 127, 129, 130
Hunt, Jim 44
Hutchins, Robert 132, 141, 146
Ireland, Innes 78, 81-83
Jarier, Jean-Pierre 177, 180, 183, 184, 186, 189
Kaback, Sy 53, 64
Kelleners, Helmut 170
Kessler, Bruce 33-37, 41
Kneeland, William 93
Kolb, Charlie 104, 124, 134, 146, 153, 159, 160
Laffeach, Jean-Pierre 178, 182
Laffite, Jacques 184
Lagier, Bernard 156
Langlois, Patrick 200
Lanier, Randy 216
Latteri, Ferdinando 151
Le Guezec, Claude 96, 97
Litchie, Spencer 78
Loos, Georg 170
Mae Mims, Donna 148, 150
Maglioli, Umberto 124
Malcher, Jean-Pierre 200
Marincovich, Carlos 171
Martin, Ed 34
Mayer, Tim 93
McCluggage, Denise 33, 53, 78, 83, 86, 150, 223
Merzario, Arturo 186
Mieusset, Robert 145, 170
Migault, Francois 170, 186-189, 204, 206
Minter, Milt 186, 187, 189, 193, 195
Morton, John 207, 218
Moss, Stirling 29, 30, 49, 61, 69, 76
Muniz, David 201
Newman, Alan 64, 71
Newman, Paul 193
O'Brien, Tom 104
O'Dell, Don 32
Pabst, Augie 51, 57, 59, 64
Paoli, Jean-Pierre 190

Parkes, Mike 164, 166, 167
Parsons, Chuck 151, 167, 169, 170
Pasquier, Francois 145
Paul Jr, John 218
Penske, Roger 89, 91, 94, 95, 97, 120
Pilette, André 44, 46, 56, 57, 68
Piper, David 95, 103, 122, 153, 164
Posey, Sam 156-157, 159, 160, 161, 164, 167, 169, 170-172, 175-176, 180, 182, 183, 186, 189, 192, 225
Publicker, Robert 64, 78, 83, 86
Redman, Brian 192
Reed, George 32, 69, 70, 71, 85
Reventlow, Lance 36, 37, 39, 46
Revson, Peter 171, 173
Rindt, Jochen 103, 125-127, 130, 132, 137
Roberts, George 76, 85, 90, 91
Rodriguez, Pedro 33, 42, 48, 53, 58, 59, 69, 71, 80, 86, 87, 89, 90-93, 95, 96, 98-103, 108, 110, 112, 114, 118, 119, 122, 124, 126, 128, 129, 132-134, 136, 138, 141, 146-155, 161, 162, 170
Rodriguez, Ricardo 33, 48, 53-56, 59, 60, 61, 69, 71, 74, 76, 86, 87
Rodriguez, Ricardo (USA) 151, 160
Rollo, Pinkie 223
Rosinski, Jose 103, 108
Rutherford, John 191
Ryan, Peter 76, 78, 84-86
Savage, Swede 172, 173
Scafiotti, Ludovico 111, 113, 114, 134, 138, 153
Schell, Harry 35, 36
Shelby, Carroll 28, 114
Schlesser, Jo 57, 96, 97, 118, 148
Serena, Fabrizio 78, 83
Sturgis, William 51, 57
Surtees, John 100, 104, 110, 116-120, 122, 127, 138
Tavano, Fernand 34, 45, 64, 104, 107
Theodoli, Fillipo 92, 93
Thiem, Doug 76, 93
Thérier, Jean-Luc 151
Tullius, Robert 209
Vaccarella, Nino 110, 126, 128, 129, 132, 145
Von Trips, Wolfgang 31, 3
Wester, Don 136
Wietzes, Eppie 195
Wilson, Desire 216
Wollek, Robert 216
Wuesthoff, William 59
Young, Gregg 171, 172, 200, 206
Zeccoli, Teodoro 160, 161, 191

Venues

Augusta 103
Bonneville 192, 193
Bridgehampton 37, 55, 57, 58, 83, 86, 97, 111, 114, 132, 146, 153-135, 161
Buenos Aires 171

Brynfan Tyddn 28
Cumberland 53, 64, 138
Daytona 76, 90, 101, 122, 136, 147, 153, 157, 164, 171, 175, 186, 189, 206, 207, 212, 215, 218
Elkhart Lake (Road America) 36, 39, 40, 59, 154, 155, 170, 184
Goodwood 95, 110
Havana (Cuba) 27, 48
Laguna Seca 146
Le Mans 33, 44, 46, 56, 67, 68, 85, 93, 95, 103, 124, 142, 151, 156, 160, 169, 173, 177, 187, 190, 195, 203, 206, 210, 212, 215, 219
Lime Rock 36, 46, 195
Lexington (Mid Ohio) 170
Mexico City 118, 134, 162, 200
Monza 34, 138, 151
Montlhéry 71-73, 86, 118
Mosport 69, 71, 86, 100, 114, 133, 153, 161
Nassau (Bahamas) 30, 41, 42, 47, 48, 59, 60, 71, 74, 87, 89, 101, 119, 134
Nürburgring 52, 53, 55, 65, 138, 139
Pescara 69
Pueto Rico 87
Reims 104, 130, 152
Riverside 71, 147
Road Atlanta 195, 206
Roosevelt Raceway 55
St Jovite 110, 141
Sebring 32, 33, 44, 49, 61-4, 76, 103, 122, 136, 149, 159, 167, 172, 176, 186, 189
Targa Florio 53, 138, 151
Thompson Raceway 33
Tour de France 97
Vineland 138
Virginia International Raceway 100, 138
Watkins, Glen 39, 114, 116, 133, 138, 154, 162, 175, 183, 189, 191
Zeltweg 132

Personnel

Baus, John 125, 130, 198, 203
Caiti, Alfredo 8, 11
Chinetti, Luigi Throughout
Chinetti, Marion 18, 204
Craige, Robert 193
De Vroom, Jan 26 29, 30
Ferrari, Enzo 14, 122, 175
Fritz, Dick 12, 157, 159, 175, 182, 193, 197, 224
Garthwaite, Al 175
Iori, Nereo 193
Johnson, Ed 183
Lebreton, Jean-Louis 161, 173, 184
Sicard, Francois 159, 173, 193, 201
Sparling, Wayne 166, 173, 184
Strong, Margaret 26

N. A.